The Theater in the Fiction of Marcel Proust

The Theater
in the Fiction of
Marcel Proust

By John Gaywood Linn

Ohio State University Press

All quotations from Marcel Proust's *Du côté de chez Swann, A l'ombre des jeunes filles en fleurs, Le Côté de Guermantes, Sodome et Gomorrhe, La Prisonnière, La Fugitive,* and *Le Temps retrouvé* are from the 1954 Gallimard edition of *A la recherche du temps perdu* in the "Bibliothèque de la Pléiade." Copyright © 1913, 1919, 1920, 1921, 1922, 1923, 1924, 1925, and 1927 by Editions Gallimard and used by permission of the publisher.

All quotations from Marcel Proust's *Pastiches et mélanges* are copyright © 1919 by Editions Gallimard, and are used by permission of the publisher.

All quotations from Marcel Proust's *Jean Santeuil* are copyright © 1952 by Editions Gallimard, and are used by permission of the publisher.

All quotations from Germaine Brée, *Du temps perdu au temps retrouvé* are used by permission of Les Belles Lettres, Paris.

All quotations from Robert Dreyfus, *Souvenirs sur Marcel Proust* are used by permission of Editions Bernard Grasset, Paris.

All quotations from Jacques Nathan, *Citations, références et allusions de Proust* and *La Morale de Proust* are used by permission of Librairie A. G. Nizet, Paris.

All quotations from Léon Pierre-Quint, *Marcel Proust, sa vie, son œuvre* are used by permission of Editions de Sagittaire, Paris.

All quotations from Marcel Proust, *Correspondance avec sa mère,* edited by Philip Kolb, are used by permission of Librairie Plon.

All quotations from Marcel Proust, *Lettres à Madame et Monsieur Emile Straus,* edited by Suzy Proust-Mante and Paul Brach, are used by permission of Librairie Plon.

All quotations from Marcel Proust, *Lettres à Walter Berry,* [et al.], edited by Robert Proust and Paul Brach, are used by permission of Librairie Plon.

All quotations from Derrick Leon, *Introduction to Proust: His Life, His Circle, and His Work* are used by permission of Routledge and Kegan Paul, Ltd., London.

All quotations from Marcel Proust's *Les Plaisirs et les jours* are copyright © 1924 by Editions Gallimard, and are used by permission of the publisher.

All quotations from Marcel Proust's *Contre Sainte-Beuve suivi de nouveaux mélanges* are copyright © 1954 by Editions Gallimard, and are used by permission of the publisher.

All quotations from Clive Bell, *Proust,* are used by permission of Harcourt, Brace, and World, Inc., New York, and The Hogarth Press, London.

All quotations from André Maurois, *Proust: Portrait of a Genius* are used by permission of Harper and Row, Publishers, Inc., New York.

All quotations from *Proust, the Early Years* by George D. Painter, Copyright ©, 1959, by George D. Painter. Reprinted by permission of Atlantic–Little, Brown and Company, publishers, Boston, and Chatto and Windus, Ltd., London.

Chapters III and VI contain two articles by John Gaywood Linn originally published in the *Romanic Review*—Vol. LII, No. 3 (October, 1961), pp. 210-25, and Vol. XLIX, No. 3 (October, 1958), pp. 179-90. They are reprinted here by permission of the Columbia University Press.

To my parents,
my wife Eleanor,
and my son John

Acknowledgments

I WISH to express my gratitude for the interest shown and the encouragement given by Professor Justin O'Brien, Columbia University, whose acceptance of two portions of the manuscript for publication in the *Romanic Review* emboldened me to proceed with the total work, and by Professor Victor Brombert, Yale University, whose careful analysis and helpful suggestions were greatly useful in the revision of the manuscript. Neither of them, of course, is to be thought of as having subscribed to my thesis, or as in any way involved with errors or inadequacies in the final manuscript. I am also grateful for the secretarial assistance provided by the office of the Division of Graduate Studies, Queens College of the City University of New York. I am beholden in various ways for the interest, encouragement, and advice of Professor George B. Parks, Professor Robert H. Ball, Professor Martha W. England, and other colleagues in the Queens College English Department. I also thank my editor, Robert S. Demorest, for his conscientious care, tactful advice, and sense of humor. My wife's work in preparing the Index is but the outward and visible sign of her contributions to the entire work, public acknowledgement of which would be superfluous and inadequate. I shall only thank her for her patience, interest, and invaluable help of all kinds when I was, to use Proust's own term, "Proustifying."

J. G. L.

January, 1965

Contents

The Theater in the Fiction of Marcel Proust

1

Proust and the Theater of His Time

THIS ESSAY, like the novel on which it focuses, ends where
it began. While teaching *Swann's Way* in a course in modern
fiction, I was attracted, as a matter of simple curiosity, to the
number of metaphors using theater and drama as their vehicles. Extending the examination of such metaphors to the
whole of *A la recherche du temps perdu* revealed not only
a large number of them, but a pattern and control in their
deployment, a pattern so significant that its understanding
required an examination of other theatrical material—allusions, quotations, and action—in the novel and Proust's other
writings.

In his essay on Goethe, written at the turn of the century,
Proust had commented somewhat prophetically on the use
of theater in Goethe's novels, presenting observations which
literally and metaphorically apply to his own later work.
Even his metaphors in the passage are a faint prediction of
his later practice:

Les arts, et les moyens par lesquels on s'y perfectionne, occupent
beaucoup les romans de Goethe. L'art de l'acteur, l'art de l'archi-
tecte, l'art du musicien, l'art du pédagogue y jouent un grand rôle,

3

et en tout ceci ce qui est vraiment l'art. La difficulté d'obtenir un ensemble où chacun soit prêt le frappe évidemment comme faisant partie de l'essence même de l'effort artistique. D'où la part faite aux comédies de société, aux comédies improvisées, à cette première représentation où Wilhelm Meister veut jouer et ne sait quoi dire. . . .[1]

Here Proust shows his awareness of materials which he was himself to carry further when he made extensive use of artists—particularly theatrical artists—and pursued the ramifications of society's comedies.

In *A la recherche*, Proust includes hundreds of metaphors drawn from theater, some brief, others extended. The metaphors are found in conjunction with a rather astonishing amount of non-metaphorical theater material. Independent of portions of the plot connected with the theater, close to seventy-five allusions to attending the theater are made—meeting at the theater, seeing friends in the audience, chatting in the lobby. A score and more characters from drama are mentioned, in comparisons, criticisms, and passing reference. Twenty-five or more actors and actresses, including what appears to be the whole of the Comédie Française troupe, are spoken of or appear in the action. Nearly fifty plays, classical and contemporary, are mentioned; half a dozen plays are quoted from, *Athalie, Esther,* and *Phèdre* more than a score of times. Close to thirty dramatists, from classical times to Proust's contemporaries, some of whom are asserted to be associates of the fictional characters, are alluded to or appear in the novel.

Much of this, of course, arises naturally from the world and culture which Proust portrayed, and from his own tastes and interests; but it is also made to serve more integrated purposes. In addition to almost five hundred metaphorical and direct allusions to theater and drama, and quotations from drama, by Marcel and other characters, the plot continually involves the theater and its people. Besides Rachel and Berma, two other important characters are actresses—the Lesbian Léa, and Odette, who played Miss Sacripant, and was painted by Elstir in her costume for this character. Two leading characters figure as playwrights, both Bloch and Bergotte being shown as writers of comedies for presentation in fashionable drawing rooms. Berma, and especially Berma as Phèdre, is made the symbol of what is admirable in theater. Berma in an absolute sense, and Rachel in a comparative one, are marked as admirable by their devotion to the theater. If Proust often uses the admirable traits of these theater characters to denigrate society by comparison, in his metaphors he equates society with what is inferior and shoddy in the theater.

Two critics have written in general terms of the methods which can be illustrated in Proust's way with theater materials. Edmund Wilson has pointed to the interweaving of details which makes up Proust's organic structure:

> . . . The "events" which may be taken arbitrarily as infinitely small or infinitely comprehensive, make up an organic structure, in which all are interdependent, each involving every other and the whole; so Proust's book is a gigantic mesh of complicated relations: cross-references between different groups of characters and a multiplication of metaphors and similes connecting the phenomena of infinitely varied fields—biological, zoological, physical, aesthetic, social, political, and financial.[2]

To this we may add "theatrical" and "dramatic." C. W. M. Johnson has dealt more specifically with Proust's methods of interweaving images:

A la recherche du temps perdu is a matrix of images related to each other in subtle ways. These images thread through the story, undergo development, and in general behave like the main characters, at times just present in a scene, at other times taking the center of the stage and delivering long monologues, and often demanding a reorientation of our thinking because of the metamorphoses they undergo. The figure is extravagant; but it points to an unrecognized source of unity in the work.

To exploit imagery in this fashion takes time and a prodigious amount of space. The reader must be occupied with other matters and allowed to forget, before conditions are right for recall and further development; but after the image has undergone several such variations it becomes so charged with associations that the slightest allusion to it is evocative.[3]

These matters were the beginning and the end of the present study, but Proust's theatrical net also catches up relationships among autobiography and fiction, art and life, the chronology of the novel, major themes of the work, the working methods of its creator, and other fish both large and small.

The legend of Proust the recluse confined to his medically smoked, cork-lined room has been so firmly established that the idea of his interest and even indirect participation in anything so active as the theater is likely at first to seem improbable. Yet one of his first efforts written for "publication," in October, 1888, when he was seventeen, was some notes on the theater for the little *Revue lilas*;[4] and in the year of his death, he wrote to Philip Sassoon of explaining to a waiter at the Ritz, who had prepared the role of Sosie, what Molière's play was about.[5] In 1897, he wrote for the *Revue d'art dramatique* a piece on theatrical criticism called "Silhouette d'artiste."[6] In 1903, he proposed to write regular theater reviews for the *Renaissance latine*, and was so annoyed when the scheme fell through that he referred to the review as "la perfide Inconstance latine," "l'ingrate Jactance latine," "la choquante Inconvenance latine," "l'Indécence latine," and "la Méconaissance latine." [7] He attended rehearsals in theaters and in drawing rooms, and on one occasion "with conspicuous lack of success, officiated as prompter." [8] He asked the help of his friends Reynaldo Hahn and Gaston de Caillavet to obtain an audition for a singer at the Apollo. [9] He suggested a passage of dialogue for insertion into a play of Antoine Bibesco's. [10]

Most tantalizing is a remark in one of his letters, when he wrote to Madame de Caillavet, "Dites à Gaston et à Robert que j'ai en vue une *assez belle* (!) idée de pièce," but—and this is all we ever read of it in his letters—he immediately added, "et que je n'ai pas le courage de la faire." [11] Though not a playwright, Proust was something of a theatrical angel: in 1922, the year of his death, he wished to sell some shares of stock he held in the Vieux Colombier theater. [12] Probably one of the most peculiar rumors about Proust, late in his life, falsely suggested an even more unexpected theatrical accomplishment: that he had designed the decoration of a Montmartre theater—a rumor he decided neither to deny nor to complain of. [13] These few particulars suggest that cork and smoke did not raise any insuperable barrier between Proust and the theater of his time. When we further consider the circles of his friends and his social life, we begin to see why theater and drama play what might have been regarded at first glance as an unexpectedly large part in *A la recherche du temps perdu*.

No reader of *Du côté de chez Swann* will be surprised to discover that the youthful Proust had a great enthusiasm for the theater. When he was thirteen, his "idea of earthly

7

happiness" was "to live in close contact with those I love, with the beauties of nature, with a quantity of books and music, and to have, within easy distance, a French theatre."[14] As a schoolboy, Derrick Leon tells us, "it was the theatre that was his great topic of conversation. He would expatiate with equal vigour on the wonderful performance Bernhardt had just given in *Hamlet* . . . or the great misfortune of not having been able to make use of an opportunity he was once offered, because his parents considered that he was too young to go out at night, of being taken to see Lemaître."[15] Robert Dreyfus writes of the same period, "Et je suis certain de son enthousiasme d'enfant pour Mounet-Sully et pour Mme Sarah Bernhardt, dont il a transmué le génie dans son personnage de la tragédienne Berma."[16] George D. Painter reports the amusement of one observer who saw the "little boy" buying the complete works of Molière.[17] Mme Proust's letters to her son, when he was away on vacations, are full of references to theater and drama, as well as of quotations from plays. She apologizes for not having sent a requested copy of *Ruy Blas* and refers to the play *Tosca*,[18] and reports on theater articles of the day: "Il paraît que le *Figaro* d'hier était amusant par Caliban et palpitant par Boulanger."[19] Proust's return correspondence with his mother is also full of references to the reading of plays and of quotations from them.

When Proust was twenty, he answered a questionnaire thus:

> *Who is your favorite hero of fiction?*
> Hamlet.

> *Who are your favorite heroines of fiction?*
> Phèdre [crossed out by Proust] Bérénice.[20]

Lucien Daudet describes an early visit with Proust which is, in several details, similar to Marcel's description in the novel of his visits at his Uncle Adolphe's, and which involves the same interest in actresses: ". . . Devinant ma timidité après un premier essai de conversation très vague, il me dit: 'Tenez, je vous ai préparé quelques photographies de gens célèbres, des actrices, des écrivains, des artistes, cela vous amusera peut-être, et aussi ce livre.'" [21]

Perhaps the clearest indication of Proust's early interest in and knowledge of the theater is the piece which he wrote for the student magazine, the *Revue lilas*, when he was seventeen. Robert Dreyfus, calling it basically a pastiche of Jules Lemaître, quotes the piece, with explanatory footnotes. It is essentially a collection of random notes such as the following:

Vu Jules Lemaître pour la première fois. Jolie tête de jeune taureau, face de faune songeur avec deux yeux d'un bleu bien pur, bleu comme un reflet de pervenche dans une source claire. . . . Presque égal au divin Mounet, il est au-dessus de toute comparaison avec n'importe quel autre tragédien. Pourquoi l'Odéon ne l'engage-t-il pas, au lieu de permettre à l'exécrable X . . . de continuer à déshonorer les vers admirables d'Athalie? . . . Excessivement remarquable, Alice Lavigne, dans les *Joyeusetés de l'Année*. Dans la Scène de la Danse, avec un sens merveilleux de l'eurythmie; très fine la charge vraiment éminente d'un entrechat imperturbablement continué et comme automatique pendant la conversation des deux danseuses. Du contraste, dirait tel maitre*, jaillit un comique imprévu, et des fusées de rire traversent la salle. . . . Bien faibles les *Pieds de Mouton*. Pour prendre une expression "que je vous cueille sur les lèvres mêmes de Mme Théo,"** on se tord à Mimi. [22]

Dreyfus is not sure whether this youthful effort of the theater-struck Proust was ever published, since the files of the review are lost, but he points to the way in which the manuscript prefigures later work:

9

Mais cet essai de chronique dramatique n'est-il point curieux? Par l'admiration de Racine et des grands interprètes de la tragédie classique (*Athalie* ou *Phèdre*), le "divin Mounet," c'est-à-dire Mounet-Sully, la Berma . . . , son auteur ressemble comme un frère à l'enfant de Swann, . . . mais un frère aîné, plus dégourdi, qui fréquente les petits théâtres et lit avec ravissement, chaque dimanche, les délicats feuilletons de ce Jules Lemaître qu'il vient d'avoir le bonheur de rencontrer "pour la première fois" (probable-ment chez Madame Straus).

Dreyfus' parenthetical remark about Madame Straus indicates the next stage in Proust's interest in the theater and its people, for his social life gave him the opportunity to meet many of the theatrical luminaries of the day, and to see many of them taking part in drawing-room presentations of various kinds.

He was a friend of Mme Aubernon, who, during the Dreyfus affair, said, "I shall keep my Jews," since she "knew too well," as Derrick Leon points out, "from which quarter came so much of the talent that made her theatrical perform-ances successful." [23] These "theatricals" were said to be the basis for those of Mme de Villeparisis in *A la recherche*.[24] Her salon included Becque, Lemaître, Sardou, and Dumas fils; but, as Leon indicates, her home became a center for more than literary and theatrical chit-chat:

The real importance of her influence was due to the theatrical performances which she staged in her house. . . . She had her own private company, and . . . organized ambitious productions, not only of the works of her "chosen," but also of hitherto un-known pieces from abroad. She was first to produce Becque's *Parisienne*, with Antoine and Réjane; and the comedy *Village*, by Octave Feuillet. It is also to her eternal credit that it was at her house that there were played for the first time in Paris Ibsen's *Doll's House* and *John Gabriel Borkman*.[25]

That Proust's friendship with Mme Aubernon included attending her theatricals we know from what he wrote about

Village to Pierre Lavallée: ". . . J'ai été obligé de partir au milieu du *Village* mais [Robert de Flers] a été étourdissant dans la première pièce."[26]

Other friends offered Proust similar opportunities to meet theater people and to see more or less elaborate private performances. One of these friends was Mme Lemaire, at whose home Réjane, Bernhardt, Coquelin, and Mounet-Sully performed on various occasions.[27] Another friend was Comte Robert de Montesquiou, the aesthete, flamboyant snob, and minor Symbolist poet who served as one of the models for the Baron de Charlus. This friendship gave Proust an entree to the worlds of society, the arts, and the tangled relationships of Montesquiou's male friends. Of the close relationship between Montesquiou and the divine Sarah, Mme Clermont-Tonnerre gives one rather grotesque bit of evidence: "Il eut pour Sarah Bernhardt une admiration éternelle, une amitié qui dura jusqu'à *l'Aiglon,* et un amour physique de 24 heures qui amena chez lui une triste réaction: huit jours de vomissements incoercibles."[28] Another friend of Proust's who was intimate with Sarah Bernhardt (apparently with less violent results) was Reynaldo Hahn, of whom Proust wrote to the Comtesse de Noailles in 1901:

. . . J'ai reçu de Bruxelles (où il est avec Sarah Bernhardt) (*confidentiel*) une lettre de Reynaldo Hahn. . . . Il a emporté avec lui le *Coeur innombrable* dont il est fou, et l'a lu à Sarah. Elle en a été enthousiasmée, vous trouve le plus grand des poètes, un grand génie, etc., et a aussitôt appris l'*Offrande à Pan* et la récitera jeudi chez M. de Montesquiou.[29]

This reading took place on May 30, at Montesquiou's Pavillon de Muses, as he called his house, with Proust's mother in the audience.[30] Derrick Leon describes Montesquiou as "surrounding himself with famous poets, actresses and professional beauties; the friend of Bernhardt, Duse, Rostand," and adds that "his poems were recited frequently by Sarah Bernhardt

11

at the exclusive receptions of the Duchesse de Rohan." [31] Clearly, Proust would have had more than public knowledge of Bernhardt of which to avail himself in the creation of Berma.

Of two of Montesquiou's evenings which Proust attended, we have some idea. Of one, Derrick Leon tells us: "The evening was a memorable one. Sarah Bernhardt recited for the first time *Le Coucher de la Mort*; and later, with Bartet and Reichenberg, as a trio, Chénier's *Ode to Versailles*." [32] One of Proust's early letters to Montesquiou includes the acknowledgment, "Vous avez bien voulu me permettre d'aller vous voir le soir où Mlle Bartet a récité vos vers chez Mme Lemaire." [33] Even had Proust never set foot in a theater, which is far from being the case, his social life would have given him an unusual knowledge of its people, and drawing-room productions some acquaintance with its workings.

Proust had been more directly involved in drawing-room theater in several capacities. Painter gives an account of Proust as an unsuccessful prompter, and of his being asked to act. His prompting was less than useful, since he was so pleased with the costumes and his friends' abilities that instead of lines, he fed them laughter and bravos. He refused the role of Pierrot in Gaston de Caillavet's *Colombine*, although (or perhaps, because) he was told, "You're just right for the part, you're so pale and your eyes are so big!" [34] To the same file that contains the play that Proust never wrote, one must regretfully consign the thought of the role Proust never acted.

Proust's most direct involvement in drawing-room theater, when he was made a character in the dramatic action, was even less fortunate. Robert Dreyfus gives a rather complete account of the affair, including the lines that offended Proust:

Enfin Marcel Proust poursuivit au loin une sorte de carrière aérienne, offrait aux salons *les Plaisirs et les Jours*. . . . Que de "scènes de revue" tentèrent notre imagination!

La revue s'intitula *les Lauriers sont coupés*. . . . Le hasard d'une scène évoquant les débuts littéraires de Marcel Proust pourrait seul sauver d'un oubli total ce divertissement éphémère.

Mais à quoi bon l'analyser, cette scène? Elle fit de la peine à Marcel Proust, voilà ce qu'il suffit de retenir. En vérité, notre pastiche de son langage et de sa politesse dans le monde, nos plaisanteries sur son "snobisme" ou sur le prix inabordable de son livre, tout cela était fort anodin. . . . Mieux armé que personne au monde pour faire rire d'autrui s'il avait voulu, Marcel Proust ne cédait qu'à regret à ce penchant condamnable. . . .

Il avait trop de dignité pour faire entendre aucune plainte, mais il s'abstint d'assister au spectacle du *Chat-Bourbon*.[35]

Dreyfus presents part of the scene in a footnote:

PROUST, *s'addressant à Ernest La Jeunesse*. —Est-ce que vous l'avez lu, mon livre?

LA JEUNESSE. —Non, Monsieur, il est trop cher.

PROUST. —Hélas! c'est ce que tout le monde me dit ... Et toi, Gregh, tu l'as lu?

GREGH. —Oui, je l'ai découpé, pour en rendre compte.

PROUST. —Et toi aussi, tu as trouvé que c'était trop cher?

GREGH. —Mais non, mais non, on en avait pour son argent.

PROUST. —N'est-ce pas! ... Une préface de Monsieur France, 4 francs ... Des tableaux de Madame Lemaire, 4 francs ... De la musique de Reynaldo Hahn, 4 francs ... De la prose de moi, un franc ... Quelques vers de moi, cinquante centimes ... Total treize francs cinquante, ça n'était pas exagéré?

LA JEUNESSE. —Mais, Monsieur, il y a bien plus de choses que ça dans l'*Almanach Hachette*, et ça ne coûte que vingt-cinq sous!

13

PROUST, *éclatant de rire.* —Ah! que c'est drôle! ... Oh! que ça me fait mal de rire comme ça!

Dreyfus concludes, "Ces 'blagues' peuvent paraître un peu grosse, mais leur gaieté était sans fiel." [36] The gaiety escaped Proust. As Derrick Leon reports, "He was rather more pained than indignant. Apparently it never occurred to him to be amused. . . . 'I don't understand it,' he remarked, with sad bewilderment. 'I simply don't understand it.'" [37]

As well as providing this example of the theatrical activities of one group of Proust's contemporaries, Dreyfus presents an account of Charles Haas (one of the originals of Swann) involved in amateur theatricals. Proust wrote, "Ta revue jouée par Haas à Mouchy m'a tiré des larmes," a remark for which Dreyfus offers the following explanation:

Or, voici que, dans ma *Petite Histoire de la Revue de fin d'anneé,* j'avais nommé les interprètes [Haas among them] d'une revue de M. de Massa—*les Cascades de Mouchy*—jouée au château de Mouchy, le 19 décembre 1863. . . .
   Swann au château de Mouchy! Swann acteur mondain! Swann jouant dans une revue de salon, avec les membres du Cercle de la rue Royale peints auprès de lui par Tissot!
   Pour tout bon lecteur de *Swann,* la petite phrase de cette lettre de Marcel Proust . . . devient évocatrice comme une autre "petite phrase" de Vinteuil.[38]

The thread of drawing-room theater runs from Swann-Haas before Proust was born, through Proust's own life, into the society, characterization, plot, and metaphors of his own life's work.

Many of Proust's friends and acquaintances worked in various areas of theater. Gaston de Caillavet was his friend before he was a playwright, and when his *Lys rouge* was produced, Proust, having seen it, sent him a congratulatory telegram,[39] and, according to Derrick Leon, "was among the small party of friends who gathered to celebrate the occasion." [40] Another playwright whom he knew well, Paul Hervieu, he took to the second night of *Le Sieur de Vergy*, by Caillavet and Flers, "where in his enthusiasm at his old friends' success he 'narrowly missed blacking Hervieu's eye three times over with my clapping hands.'" [41] "The name Doncières," we are told, "comes from a character in *Connais-toi*, a play by Paul Hervieu, whom Proust knew well, produced at the Comédie Française in 1909." [42] Of Reynaldo Hahn, Proust wrote to Mme Straus, "Il est venu une fois ou deux auprès de mon lit, composer la musique de son ballet pour l'Opéra. . . . " [43] The ballet was *Le Dieu bleu*, composed for Diaghileff, whom Proust also knew.

When Proust was forced to move in 1919, Jacques Porel arranged for Proust to rent a furnished apartment in the house of his mother, the celebrated actress Réjane. Porel apparently felt that Proust knew his mother well enough to be asked to write a memorial piece after her death, but Proust declined because of his health.[44] Besides Bernhardt and Réjane, Proust was well acquainted with a third and younger actress, Louisa de Mornand.

"We know, too," Derrick Leon writes, "that . . . Robert's affair with Rachel was based on the liaison of one of [Proust's] friends with Louisa de Mornand." [45] But Robert Vigneron asserts a less remote liaison in a discussion of Proust's mother:

She had favored his affair with Louisa de Mornand, the young actress from the Vaudeville, who sometimes came to see him late at night, after the theatre: when she knew in advance of such a visit, Mme Proust obligingly retired early, in order to leave in complete freedom these two young people whom she could not help believing to be lovers. Perhaps she hoped that normal love affairs would succeed in curing Marcel of the sordid aberrations that she suspected; but, aside from a few spicy interludes, it seems that Marcel did not make of Louisa, who had a real protector anyway, anything more than a sort of *fausse maîtresse* designed to ward off any overt suspicion of his less orthodox amusements.[46]

Proust's brother, ignoring this aspect of her life, asserts that Louisa's theater career provided the basis for Rachel's career in the theater:

On voit Marcel s'intéresser à l'évolution du talent artistique de Louisa de Mornand. . . . Il y a quelque chose d'analogue, quoique bien entendu je ne veuille susciter aucune comparaison ni aucune recherche de clef (puisque j'ai dit qu'il n'y en avait pas), à la façon dont a progressé le talent de *Rachel* depuis ses premiers essais incompris jusqu'à l'affirmation définitive de son talent, ceci bien entendu si on dissèque le personnage de *Rachel* et qu'on n'en considère que le côté artistique.[47]

In the preface to the Mornand letters in the same volume, Fernand Nozière gives an account of Louisa de Mornand, with a slightly different reaction from Leon's or Robert Proust's:

Marcel Proust était un ami de sa famille et, comme Mlle de Mornand voulait être comédienne, il la présenta à Henry Bataille. Ainsi les premiers pas de la petite actrice unissent le dramaturge audacieux et pathétique au romancier qui ne fut ni moins pathétique ni moins audacieux. . . .
Ainsi Mlle Louisa de Mornand entra au Vaudeville. . . .
Ces comédiennes du Vaudeville auraient dû fournir à Marcel Proust des sujets, des caractères d'un modernisme aigu. . . . Je ne crois pas qu'il soit possible de trouver dans son œuvre un croquis de femme qui ressemble nettement à Louisa de Mornand. C'est pourtant un type qui aurait du l'intéresser. . . . Mais la banalité de l'existence les sépara.[48]

16

They may have become separated, but not before an acquaint-anceship of some duration, during which she had appeared in several plays, "would sometimes look in, after the theatre, to say good night," [49] and Proust had written her a number of letters that show him to have been *au courant* with her theater career and to have seen her act several times.

In several of his letters, he asks for news of her progress and pays her compliments: "Dites-moi aussi si Mlle de Mornand a été dans *Maman Colibri* une aussi exquise 'Louisa' qu'elle l'est dans la vie réele et si le public a paru être de l'avis de ses amis." [50] He also reports compliments which he has heard: "On m'a dit que vous étiez radieuse de beauté dans la pièce de Prévost." [51] He sends messages to the theater by his friends and offers good wishes for her success. He several times tries to arrange meetings, either after or at the theater. [52] Their relationship may have been as brief as Nozière suggests, but the tone of Proust's letters shows that he knew well what remarks would please and encourage a young actress.

Proust also took an active part, if a minor one, in further-ing her career by getting "puffs" on her behalf into various publications: "Il paraît que je vais peut-être pouvoir faire passer au *Gil Blas* quelques mots sur vous, j'en suis content." "Dites-moi le nom de la pièce où vous allez jouer et les noms des journaux où vous désirez une mention aimable." "J'ai fait le 'médaillon' Louisa de Mornand pour le *Gil Blas*. Je ne sais quel jour il paraîtra." [53] At least once, she was able to do a theatrical favor for him, and she received a charming acknowledgment:

Grâce à vous la jeune personne est placée! . . . Cette action va avoir un grand retentissement dans le monde des théâtres et dans le monde où Mlle N... comptait des protectrices. A l'heure qu'il est, Sarah Bernhardt, Mme le Bardy, Mme Georges Menier

17

doivent se dire: "Quelle puissance, quelle grâce, quelle charité a cette exquise Mlle de Mornand!" [54]

The plays mentioned in all of this correspondence being of the first decade of the century, it is evident that Proust's interest in and knowledge of the theater continued to be direct and personal at least into his thirties.

In his youth, attendance at the theater was evidently one of Proust's frequent and favorite pastimes, shared with the circle of his friends. There were "visits to the opera and the theatre with Jacques Bizet and Jacques Baignères," [55] and "Lucien Daudet would fetch him from the Institut and take him off to spend a few hours at the Louvre, or to a matinée of classical drama at the Comédie Française." [56] Daudet wrote of these latter occasions, "D'autres jours, nous allions au théâtre, voir une pièce dont je le prévenais d'avance 'que je la détesterais,' quelque Classique au Théâtre Français. (Je me souviens, entre autres, d'une matinée de l'*Avare*. Peut-être, sans lui, je n'aurais jamais compris Molière.)" [57]

In several Proust letters of this period (1889-1901), there are references to visits to the theater. His mother wrote to him when he was away on vacation, "Malgré ta lettre reçue ce matin . . . où tu me parles retour et *Tosca* je me berce de l'espoir que . . . tu pourras prolonger." [58] In an itemization of his expenses, Proust explained to his mother, "Places de théâtre signifie *Tour du Monde* et *Guillaume Tell* je pense que je t'ai parlé de cela." [59] Several of Proust's letters to Montesquiou, written from the Boulevard Malesherbes, where Proust lived from 1893 to 1900, allude to attendance at plays or other theatrical performances. In three letters, he inquires about arrangements for seeing the Folies Bergères. [60] Twice he refers to theater engagements as reasons for not having met Montesquiou.[61] Even these few allusions to visits to the theater are significant, since Proust later gives the impression that he never went to the theater at all after the turn of the century, although additional allusions in the letters contradict this.

Georges de Lauris cites instances of Proust's attending the theater after 1907. He writes, referring to the time when Proust moved to the Boulevard Haussman, which was in 1907, "Il lui plaisait d'offrir une soirée au théâtre. Alors, il prenait magnifiquement loges ou baignoires. Le nombre des invités augmentait toujours." [62] Proust's arrangements for a theater party appear in a letter of 1909.[63] A letter of the following year suggests, although it does not prove, another occasion when Proust attended the theater: ". . . Je l'ai rencontré au Casino [Cabourg] où on jouait *Arsène Lupin*." [64]

That Proust could, and did, still attend the theater is shown by a remark in a 1910 letter: "J'ai été aux Ballets Russes, vous sans doute aussi, c'est bien joli n'est-ce pas?" [65] This was not a unique occasion; according to Derrick Leon, "When he was well enough to go out, he would sometimes accompany Mme Sheikevitch and Jean Cocteau to the Diaghileff ballet." [66] Despite the difficulties caused by his health, Proust attended the theater on at least four more occasions, two of them mentioned in his correspondence with Mme Straus. The first of these was the *Martyre de Saint Sébastien*, May 21, 1911.[67] The second of these occasions, the dress rehearsal of *Kismet*, December 17, 1912, suggested—as will be shown later—the basis for an important scene in *A la recherche*.[68] Although it is known that Proust attended the theater as late as 1920, there is evidence of only infrequent attendance during the ten years preceding his death. In 1914, he writes to Jacques Rivière, "Déplorable représentation des Ballets Russes hier soir!" [69]

Proust, in 1919, protested the limitations of his life, in a letter to Paul Souday, saying that he had not visited the Louvre for ten years, and had attended only one concert in that time.[70] As early as 1912, he wrote to Mme Straus, "Moi qui vais si rarement au théâtre, le hasard fait que j'ai connu dans une loge une de vos amies, . . . Mme Standish." [71] But two letters to Mme Straus in 1912-13 show him as still seriously considering the possibility of accepting her invitations to a theater party:

Que vous avez été gentille de m'inviter pour la centième de *"La Gifle"*. . . . Je ne suis pas venu pour beaucoup de raisons, dont l'une est que si cela m'amuse infiniment d'aller au théâtre avec vous, c'est parce que c'est avec vous et pas du tout parce que c'est au théâtre. Je veux dire que si c'était au théâtre sans vous, cela m'ennuierait.[72]

Despite the boredom with theater registered here, which is also reflected in the handling of theater material in *A la recherche*, Proust in a later letter honestly seems to regret being unable to see certain productions. In 1917, he wrote to Walter Berry, "Je vous envie beaucoup d'avoir été à *Cléopâtre*. Ces spectacles de Gémie sont la seule chose que j'aie eu envie de voir au théâtre depuis bien des années." [73] And in 1920 he managed to go to the theater at least twice.

In a footnote to a letter from Proust to Jacques Rivière in July, 1920, mentioning Gide's translation of Shakespeare's *Antony and Cleopatra*, Philip Kolb writes, "On avait donné, le 14 juin 1920, la répétition générale de la pièce à l'Opéra. . . . Proust assista à cette représentation de gala dans la loge de la princesse Soutzo; il apprit pendant l'entr'acte, la mort de

Réjane." [74] The daily press treated Gide's play so badly that it made of Régis Gignoux, who reviewed it unfavorably in the *Figaro*, what Proust called "un véritable ennemi personnel, un démolisseur de beauté." [75] In the year of his death, he was equally distressed at the reception of Gide's *Saul*. [76] Proust, in a letter to Mme Straus, dated April 20, 1920, describes his distress at an opera gala:

. . . Je suis allé à cause des heures tardives, à l'absurde soirée de gala à l'Opéra où j'étais invité. Quelle tristesse d'y apprendre—si le renseignement est exact—que Bakst qui a fait cette géniale Schéhérazade . . . serait enfermé et pour une maladie qui ne peut durer que quelques années (paralysie générale). On ne donnait pas de beaucoup meilleures nouvelles de Nijinski qui fut le bondissant créateur de ces ballets russes. . . . Le spectacle de l'Opéra était affreux . . . Schéhérazade même défigurée, ce qui, si l'état de Bakst est vrai, est, devant son impuissance à défendre son œuvre un terrible sacrilège. [77]

Thus we have Proust within two years of his death, despite the seclusion imposed upon him by his health, still able on occasion to attend the theater, and still very much—and personally—interested in the various creators of the ballet.

The idea of a real connection between Proust and the theater is far less improbable than visions of the cork-lined room make it first appear, and his knowledge of theater and drama, like all other aspects of his life, plays its part in *A la recherche*. And like the other aspects, it is transformed to artistic ends and becomes another instrument of his literary purposes.

Drama and Theater Allusions in "A la recherche du temps perdu"

A DETAILED CONSIDERATION of Proust's extensive use of theatrical and dramatic allusions in *A la recherche du temps perdu* opens up two main questions: Why does Proust make such allusions and so many of them, and what can his readers gain by attending to them? Although Jacques Nathan in his *Citations, références et allusions de Proust*[1] raises both questions about Proust's allusions in all fields, he gives most emphasis to the first question.[2] As Nathan's introduction points out, Proust does not make citations by chance: ". . . Chaque cas révélait des préférences artistiques et aussi des tendances parfois profondes de son esprit et de son caractère, certaines particularités de ses conceptions littéraires, et jetaient même quelques lumières sur ses méthodes de création."[3] This opinion is borne out when one thoughtfully examines Proust's use of theater allusions.

While one might suppose that any novelist would wish to include references to events in real life merely to establish verisimilitude, Nathan shows biographical reasons why

Proust would have been especially likely to use this device:

> N'oublions pas d'autre part que Proust a été tourmenté très tôt par la crainte de ne pas pouvoir communiquer avec la réalité. . . . Cette crainte . . . devient une hantise quand la maladie, et la claustration qu'il s'impose, séparent graduellement Proust du monde extérieur. . . .
>
> Heureusement, pour retenir ce monde extérieur qui lui échappe, le reclus dispose d'une table de références fixe, accessible à ses lecteurs, constituée par les œuvres littéraires et les œuvres d'art.[4]

Whatever psychological need Proust may have had to make such allusions, for the reader they serve to attach the fiction to everyday life at numerous points, however seemingly insignificant. They are parts of the chain connecting fact to disguised or transposed fact, in turn connected to fiction. Proust's method may blur both the facts and the points of connection, but the accumulation of allusions maintains a relationship between historical chronology and Time Remembered.

One non-biographical explanation of the use of allusions, as Nathan points out, is that since Proust wrote about a period when "everyone" was given to allusions, his characters other than the narrator also have the habit, and their allusions play a part in characterizing them.[5] The theatrical allusions function in this fashion in *A la recherche,* as they do to some extent in all Proust's fictions, and many facets of characterization, particularly satirical ones, are lost if the content of the allusions is missed. Not only are separate individual allusions not unplanned, but Proust seems to me to employ a consistent system in their application and their interrelationships, so that they cast light not only on individual points but upon one another.

A large number of the theatrical and dramatic allusions serve purposes indicated by Nathan: establishing verisimilitude or contact with reality, and characterizing their users, whether they be Marcel or other characters.[6] But many additional purposes are also served by these references. The limitations respected by Proust on his range of appropriate sources show the tastes of the narrator and the other characters, thereby contributing to the sense of the milieu. This might be described as verisimilitude carried a step further, since it involves fidelity to both actuality and characterization. Some allusions provide recognizable points of chronological reference. Some, and these may be accidental, enable the reader to see through the fictional disguise. If this is not accidental, then it is a special device of verisimilitude: if we are allowed to suspect that one character is "really" Sarah Bernhardt, then we may begin to assume that Saint-Loup's Rachel has an equally "real" existence.

In combination, certain of the allusions begin to establish a particular tone without ever stating it. If a number of characters from different levels of society are allowed to make the same or similar allusions, some social distinctions begin to disappear. The constant equation of social attitudes and behavior with theatrical expression has a cumulative effect of making society seem theatrical (sometimes in the pejorative sense) and, with Proust's stress on Molière, comic. This effect is sometimes intensified by those ironic comparisons in which things or persons theatrical are made to seem superior to the people discussing them, or to the situation to which they refer. When theatrical references provide the basis for a concatenation of metaphors and comparisons, all or most of the members of the series come to be thought of as theatrical. When the metaphors and comparisons continually make the subjects of comparison inferior to the theater material, or make the subjects "theatrical," the references become the vehicle for an enormous and inclusive metaphor, eventually to be subsumed under the great final *coup de théâtre* scene near the end of the novel. Marcel's allusions to drama and theater may in the first instance appear "naturally" in the milieu, but Proust has as usual made the natural serve his artistic ends.

Although Nathan suggests that Proust's allusions are a guide to his artistic preferences, the limitation of Marcel's references creates only a partial index of Proust's own tastes and interests. Since many of the allusions are to provide reference points for verisimilitude and chronology, to show the connections between real and fictional life, Proust is doubly limited—by the tastes of his characters and by the presumed knowledge of his readers. He is not, after all, writing a novel about the theater or to express his views on matters theatrical, but presenting views of his characters, including the narrator, in terms of the theater. Allusions in the dialogue must rest, if their value as characterization is to be clear, on standards which the author can assume that his readers will understand and, presumably, accept. Marcel's own metaphors must also characterize the narrator by employing references to theaters, actors, and plays that are immediately recognizable to the reader. It is therefore not surprising that the theaters named are either the state or smart theaters, the actors and actresses largely those of the Comédie, the plays and playwrights usually classical and neoclassical, the characters from Molière, Shakespeare, and the Greeks far more often than from contemporary plays.

Proust's omissions are almost as interesting as his inclusions. For instance, although he mentions a number of theaters by name, he makes only a single passing reference, in a metaphor, to Antoine's Théâtre Libre, and the reference is a slighting one: "Elle disait cela parce qu'elle trouvait que c'était curieusement théâtre libre, et aussi que c'était joliment commode."[7] There is no direct mention of Antoine himself, one of the most significant experimenters of the time, nor any note of the theater in which he introduced the plays of Ibsen, Hauptman, Strindberg, and other naturalists, and led the way to realism in acting and scene design. Proust shows no interest in whatever would have been the Parisian equivalent of "off-Broadway" theater, confining himself in his allusions almost exclusively to the subsidized theaters and the fashionable boulevard theaters.

In the whole novel, only one thread, and that a tiny and almost concealed one, leads even remotely to Antoine. It appears when Saniette admits that he has been to a matinee of the *Chercheuse* at the Odéon, and the company is amused to realize that he means Favart's *Chercheuse d'esprit*, leading Brichot to observe: "Mais, soit dit sans manquer de respect aux mânes du gentil Favart, il n'était pas de tempérament ibsénien. . . . D'ailleurs, la satrapie de Porel étant maintenant occupée par un fonctionnaire qui est un tolstoïsant de rigoureuse observance, il se pourrait que nous vissions *Anna Karénine* ou *Résurrection* sous l'architrave odéonienne" (*Sodome et Gomorrhe*; II, 935). The reference to the "functionary" would seem to be to Antoine, although the chronology is somewhat shaky. Porel, husband of the celebrated Réjane, was director of the Odéon from 1884 to 1891. Antoine, who had worked at the Odéon, established the Théâtre Antoine in 1897, and was not to become director of the Odéon until 1906. *Résurrection* was produced at the Odéon—but in 1902 when neither Porel nor Antoine was director—and *Anna Karénine* in 1907, but at the Théâtre Antoine. Despite the muddiness of the chronology and the prophecy by Brichot, the presentation of the conservative attitude toward Antoine's experiments is evident. Brichot, of course, is not presented as an example of critical acumen or perceptiveness, but this passage of mild satire of a man unnamed constitutes Proust's only recognition of Antoine, and a passing metaphor his only acknowledgment of the Théâtre Libre.

Proust's admiration for Ibsen's work seems to have been less than burning, although Ibsen was admired in one of the salons to which he had entree, that of Mme Aubernon, who presented at her house the first Paris performances of *A Doll's House* and *John Gabriel Borkman*. The reasons Proust was less interested in Ibsen than was Mme Aubernon are credibly presented by Jacques Nathan. He first indicates that Ibsen was not generally well received by French audiences, who preferred easy pleasure to puzzlement with Ibsen's symbolism, and were bored with thesis plays after the abuses of Dumas fils and his successors.[8] Turning to Proust in particular, for whom Ibsen's "philosophy" would have little appeal, Nathan adds:

Signalons enfin deux faits significatifs: 1, Proust n'a jamais parlé d'Ibsen. Il a cependant publié dans la *Revue blanche* le 15 juillett 1896 un article intitulé "Contre l'obscurité," où il prend parti au nom de la clarté contre le symbolisme. Il aurait été particulièrement indiqué, surtout à cette date, de mentionner Ibsen, qui passait encore pour très obscur, et dont les symbolistes se réclamaient. Il n'en a rien fait. 2, Proust s'est montré extrêmement ironique tout au long de son livre pour les pièces et les romans à thèse.[9]

Marcel includes Ibsen and other dramatists in an illustrative list to show his opinion of the journalistic mind: "Chaque fois que se produit un événement accessible à la vulgarité d'esprit du journaliste philosophe, c'est-à-dire généralement un événement politique, les journalistes philosophes sont persuadés qu'il y a quelque chose de changé en France, qu'on ne reverra plus de telles soirées, qu'on n'admirera plus Ibsen, Renan, Dostoïewsky, Annunzio, Tolstoï, Wagner, Strauss" (III, 264–65).

Ibsen again turns up in company when Charlus accuses Marcel of taking part with Robert de Saint-Loup in an orgy, and Marcel reflects, "J'aurais voulu répondre qu'au déjeuner avilissant on n'avait parlé que d'Emerson, d'Ibsen, de Tolstoï" (II, 278). Three of the same names, including Ibsen's, appear in a list of Bergotte's dislikes: "Il détestait Tolstoï, George Eliot, Ibsen et Dostoïewski" (I, 556). These references to Ibsen, along with one mention of his name in a metaphor— and that concerned with the difficulties of a theatrical reporter's describing one of his plays, (III, 364)—the offer of Ibsen manuscripts to the Duchesse de Guermantes, and a passing remark at the Verdurins' are Proust's only notice in the novel of the Norwegian dramatist. He is consigned to an obscurity only somewhat less complete than that of Antoine, who was most closely associated with the early presentation of Ibsen's work in Paris. The beginnings of modern realistic drama in France are no important part of Marcel's milieu or cause for his admiration, which was reserved for the conservative and classical—and the uncontroversial.

Whatever Proust's tastes, he seldom lets the force of his metaphorical allusions depend on them. The vehicles of Marcel's metaphors are either easily recognizable or clearly explained. Particular performances mentioned are well-known performances, like a contemporary Gielgud Hamlet, or Anderson's Medea. "Et tous deux," Marcel reports, "cherchaient à reproduire la manière dont M. de Norpois avait dit cette phrase, comme ils auraient fait pour quelque intonation de Bressant ou de Thiron dans *l'Aventurière* ou dans *le Gendre de M. Poirier*" (I, 483). Similarly, in describing the resemblance between Saint-Loup and Charlus, Marcel says that it is "comme un acteur que reprend le rôle joué jadis par Bressant ou Delaunay" (III, 761). A foreign actor mentioned is one who is internationally known, and he is bracketed with a French actor who specialized in melodrama and never appeared at the Comédie. The comparison is applied, not to one of the aristocrats, but to Françoise: "Elle excellait à régler ces mises en scène destinées à instruire si bien le spectateur. . . . Elle avait, pour faire parler ainsi un objet inanimé, l'art à la fois génial et patient d'Irving et de Frédérick Lemaître" (II, 360). When the only other foreign actor is mentioned, one who had played in Paris early in the century, the allusion is carefully explained: " . . . Plus même qu'à l'art de l'acteur, c'était à celui de certains prodigieux mimes, dont Fregoli reste le type, que faisaient penser ces fabuleuses transformations" (III, 947).

In his metaphorical allusions to playwrights, Proust cites only four who were his own contemporaries, and one of these, Wilde, is chosen because of his actual, not his artistic life. More directly using drama as its vehicle is a comparison made by Swann on the introduction of contemporary figures into biblical paintings: "Il n'y avait pas selon Swann, dans ces cortèges, un seul Parisien de marque qui manquât, comme dans cet acte d'une pièce de Sardou où, par amitié pour l'auteur et la principale interprète, par mode aussi, toutes les notabilités parisiennes, de célèbres médecins, des hommes politiques, des avocats, vinrent pour s'amuser, chacun un soir, figurer sur la scène" (I, 535). Edward VII, when he was Prince of Wales, was one of the notables who assisted Sarah Bernhardt in *Fedora*. "During one scene," we are told, "the actress had to weep by the bedside of a murdered prince. A number of Parisians amused themselves by playing for one night this mute and invisible part, and the Prince delighted French society by taking his turn at filling the role."[10] Two metaphors about French playwrights would work almost as well without mention of their names, or with other names substituted. Their effect depends not on the dramatists cited, but on the equation of social behavior with theatrical. Marcel writes of actual royalty "comme les reines dans Sardou" (II, 426), and later observes M. d'Argencourt "dans son incarnation de moribond-bouffe d'un Regnard exagéré par Labiche" (III, 922). Marcel uses ten metaphors involving names or indications of Greek or French classical playwrights, Molière's name appearing six times. These metaphors are all comparatively brief, establishing a kind of one-for-one shorthand relationship. Françoise "avait pour les liens invisibles que noue entre les membres d'une famille la circulation d'un même sang, autant de respect qu'un tragique grec" (I, 53). Shakespeare is also called upon for metaphorical aid: Women in love with inverts are doomed to the "même désappointement que celles qui, dans les comédies de Shakespeare, sont deçues par une jeune fille déguisée qui se fait passer pour un adolescent" (II, 621).

The names of characters in plays, with the exceptions of the mention of Phèdre as a Berma role and the names which appear in direct quotations, appear most frequently in Marcel's metaphors. Molière's characters are the most often named, followed by those of Shakespeare and the Greek dramatists. Their immediate recognizability is obvious, as is that of characters from Goethe, Racine, Hugo, Voltaire, and one from Sardou. The last is the only character from a contemporary play among the metaphors, and is in any event recognizable as historical. Most of Marcel's metaphors referring to characters are brief, for once he has made the identification, he has also made his point, as when "quelques sporades de la bande zoophytique des jeunes filles" appear "tout d'un coup, tel Méphistophélès surgissant devant Faust" (I, 855). In the theater-aquarium description, the princess is turbanned "comme quelque merveilleuse tragédienne costumée en Zaïre ou peut-être en Orosmane" (II, 44). The "nez rebelle" of a Jew "fait penser au nez de Mascarille plutôt qu'à celui de Salomon" (II, 190), making the "rebellious nose" more like the famous nose in *Les Précieuses ridicules* than like a racial characteristic. In a slightly longer metaphor, "on eût pu croire que le baron cherchait à découvrir l'énigme du Sphinx, si ce n'avait pas été plutôt celle d'un jeune et vivant Œdipe" (II, 689). The invert is "obligé, comme Harpagon, de veiller sur son trésor et se relève la nuit pour voir si on ne le lui prend pas" (II, 921). A reference presumably to a Sardou creation for Bernhardt in 1884 is mentioned when Gilberte's appearance has so changed that Marcel remarks, " . . . Je restai stupéfait comme si j'avais eu devant moi une actrice, une espèce de Théodora" (III, 702). Even if the reference is to the early career of the historical Theodora, the famous Sardou role helps clarify the import of the metaphor. The aged Charlus is briefly compared to King Lear, once for Shakespearian majesty (III, 859), once for affability (III, 922). His downfall is likened to that of Oedipus (III, 860). Bloch's

32

anxious face is described as that of an old Shylock (III, 967). These brief metaphorical references almost become epithets identifying Proust's characters, rather than means of comparison.

Some metaphors based on characters are developed at greater length, not because the dramatic characters are less familiar, but rather because Marcel wishes to particularize somewhat more clearly the terms of his reference. The comparison, for example, between the hotel page-boys and a classical chorus is not a matter of character, but of stage behavior: they are always on duty in the lobby, during and between the greater actions (I, 706). Similarly, a comparison of Charlus and Jupien with Romeo and Juliet hardly establishes a "one for one" relationship: "La haine des Capulet et des Montaigu n'était rien auprès des empêchements de tout genre qui ont été vaincus . . . avant qu'un ancien giletier, qui comptait partir sagement pour son bureau, titube, ébloui, devant un quinquagénaire bedonnant; ce Roméo et cette Juliette peuvent croire à bon droit que leur amour n'est pas le caprice d'un instant, mais une véritable prédestination" (II, 627).

Of the almost twenty play titles in metaphorical observations, only one is to a play written during Proust's lifetime, while at least a dozen are to classics, French and Shakespearian. Vegetables play parts "dans leur farces poétiques et grossières comme une féerie de Shakespeare" (I, 121); disappointing dinner guests give "l'impression de plate vulgarité que peut donner l'entrée dans le port danois d'Elseneur à tout lecteur enfiévré d'*Hamlet*" (II, 532); the attitude of a businessman to a writer would be contemptuous "si votre divertissement était d'écrire *Hamlet* ou seulement de le lire"

(II, 1036). Another metaphorical pairing of plays is used to clarify a change in the Baron's illness: "Une rechute le faisait taire. Cette chrétienne douceur, où s'était transposée sa magnfique violence (comme en *Esther* le génie, si différent, d'*Andromaque*), faisait l'admiration de ceux qui l'entouraient" (III, 323). In almost all of Marcel's metaphors, his character and the recognizability of the references, rather than Proust's tastes, control Proust's choices.

Since attendance at the theater is a natural and frequent part of the lives of Proust's characters, a fair portion of the characterization is based upon their reactions to this part of their milieu, which is, of course, Proust's milieu. His characters do at least three things that characters in our contemporary novels seldom seem to do: they go to the theater, they read books, and they occasionally tell jokes. This is true of his fiction from the short stories in *Les Plaisirs et les jours* through *Jean Santeuil* to *A la recherche*. Were it not for the much greater use which Proust makes of theater occasions in *A la recherche*, the instances in *Les Plaisirs* might hardly be worth noticing, but they do show the seeds of later developments. In "La Mort de Baldassare Silvande," Alexis' moribund uncle still promises visits to the theater.[11] Attendance at the theater is equated with Baldassare's love of life: "Maintenant il ne douta plus . . . que dans la gaieté du malade, dans son désir d'aller au théâtre, il n'entrait ni dissimulation ni courage, et qu'arrivé si près de la mort, Baldassare continuait à ne penser qu'à la vie" (p. 25). To a young man of fashion is directed the question, "Pourquoi vous voit-on chaque soir, Olivian, vous rendre à la Comédie?" (p. 91). Of a woman of fashion we are told, "Elle lança des comédies, des parfums et des robes" (p. 59). An attractive young duchess is described as "cette puissante amante de la vie sous toutes ses formes, bonté, littérature, théâtre, action, amitié," and Proust adds, "Combien des fois, dans la rue, au théâtre, des passants songeurs avaient allumé leur rêve à ces astres [ses yeux] changeants! Maintenant la duchesse . . . se souvenait d'un vaudeville ou combinait une toilette . . . " (pp. 166–67).

Theatergoing is a regular part of Jean Santeuil's life, a product of the same opportunity for leisure which allows him to be an habitué of salons. The pastime was apparently not without its perils: "Ayant été publiquement insulté au théâtre par un monsieur, Jean résolut de lui envoyer deux témoins." [12] He continues to have "parties de théâtre" (III, 272) for his mistress (p. 173). Theatergoing is not merely a special taste of Jean's, but an activity of many of the other characters. M. Sandré, Jean's grandfather, remembers, "Oui, j'ai encore vu Mme Récamier, c'était au théâtre, elle était avec Chateaubriand, l'Empereur était dans la salle, en 1806, voilà soixante ans de cela" (I, 79). As a bit of gossip about another man, it is reported, "Pas une fois dans la suite il ne lui [sa femme] permet d'aller au théâtre . . . " (p. 110). Drawing-room comedy, in the literal sense of plays in salons, is also a part of the milieu, as it was of Proust's. One father encourages his son's theatergoing, with drastic, if irrelevant, results. We are told that Edouard Marie, "dans la vingt-cinquième année de sa vie étant sorti un soir du théâtre," caught cold, and died (II, 90). Despite the perils of duels and disease, casual invitations are still issued. It is precisely the fact that theatergoing is so ordinary a part of his and his characters' milieu which makes possible Proust's unobtrusive use of it.

The theaters which Proust names as part of the milieu of *A la recherche* are, as has been indicated, naturally either the state theaters or the smart theaters.[13] One of the earliest clusters of theater allusions in *A la recherche* is the description of the playbills which seemed so mysterious to the young Marcel: "Si ce n'est une des œuvres étranges comme *le Testament de César Girodot* et *Œdipe-Roi* lesquelles s'inscrivaient, non sur l'affiche verte de l'Opéra-Comique, mais sur l'affiche lie de vin de la Comédie-Française, rien ne me paraissait plus différent de l'aigrette étincelante et blanche des *Diamants de la Couronne* que le satin lisse et mysterieux du *Domino Noir* . . ." (I, 73). Swann's unexpected connection with "distinguished" friends is revealed to the Verdurins when he offers to get Mme Verdurin a permit that will admit her to the Opéra without having to wait in the crowds; this he promises "pour la reprise des *Danicheff*" (I, 216). M. de Guermantes, in the green room of the Comédie Française, invites Reichenberg to recite before the King of England (II, 430), and Mme Verdurin adopts the tone of a marquise in the Théâtre Français (II, 912). Odette defines the Eden Théâtre as one of the smart places, and a young girl looks forward to the time when she will be old enough to be allowed to go to the Palais Royal (I, 909). That her attitude was typical can be shown from a description published in 1880: "Its plays were the most risky, not to say reckless, in Paris. From the careful manner in which the morals of French girls are guarded, this theater has all the flavor of forbidden fruit. . . . It is said that the first favor a young Parisian bride asks from her husband is to take her to the Palais-Royal Theatre."[14]

Two theaters are mentioned to establish the kind of atmosphere which is associated with the Empire promenade in London: Saint-Loup's friends seek to alarm him by suggesting that his mistress would be in the promenade at the Folies Bergères (II, 282); and when Marcel fears that Albertine may be renewing her old ways, his jealousy is bound up in her visits to the Trocadéro, where Léa is acting (III, 144, 462 ff.). In all these references, the theaters which Proust has Marcel name are those which would be most familiar to the characters in his milieu. They are given for verisimilitude; the reader's knowledge is taken for granted. The only detailed description of a theater—or of an audience in a theater—is the well-known theater-aquarium passage (in which members of the audience are likened to exotic fish) that occurs in the novel on a gala night when Berma appears in one act of *Phèdre* at the Opéra Comique.

In his allusions to actors and actresses, Proust is again most loyal to the Comédie Française. Half the actors mentioned were associated with the Comédie, and several of the others are named explicitly to show their inferiority; the same is true of the actresses. When Marcel as a schoolboy discusses his own hierarchy of actors, like an American boy classifying baseball players, all the names he mentions—Coquelin, Delaunay, Febvre, Got, Maubant, Thiron—are of Comédie Française actors (I, 74). Jacques Nathan points out that these are actors of whom Proust would have known only by hearsay.[15] The rankings which he assigns them are not significant, for it is precisely Marcel's point that they constantly shift. Marcel's hierarchy of actresses is also chosen entirely from the Comédie, with the addition of his own distinguished creation, Berma: "Je classais par ordre de talent les plus illustres: Sarah Bernhardt, la Berma, Bartet, Madeleine Brohan, Jeanne Samary, mais toutes m'intéressaient" (I, 75). Berma's distinction is thus made clear early in the novel by the company in which she is placed, but Proust shows a certain gallantry in placing her second only to her original.

Bernhardt is mentioned several more times in the novel, enough perhaps to maintain the polite pretense that Berma is not she. Charlus dismisses her *L'Aiglon*, like Mounet-Sully's *Œdipe*, as tripe (II, 1070), and Marcel mentions Sarah in *Phèdre* in a list of things which, like Venice, the Prado, and the Dresden gallery, he has not yet seen (II, 1084). Cottard speaks of her inanely (I, 201), and Charlus disapproves of one of her wartime statements (III, 825–26). If her appearances in the novel are less distinguished than those on the real stage, they nonetheless fulfil Proust's purposes of providing recognizable reference points and showing that the lives of his fictional characters impinge upon a familiar real life. With similar effect, Coquelin appears fleetingly in the novel: "Coquelin passait en discourant au milieu d'amis qui l'écoutaient et faisait avec la main, à des personnes en voiture, un large bonjour de théâtre" (I, 420); and twice is referred to as a person known by the characters. Bloch père observes, "Le gouvernement a été impardonnable. Il n'a pas consulté M. Coquelin! M. Coquelin a fait savoir qu'il était mécontent," to which Marcel adds the parenthetical remark, "M. Bloch se piquait d'être réactionnaire et méprisant pour les gens de théâtre" (I, 776). Marcel speculates on being seen with Mme Swann by the "mulâtre ami de Coquelin" (I, 536), and speaks of Coquelin the elder accepting small parts (II, 1084).

Six contemporary playwrights similarly appear as part of the milieu of the novel, providing verisimilitude. Three of them are claimed by Nissim Bernard as social lions: "Je me rappelle un diner chez moi, à Nice, où il y avait Sardou, Labiche, Augier" (I, 775). These three have obviously been

38

chosen as socially acceptable popular playwrights. Edmond Rostand is cited as certain to be one of Mme de Guermantes' guests (II, 213), and "l'auteur dramatique Grandmougin" is mentioned as one of her guests at the party for the King of England (II, 452). Hervieu, who was anti-Dreyfus, is mentioned by the Duchesse as being part of the plot (III, 235).

Scene designers are mentioned in the milieu, but largely, as the following passage shows, to provide a chronological reference point: "Elles étaient plutôt à la façon des décors de Sert, de Bakst et de Benoist, qui en ce moment évoquaient dans les ballets russes [which first visited Paris in 1909] les époques d'art les plus aimées" (III, 369). Bakst and Benoist[16] had been mentioned in an earlier passage, which gives Mme Verdurin an unexpected role:

. . . Quand, avec l'efflorescence prodigieuse des ballets russes, révélatrice coup sur coup de Bakst, de Nijinski, de Benoist, du génie de Strawinski, la princesse Yourbeletieff, jeune marraine de tous ces grands hommes nouveaux, apparut portant sur la tête un immense aigrette tremblants . . . on put croire que cette merveilleuse créature avait été apportée dans leurs innombrables bagages, et comme leur plus précieux trésor, par les danseurs russes; mais quand à côté d'elle, dans son avant-scène, nous verrons, à toutes les représentations des "Russes," siéger comme une véritable fée, ignorée jusqu'à ce jour de l'aristocratie, Mme Verdurin, nous pourrons répondre aux gens du monde qui croiront aisément Mme Verdurin fraîchement débarquée avec la troupe de Diaghilew, que cette dame avait déjà existé dans des temps différents. . . . (II, 743)

Here the suggestion of the passage of time is given along with one of time's effects, the progress of Mme Verdurin. Proust's theater allusions do not merely help to establish and clarify

39

the milieu of his characters: they also suggest the changes which time works on both milieu and characters.

Proust's most significant and most frequent use of theater allusions is to provide viable evidence for characterizing individuals, social groups, and society as a whole. Only once or twice in *Les Plaisirs* does Proust use theater material for specific characterization, as he later uses the views of the Duchesse on *Les Septs Princesses* to show her pretentiousness and her ignorance of Maeterlinck. In "Mondanité et Mélomanie," we are shown a similar lack of understanding on the part of Pécuchet:

Maeterlinck effraye, mais par des moyens matériels et indigne du théâtre; l'art émeut à la façon d'un crime, c'est horrible! D'ailleurs, sa syntaxe est misérable.
Ils en firent spirituellement la critique en parodiant dans la forme d'une conjugaison son dialogue: "J'ai dit que la femme était entrée. —Tu as dit que la femme était entrée. —Vous avez dit que la femme était entrée. —Pourquoi a-t-on dit que la femme était entrée? (p. 101)

Similar comments are used in *A la recherche* to characterize Charlus, the Duchesse, the Verdurin circle, Bloch, and others, but with far greater subtlety, and, as cannot be done in shorter pieces, great amounts of cross-referencing by Marcel and self-contradicting by the characters.

Theater, besides being a natural part of Jean Santeuil's milieu, also becomes in a modest way a standard by which characters and actions in the novel may be judged. (In *A la recherche*, Proust makes greater and more systematic use of this method, which here seems almost accidental and inorganic.) A nice piece of snobbism is registered in *Jean Santeuil*: "Il était des gens à qui on donne en échange d'un service rendu une place de théâtre parce qu'il est impossible de les inviter chez soi" (I, 251). Social conservatism is several times limned by attitudes to theater, as in this example: "Dans le monde qu'elles enferment commes les statues des dieux entouraient le foyer romain, la femme adultère n'entre jamais. . . . On n'y admettra pas le poète, est-il besoin de dire qu'on n'y admettra pas l'acteur. Le fils, s'il se faisait acteur, serait jeté par la fenêtre" (III, 326). In line with this latter attitude is the observation that "ce qui fait que la plus grande joie d'un acteur, qui en a connu pourtant de si vives, est d'être décoré comme un sous-chef de bureau . . . " (I, 251).

Minor theater actions are used to characterize women friends of Jean. The first is an example of Proust's observation of the way in which people unconsciously betray themselves by constant allusion which they believe to sound casual or disguised. (Charlus' conversation about inverts shows this most strikingly in *A la recherche*.) Here, the reference is to a girl involved with a Dutch tenor at the Opéra-Comique: "Et quand un ami venait la voir, elle parlait sans cesse de l'amour, de l'Opéra-Comique, de la Hollande et du chant . . . " (III, 168). The second passage is an anecdote which runs through several pages, but to not much greater point, involving the use of some theater tickets given to Jean's mother (III, 236–38). Except for characterization of snobbery, nothing more comes of this, and Proust seems content with the single point he has made. Another anecdote reads like a passage from *La Prisonnière,* with Jean checking up on a friend who evades an engagement by claiming that she is to go to the theater with her brother-in-law (III, 218–20).

Specific references to particular plays, actors, or dramatists are used in the same way, again with no notable system. Of an innkeeper's daughter we are told, " . . . On lui donne à lire *le Bourgeois gentilhomme*: elle ne comprend pas, mais on lui dit de continuer tout de même" (I, 48). Some consistency is determinable among the illusions attaching to Jean, which largely concern classical French drama. Jean's own reading, which is obviously Proust's, is indicated: " . . . Il s'efforçait sans cesse de relire *Phèdre*, *Cinna*, les *Fables* de la Fontaine. . . . Les images brillantes, le style enflammé du dernier des romantiques excitaient en lui une ardeur matinale qui, glacée par la lecture de *Britannicus* ou de *Cinna*, n'en était ensuite que plus passionément recherchée" (pp. 123–24).

Perrotin, who sounds like a candidate for the Verdurin circle, is characterized partly by his behavior in regard to the theater:

Stupide, il paissait dans le monde pour un homme étourdissant d'esprit, parce qu'on l'apercevait toujours en train de faire rire des actrices. . . . Comme au théâtre il disait des choses qui doivent faire rire, où on a l'air d'être dupe. "Moi je veux bien, c'est convenu, non, non, non," puis faisant subitement de l'acteur le public, riait en se tordant et en regardant tout le monde. . . . Puis il parla art, de la pièce de M. Donnay, et de M. Lemaître, de M. Pailleron, car en homme bien élevé, il disait Monsieur en parlant de gens qu'il ne connaissait pas. . . . (II, 36–38)

The same point as that of the last sentence is also made in *Sodome et Gomorrhe*, and again with theatrical examples (II, 1087). The point is small enough, but the theatrical references make the game slightly more interesting.

Jean, in two passages, has reactions to theater posters which resemble Marcel's, but the material is put to less use than in *A la recherche*. The two passages are independent, the first reading,

Il passa devant des affiches; chacune d'une couleur étrange avec les noms de pièces qu'il n'avait pas encore vues, et d'acteurs qu'il aimait, semblait déjà lui donner l'avant-goût de la représentation, l'odeur de la salle, le lever du rideau. Comme cela allait être amusant de revoir tel ami, tel autre. (II, 61–62)

The second passage appears in the next volume:

Mais en revenant de chez sa tante, ayant passé devant une affiche où *le Cid* était annoncé, Jean pensa à Corneille puis à Racine, puis à Molière puis aux *Femme savantes*. Là, son imagination, comme une toupie qui tourne longtemps sur elle-même et semble oublier l'objet qu'elle ira vivement frapper tout à l'heure, s'attarda sur le personnage de Philaminte, parut se rapprocher de celui de Bélise, revint à Philaminte, quand tout d'un coup reprenant sa course elle donna dans Henriette et fut renvoyé immédiatement comme à un point symétrique à sa tante Henriette. (III, 178)

These two rather simple trains of association, from posters to the imagined rising of the curtain, and from play title back to his aunt, may be contrasted with the passage from *A la recherche* dealing with posters. Although the basic premise is the same as that of the first cited passage from *Jean Santeuil,* the details and texture are far richer:

Tous les matins je courais jusqu'à la colonne Morris pour voir les spectacles qu'elle annonçait. Rien n'était plus désintéressé et plus heureux que les rêves offerts à mon imagination par chaque pièce annoncée, et qui étaient conditionnés à la fois par les images inséparables des mots qui en composaient le titre et aussi de la couleur des affiches encore humides et boursouflées de colle sur lesquelles il se détachait. . . . J'arrivais à me représenter avec tant de force, d'une part une pièce éblouissante et fière, de l'autre une pièce douce et veloutée que j'étais aussi incapable de décider laquelle aurait ma préférence, que si, pour le dessert, on m'avait donné à opter entre du riz à l'Impératrice et de la crème au chocolat. (I, 73–74)

Two reasons for the greater complexity of this latter passage may now be mentioned: the more analytical approach of the mature novel, which enriches the material, and the fact that since the passage is "planted" to serve later for backward time references, it cannot be presented too casually. *Jean Santeuil* shows us Proust's ideas and observations; *A la recherche* shows what happens when the basic ideas are used to serve several simultaneous purposes.

Details—an expletive, an example, and an attitude—are transferred from a discussion of Racine by Rustinlor in *Jean Santeuil* to another by Bloch in *Du côté de chez Swann*. It appears thus in the earlier work:

Racine est un assez vilain coco, dit M. Rustinlor . . . et d'ailleurs on a toujours tort d'essayer d'aimer: on aime ou on n'aime pas. Ses tragédies sont fort embêtantes, mais il a dans *Phèdre* quelques beaux vers comme celui-ci; "La fille de Minos et de Pasiphaé" que Gautier déclarait être le seul beau vers qu'il eût jamais trouvé chez Racine. —Le seul? demanda Jean qui cherchait inutilement à deviner la beauté de ce vers. —Le seul, répondit M. Rustinlor. . . . Il [Gautier] était de la dernière sévérité pour Racine, dont d'ailleurs les rimes sont pitoyables. Sa vision de l'antiquité juive et grecque n'est pas à mépriser, mais j'aime mieux qu'*Esther* deux pages sur Esther de Paul de Saint-Victor . . . et que *Phèdre* un conte de Pierre Louÿs appelé *Ariane*.

. . . Il [Jean] ne percevait pas alors les belles sonorités mythologiques du vers de Racine. (I, 128–29)

Bloch, in the same vein, tells Marcel: "Je dois confesser, d'ailleurs, que lui et même le nommé Racine, ont fait chacun dans leur vie un vers assez bien rythmé, et qui a pour lui, ce

44

qui est selon moi le mérite suprême, de ne signifier absolument rien. C'est: "La blanche Oloossone et la blanche Camyre" et "La fille de Minos et de Pasiphaé" (I, 90). It is not suprising that these materials to characterize a silly and precious person should have been carried over from the early work to the mature one, for Proust's opinions of drama remain conservative: his highest praise is always reserved for the most classical of the French classics. The difference between the passages in the two novels is that the Rustinlor episode is isolated, while the Bloch episode is one bead on a long string that includes Bergotte on *Phèdre*, Berma as Phèdre, and numerous other episodes.

In addition to the indirect characterization of Marcel which Proust establishes with Marcel's choice of theater allusions to characterize others in references and metaphors, and the indirect characterization of other individuals by the same means, Proust uses patterns of resemblance to suggest and adumbrate various interrelationships. Family resemblances are brought out; interest in theater is one of the parallels that underline the similarities between Swann and Marcel; and the Verdurin "wit" appears, on comparison, not unlike the Guermantes "wit" in content, method, and quality.

Swann resorts to dramatic works to define to himself the boredom he feels with the Verdurin circle after he has lost interest in it: "Vraiment ces gens sont sublimes de bourgeoisisme, ils ne doivent pas exister réellement, ils doivent sortir du théâtre de Labiche!" (I, 286). Swann's infatuation with Odette is partly indicated by his going to inferior plays or operettas because she liked them: " . . . Elle avait l'air heureux parce qu'elle devait aller à la *Reine Topaze.* . . . S'il retournait à *Serge Panine* . . . c'était pour la douceur d'être initié dans toutes les conceptions d'Odette, de se sentir de moitié dans tous ses goûts" (I, 245–46). Shortly afterward, we are shown that Odette idolizes *Serge Panine,* while Swann's lack of admiration is almost equally divided between it and the *Maître des forges* (p. 257). Swann also makes an issue of Odette's desire to see *Une Nuit de Cléopâtre,* an 1885 comic opera by Victor Massé. He says, "Vois-tu, *Une Nuit de Cléopâtre* (quel titre!) n'est rien dans la circonstance. . . . Evidemment j'aurais mieux aimé te demander comme une chose sans importance de renoncer à *Une Nuit de Cléopâtre* (puisque tu m'obliges à me souiller les lèvres de ce nom abject) dans l'espoir que tu irais cependant" (I, 290–91). Odette, who found this over her head, ends the discussion in order to get to the theater in time for the overture. Odette, some years later, makes a theatrical allusion when she says to Marcel, "C'est très bien de venir voir Gilberte, mais j'aimerais aussi que vous veniez quelquefois pour *moi,* pas à mon Choufleury, où vous ennuieriez . . . mais les autres jours" (I, 592). (The allusion is to *Monsieur Choufleury restera chez lui,* by the Duke de Morny, 1861, under the pseudonym of Saint-Rémy.) [17]

Later, Swann's doubts and jealousy are stirred (like Marcel's when he reads that Léa is to play *Les Fourberies de Nerine;* III, 144) by the mere reading of a play title:

Ayant ouvert le journal, pour chercher ce qu'on jouait, la vue du titre: *Les Filles de Marbre* de Théodore Barrière le frappa si cruellement qu'il eût un mouvement de recul et détourna la tête. . . . Ce mot de "marbre" . . . lui était soudain redevenu visible et l'avait aussitôt fait souvenir de cette histoire qu'Odette lui avait racontée autrefois, d'une visite qu'elle avait faite au Salon du Palais de l'Industrie avec Mme Verdurin et où celle-ci lui avait dit: "Prends garde, je saurai bien te dégeler, tu n'est pas de marbre." Odette lui avait affirmé que ce n'était qu'une plaisanterie, et il n'y avait attaché aucune importance. . . .

Sans oser lever les yeux vers le journal, il le déplia, tourna une feuille pour ne plus voir ce mot: "Les Filles de Marbre." . . . (I, 360)

Toward the end of *Du côté de chez Swann* (I, 408), Gilberte is shown jumping for joy at the prospect of going to see *Michel Strogoff*. Whatever the varying levels of their tastes, all of the family Swann are theatergoers, and this interest is one of several which Marcel shares with Swann.

Charlus' toploftiness is typified by the remark, "Voir Sarah Bernhardt dans *l'Aiglon*, qu'est-ce que c'est? du caca. Mounet-Sully dans *Œdipe*? caca" (II, 1070). Charlus thinks as little of Bernhardt as a person as in *L'Aiglon,* judging from a conversation during the war. A young man asks him, "Vous n'avez pas vu que Sarah Bernhardt l'a dit sur les journaux: La France, elle ira jusqu'au bout. Les Français, ils se feront plutôt tuer jusqu'au dernier." Charlus' reply is, "Je ne doute pas un seul instant que les Français ne se fassent bravement tuer jusqu'au dernier. . . . Je n'en doute pas, mais je me demande jusqu'à quel point *Madame* Sarah Bernhardt est qualifiée pour parler au nom de la France" (III, 825–26). He is equally definite about his critical opinions, as when he supports his admiration for Racine in the face of an attack from Saint-Loup:

Ce que ressentait Mme de Sévigné pour sa fille peut prétendre beaucoup plus justement ressembler à la passion que Racine a dépeinte dans *Andromaque* ou dans *Phèdre*, que les banales relations que la jeune Sévigné avait avec ses maîtresses. . . .
—Tu aimes beaucoup *Andromaque* et *Phèdre*? demanda Saint-Loup à son oncle, sur un ton légèrement dédaigneux.
—Il y a plus de vérité dans une tragédie de Racine que dans tous les drames de Monsieur Victor Hugo, répondit M. de Charlus.
—C'est tout de même effrayant, le monde, me dit Saint-Loup à l'oreille. Préférer Racine à Victor, c'est quand même quelque chose d'énorme! (I, 763)

47

Charlus brings Racine into his diatribe in which he suggests that Bloch might provide him with some Jewish entertainment: "Il pourrait peut-être louer une salle et me donner quelque divertissement biblique, commes les filles de Saint-Cyr jouèrent des scènes tirées des *Psaumes* par Racine pour distraire Louis XIV" (II, 288). He is equally superior when, in a conversation with Brichot, he advances his claim on Molière as an invert, listing "le petit Vermandois, Molière, le prince Louis de Baden, Brunswick, Charolais, Boufflers, le Grand Condé, le duc de Brissac" (III, 303).

Charlus' allusions are marked by elaboration and self-consciousness; he does not merely allude, but pontificates with allusions, even when they are obvious: " . . . Voilà le moment agréable des fêtes, le moment où tous les invités sont partis, l'heure de Doña Sol; espérons que celle-ci finira moins tristement" (III, 287). He expresses his contempt for Morel's ignorance of Molière: " 'Du Bon Chrétien? je ne comprends pas.—Vous voyez bien que nous sommes au fruit, c'est une poire. Soyez sûr que Mme Cambremer en a chez elle, car la comtesse d' Escarbagnas, qu'elle est, en avait.' M. Thibaudier la lui envoie et elle dit: 'Voilà du Bon Chrétien qui est fort beau.'—Non, je ne savais pas.—Je vois, du reste, que vous ne savez rien. Si vous n'avez même pas lu Molière ... " (II, 1010). He makes another allusion somewhat more obscure: "Je déteste le genre moyen, disait-il, la comédie bourgeois est guindée, il me faut ou les princesses de la tragédie classique ou la grosse farce. Pas de milieu, *Phèdre* ou *Les Saltimbanques*" (III, 830). Nathan glosses this: "Nous pensons qu'il ne s'agit pas ici de l'opéra-comique de Louis Ganne (1899), mais d'une grosse farce beaucoup plus ancienne de Dumersan et Varin (1831) qui a connu un grand succès."[18] Extending an invitation to Cottard, the Baron elaborates: "Vous allez prendre quelque chose avec nous, comme on dit, ce qu'on appelaît autrefois un mazagran ou un gloria, boissons qu'on ne trouve plus, comme curiosités archéologiques, que dans les pièces de Labiche et les cafés de Doncières" (II, 1072). In another comparison of past and present, Charlus cites another contemporary: " . . . Les 'Dames' des chevaliers au moyen âge et la Béatrice de Dante étaient peut-être placées sur un trône aussi élevé que les héroïnes de M. Becque" (III, 798). To Charlus is given the only metaphor in the novel involving an actress, which he as usual explains when he sneers at Mme Verdurin's suggestion that there be invited to his party Madame de Molé, who, he says, "a la folie de croire qu'elle est capable de jouer les duchesses de Guermantes et les princesses de Guermantes, cumul qui en lui-même est une sottise, puisque la duchesse de Guermantes et la princesse de Guermantes, c'est juste le contraire. C'est comme une personne qui prétendrait être à la fois Reichenberg et Sarah Bernhardt. En tous cas, même si ce n'était pas contradictoire, ce serait profondément ridicule" (III, 234). (Reichenberg was a *sociétaire* of the Comédie from 1872 to 1898, and specialized in ingénue roles. It was she whom M. de Guermantes invited to recite before the King of England.)

Much of the quality of the Verdurin circle is conveyed by their conversation about plays, as in the following characterizations of Mme Cottard and Swann:

—Ce n'est pas de la salade japonaise? dit-elle à mi-voix en se tournant vers Odette.

Et ravie et confuse de l'à-propos et de la hardiesse qu'il y avait à faire ainsi une allusion discrète, mais claire, à la nouvelle et retentissante pièce de Dumas, elle éclata d'un rire charmant d'ingénue. . . .

.   .   .   .

—Je vais vous paraître bien provinciale, monsieur, dit Mme Cottard à Swann, mais je n'ai pas encore vu cette fameuse *Francillon* dont tout le monde parle. . . . Je suis toujours sûre de voir *Francillon* un peu plus tôt ou un peu plus tard, et de pouvoir me former une opinion. . . . Ainsi j'ai une de mes amies qui est très originale . . . et qui prétend qu'elle a fait faire chez elle cette salade japonaise, mais en faisant mettre tout ce qu'Alexandre Dumas fils dit dans la pièce. . . . Il paraît que c'était détestable. . . .

Et supposant que c'était peut-être parce qu'il n'aimait pas *Francillon*:

—Du reste je crois que j'aurai une déception. Je ne crois pas que cela vaille *Serge Panine*, l'idole de Mme de Crécy. Voilà au moins des sujets qui ont du fond, qui font réfléchir; mais donner une recette de salade sur la scène du Théâtre-Français! Tandis que *Serge Panine*! Du reste, c'est comme tout ce qui vient de la plume de Georges Ohnet, c'est toujours si bien écrit. Je ne sais pas si vous connaissez *le Maître des Forges* que je préférais encore à *Serge Panine*.

—Pardonnez-moi, lui dit Swann d'un air ironique, mais j'avoue que mon manque d'admiration est à peu près égal pour ces deux chefs-d'œuvre. (I, 256–57)

In attempting to portray the inanity of his characters here, Proust barely escapes the charge of employing fallacious imitative form to achieve his effect. M. Verdurin is as inane in conversations with Saniette:

—Quoi? c'est *la Chercheuse d'espirit* que vous appelez *la Chercheuse*? Ah! c'est magnifique, j'aurais pu chercher cent ans sans trouver," s'écria M. Verdurin qui pourtant aurait jugé du premier coup que quelqu'un n'était pas lettré, artiste, "n'en était pas," s'il l'avait entendu dire le titre complet de certaines œuvres. Par exemple il fallait dire *le Malade, le Bourgeois;* et ceux qui auraient ajouté "imaginaire" ou "gentilhomme" eussent témoigné qu'ils n'étaient pas de la "boutique." . . . (II, 934)

The rest of this conversation leads into the discussion of Ibsen, Tolstoy, Porel, and the single, buried reference to Antoine, after which the same point is made over again:

"Je me rappelle seulement que c'était Mme Samary qui faisait la Zerbine," dit Saniette. —La Zerbine? Qu'est-ce que c'est que ça? cria M. Verdurin comme s'il y avait le feu. —C'est un emploi de vieux répertoire, voir *le Capitaine Fracasse,* comme qui dirait le Tranche-Montagne, le Pédant. —Ah! le pédant, c'est vous. La Zerbine! Non, mais il est toqué," s'écria M. Verdurin. Mme Verdurin regarda ses convives en riant comme pour excuser Saniette. "La Zerbine, il s'imagine que tout le monde sait aussitôt ce que cela veut dire." (II, 936)

Cottard is shown as a worthy member of this circle, to whom Proust makes his reader feel comfortably superior, when the divine Sarah becomes a bone of contention between Cottard and Mme Verdurin:

. . . Quand elle l'invitait dans une avant-scène à entendre Sarah Bernhardt, lui disant, pour plus de grâce: "Vous êtes trop aimable d'être venu, docteur, d'autant plus que je suis sûre que vous avez déjà souvent entendu Sarah Bernhardt, et puis nous sommes peut-être trop près de la scène," le docteur Cottard . . . lui répondait: "En effet on est beaucoup trop près et on commence à être fatigué de Sarah Bernhardt. . . . Sarah Bernhardt, c'est bien la Voix d'Or, n'est-ce pas? On écrit souvent aussi qu'elle brûle les planches. C'est une expression bizarre, n'est-ce pas?" (I, 201)

The members of this circle certainly deserve each other.

In another passage Proust introduces real but rather undistinguished actors to characterize a minor member of the Verdurin circle:

. . . Il connaissait les choses de Paris avec ce détail particulier aux gens qui y viennent rarement. . . . C'est ainsi que, parlant de tout sur le même plan, il nous disait: "Nous sommes allés une fois à l'Opéra-Comique, mais le spectacle n'est pas fameux. Cela s'appelle *Pelléas et Mélisande.* C'est insignifiant. Périer joue toujours bien, mais il vaut mieux le voir dans autre chose. En

51

revanche, au Gymnase on donne *La Châtelaine*. . . . C'est joué
à ravir; vous avez Frévalles, Marie Magnier, Baron fils"; il me
citait même des noms d'acteurs que je n'avais jamais entendu
prononcer. . . . Il disait Cornaglia et Dehelly, comme il eût dit
Voltaire et Montesquieu. (II, 1086–87)

Frévalles is identified by Jacques Nathan as probably being
Simone Frévalles, notably associated with the Théâtre de la
Porte Saint-Martin;[19] Baron fils played at the Palais Royal
and in the cinema; Périer played chiefly in operetta. Cornaglia
and Dehelly may be left in the obscurity where Proust placed
them, although in 1889, some thirteen years earlier, Ernest
Cornaglia had appeared at the Odéon in *Révoltée*. That these
unfortunate actors were brought in to underline their admirer's poor taste can be shown by the following description of
the theaters with which they were associated: "The Porte-
Saint-Martin, once the home of the broadest sort of vaudeville,
welcomes Sardou. . . . More and more, the first-night audience degenerated, the cultivated public of an earlier day
being replaced by fashionable idlers avid of sensation."[20]
Thus, facts about real actors and theaters become a standard
by which the pretensions of imaginary characters are exposed.
Admiration for what the cultivated public has abandoned
gives insight into one sort of character, just as failure to
appreciate Maeterlinck gives insight into another, but similar,
sort.

Marcel repeats the story of Mme Verdurin's infatuation
with the Russian ballet, underlining, not that her taste is
faulty, but that her desire is to be *chic*:

Chez Mme Verdurin la troupe était parfaite, entraînée, le répertoire de premier ordre, il ne manquait que le public. . . . Mme
Verdurin, sorte de correspondant attitré à Paris de tous les
artistes étrangers, allait bientôt, à côté de la ravissante princesse

52

Yourbeletief, servir de vieille fée Carabosse, mais toute-puissante, aux danseurs russes. . . . On allait chez Mme Verdurin, où . . . des soupers exquis réunissaient chaque soir les danseurs . . . leur directeur, leurs décorateurs, les grands compositeurs Igor Stravinski et Richard Strauss, petit noyau immuable autour duquel . . . les plus grandes dames de Paris et des Altesses étrangères ne dédaignèrent pas de se mêler. Même ceux des gens du monde qui faisaient profession d'avoir du goût . . . étaient enchantés de voir de près ces grandes rénovateurs du goût, du théâtre, qui, dans un art peut-être un peu plus factice que la peinture, firent une révolution aussi profonde que l'impressionnisme. (III, 236–37)

This passage is typical of Proust's way of using theater materials to characterize his individuals by placing them in a recognizable historical context, sketching in the whole social milieu in which they find themselves, and then relating it all to an episode of theater art—an episode that establishes a more reliable standard than the standards of the society and the characters who set themselves up to judge and take advantage of it.

The "wit" of the Guermantes, "où survivait quelque chose de l'esprit alerte, dépouillé de lieux communs et de sentiments convenus, qui descend de Mérimée et a trouvé sa dernière expression dans le théâtre de Meilhac et Halévy" (I, 334), is first compared to drama in "Un Amour de Swann," but drama is frequently associated with the Duchesse, her favorite writers being listed precisely as Mérimée, Meilhac, and Halévy (II, 43, 207, 495). When Marcel is still impressed with Oriane's wit, he discusses it with the only one of his metaphors which refers to a play written during Proust's lifetime:

J'aurais trouvé d'un délicieux raffinement la sécheresse voulue, à la Mérimée ou à la Meilhac, de ces mots adressés par une déesse à un demi-dieu. . . . Et j'aurais écouté ce dialogue avec la même avidité que telle scène du *Mari de la Débutante,* où l'absence de poésie, de grandes pensées . . . que je suppose que Meilhac eût été mille fois capable d'y mettre, me semblait à elle seule une élégance, une élégance conventionelle, et par là d'autant plus mystérieuse et plus instructive. (II, 43)

Later, Marcel observes,

Ainsi, par ces diverses formations, Mme de Guermantes exprimait à la fois la plus ancienne France aristocratique, puis, beaucoup plus tard, la façon dont la duchesse de Broglie aurait pu goûter et blâmer Victor Hugo sous la monarchie de Juillet, enfin un vif goût de la littérature issue de Mérimée et de Meilhac. (II, 496)

This reference is repeated at almost the end of the novel when the Duchesse singles out "l'élément drôle, assimilable à la littérature genre Meilhac, esprit des Guermantes" (III, 1009). It is interesting to observe the disappearance of Halévy from the equation, although Meilhac and Halévy were as strongly associated as Gilbert and Sullivan, having collaborated on, among numerous other things, the libretti of Offenbach's *Belle Hélène* and *Grande Duchesse de Gerolstein.* The allusion to Halévy was perhaps as strong as Proust wished to make it, for Ludovic Halévy was the cousin of Mme Straus, one of the originals for the Duchesse de Guermantes. Mme Straus, née Halévy, was also the widow of Georges Bizet, for whose *Carmen* Meilhac and Halévy adapted Mérimée's story. She lived with her uncle and his son Ludovic for eight years after Bizet's death. (It was Jacques Bizet who introduced Proust to Mme Straus, his mother.) Proust's partial identification of Oriane by way of the source of her wit is complicated, but hardly subtle.[21]

The Duchesse's position in the world is underlined by a reference to the admiration of one playwright, and the offer of a gift of the manuscripts of another. The same episode is also used to characterize her husband. "Une petite dame brune, extrêmement jolie" speaks to the Duchesse:

"Je voudrais bien vous voir. D'Annunzio vous a aperçue d'une loge. . . . Il donnerait toute sa vie pour dix minutes d'entretien avec vous. . . . J'ai un cadeau à vous faire, chérie . . . et que je ne ferais à personne qu'à vous. Les manuscrits de trois pièces d'Ibsen, qu'il m'a fait porter par son vieux garde-malade. J'en garderai une et vous donnerai les deux autres."
Le duc de Guermantes n'était pas enchanté de ces offres. Incertain si Ibsen ou d'Annunzio étaient morts ou vivants, il voyait déjà des écrivains, des dramaturges allant faire visite à sa femme et la mettant dans leurs ouvrages. . . . Toujours est-il que les noms d'Ibsen et d'Annunzio, et leur survivance incertaine, firent se froncer les sourcils du duc. . . . (II, 666–67)

The Duchesse claims another playwright, saying, "C'est curieux, vous dites justement ce que Dumas me disait autrefois" (III, 1012). This remark is made as the Duchesse is preening herself on having appreciated before anyone else the talents of Saint-Loup's mistress and the merits of Maeterlinck, and on having aided in their "discovery."

The complex of allusions regarding Rachel and her unsuccessful drawing-room performance in Maeterlinck's *Les Sept Princesses* is so extended that it becomes part of the action of the novel, since the Duchesse completely reverses herself with the much later success of Rachel. In the passages dealing with both occasions, we gain illustration of the wit of the Guermantes, the Duchesse's self-satisfaction, self-delusion, and lack of critical perception, as well as incidental characterization of the Duc, M. d'Argencourt, the narrator, and "polite society," all based on the assumption, underlined by Marcel, that Maeterlinck's merits exceed those of his detractors.

Henri de Bornier is another playwright whose acquaintance the Duchesse claims, and who becomes a vehicle for her wit and satisfaction with her own opinions, neither of which is superior to the Verdurin examples:

—Mais, Basin, interrompit la duchesse, si vous voulez me dire que j'ai connu M. de Bornier, naturellement, il est même venu plusieurs fois pour me voir, mais je n'ai jamais pu me résoudre à l'inviter parce que j'aurais été obligée chaque fois de faire désinfecter au formol. Quant à ce diner, je ne me le rappelle que trop bien, ce n'était pas du tout chez Zénaïde, qui n'a pas vu Bornier de sa vie et qui doit croire, si on lui parle de *la Fille de Roland* [Bornier's verse play of 1875], qu'il s'agit d'une princesse Bonaparte . . . ; non, c'était à l'ambassade d'Autriche. Le charmant Hoyos avait cru me faire plaisir en flanquant sur une chaise à côté de moi cet académicien empesté. Je croyais avoir pour voisin un escadron de gendarmes. J'ai été obligé de me boucher le nez comme je pouvais pendant tout le dîner, je n'ai osé respirer qu'au gruyère!

. . . .

—Mon Dieu, c'était bougrement embêtant, *la Fille de Roland*, dit M. de Guermantes. . . . Mais il y avait quelques beaux vers, un sentiment patriotique.

J'insinuai que je n'avais aucune admiration pour M. de Bornier.

—Ah! vous avez quelque chose à lui reprocher? me demanda curieusement le duc. . . . C'est long, *la Fille de Roland,* mais c'est assez senti.

—"Senti" est très juste pour un auteur aussi odorant, interrompit ironiquement Mme de Guermantes. (II, 489–90)

Soon after this toploftiness, the Duchesse offers the useful dictum that "Wagner avait du génie. *Lohengrin* est un chef-d'œuvre. Même dans *Tristan* il y a çà et là une page curieuse" (p. 491). Merely on the basis of her dramatic criticism, it is easy to see why Marcel became disillusioned with the Duchesse's wit, charm, and intelligence.

A conversation between Mme de Villeparisis and a rival sounds, on the one hand, like the Verdurin circle, and, on the other, like the Guermantes:

—Ma chère, Mme de Luynes me fait penser à Yolande; elle est venue hier chez moi; si j'avais su que vous n'aviez votre soirée prise par personne, je vous aurais envoyé chercher; Mme Ristori, qui est venue à l'improviste, a dit devant l'auteur des vers de la reine Carmen Sylva, c'était d'une beauté!

"Quelle perfidie!" pensa Mme de Villeparisis. . . .

—J'étais libre, mais je ne serais pas venue, répondit-elle. J'ai entendu Mme Ristori dans son beau temps, ce n'est plus qu'une ruine. . . . La Ristori est venue ici une fois, amenée par la duchesse d'Aoste, dire un chant de *l'Enfer,* de Dante. Voilà où elle est incomparable.

Alix supporta le coup sans faiblir. (II, 202)

Her criticism has all the penetration of Cottard or Charlus on Bernhardt, or the Duchesse on Rachel.

In giving examples of foolish, precious criticism, Marcel alludes to several plays to explain the Duchesse's pleasure in expressing unusual opinions:

. . . La duchesse eût éprouvé à déclarer cela le même genre de rafraîchissement que le critique qui, depuis soixante-dix ans qu'on admire *Hernani,* confesse lui préférer *Le Lion amoureux* [an 1866 drama of the Revolution by François Poinsard]. . . . Sans doute certains essayists ont tort de mettre au-dessus des scènes les plus célèbres du *Cid* ou de *Polyeucte* telle tirade du *Menteur* . . . mais leur prédilection . . . est encore trop rationelle pour la critique folle. (II, 470–71)

Marcel cites an improbable judgment about Molière as an example of this misguided criticism: "La critique folle . . . donne tout Molière pour un vers de *l'Étourdi*" (p. 471). This is the kind of criticism, as this passage indicates, which surrounds Oriane, and provides the basis for her critical ineptitude, the antithesis of Proust's critical stance. It is the kind of criticism which substitutes fashion for understanding, the *chic* for the intelligent, which prefers to Racine the playwright who is known only because he was a rival of

Racine, believing that "la véritable *Phèdre* [est] celle de Pradon" (p. 470).

Oriane's allusions, like those of Charlus, are somewhat elaborate and self-conscious, as in this backhanded defense of one of her husband's relatives: "Je ne crois pas que j'aie jamais connu une créature pareille; c'est un cas pour un médecin, cela a quelque chose de pathologique, c'est une espèce d'"Innocente,' de crétine, de 'demeurée' comme dans les mélodrames ou comme dans *l'Arlésienne*" (II, 485).[22] Oriane also resorts to drama for a comparison in an observation about Saint-Loup: " . . . Robert a jeté cela sans reprendre haleine, on pouvait à peine distinguer qu'il y avait du latin là-dedans, il avait l'air d'un personnage du *Malade imaginaire*" (II, 509). In a somewhat extended analysis of the Duchesse's quotations from Hugo, Marcel draws on a comparison with Corneille:

De même les vers de Victor Hugo qu'elle m'avait cités étaient, il faut l'avouer, d'une époque antérieure à celle où il est devenu plus qu'un homme nouveau. . . . Des "pensées," il en exprimait alors sous la forme la plus directe. . . . Or, c'étaient ces "pensées" de Victor Hugo . . . que Mme de Guermantes aimait dans le premier Hugo. . . . Elles étaient touchantes, et déjà autour d'elles . . . le déferlement des mots nombreux et des rimes richement articulées les rendait inassimilables à ces vers qu'on peut découvrir dans un Corneille, par exemple. . . . (II, 549)

A more singular view of the Duchesse's literary taste is offered by a dowager duchess who, "n'ayant pas été en cinq ans honorée d'une seule visite d'Oriane, répondit à quelqu'un qui lui demandait la raison de son absence: 'Il paraît qu'elle récite de l'Aristote (elle voulait dire de l'Aristophane) dans le monde. Je ne tolère pas ça chez moi!' " (II, 447). The

Duchesse is hardly as odd as this observer suggests, but Marcel's theater allusions show her as quite odd enough.

Throughout his fiction, and in essays as well, Proust uses the comparison between life and theater to underline the familiar idea that fact may be more false and more artificial than fiction, but in *A la recherche* he carries this idea to less familiar extremes. As he develops the idea, he uses a leveling process in which allusions to theater involve almost all social ranks and situations, and, with further ironic effect, in his metaphors equates them with comic drama or shows them as inferior to tragic drama. The tone of irony suffuses the whole social structure until, in the great *coup de théâtre*, the reversals are themselves reversed.

Proust's most extensive use of theater material in *Les Plaisirs et les jours* was in the metaphorically titled "Fragments de comédie italienne" (pp. 67–97), in which he first employed the fairly conventional metaphor of society's resemblance to drama, its people playing parts, and its activities resembling comedies. Later, Proust was to add considerable complexity to the process of viewing life in terms of art, particularly the art of theater, by introducing a shifting pattern of value judgments in which life and theater are first equated, then made to appear inferior or superior to one another. At this early stage, Proust stopped at making the equation, in order to illustrate a point rather than to provide a standard of judgment.

In "Personnages de la comédie mondaine," he begins by asserting that in society, as well as in the theater, the actors are cast according to type: "De même que dans les comédies Scaramouche est toujours vantard et Arlequin toujours balourd . . . de même la société a décrété que Guido est spirituel mais perfide . . . que Girolamo capitalise, sous les dehors d'une rude franchise, des trésors de sensibilité; que Castruccio, dont on peut flétrir les vices, est l'ami le plus sûr et le fils le plus délicat . . ." (p. 93). Proust goes on to point out that these arbitrary characterizations are so inaccurate that the "actors" not only differ from their "masks," but are able to do as they like because their false masks are immutably accepted. Type-casting has its social advantages, whatever its theatrical weaknesses: "Cette divergence entre le caractère véritable . . . et le type qu'ils incarnent irrévocablement aux yeux sagaces de la société, est sans danger pour eux, puisque cette divergence, la société ne veut pas la voir. . . . Girolamo en disant à un ami 'ses vérités,' lui sait gré de lui servir ainsi de comparse et de lui permettre de jouer, en le 'gourmandant pour son bien,' un rôle honorable, presque éclatant, et maintenant bien près d'être sincère" (p. 95). Society not only accepts the masks: it insists on them.

Finally, Proust adds two more points to his rather simple comparison. The first point contains a germ of his later treatment of fragmented personality. The statement that the actors are differently seen by different audiences when they appear on different stages makes one think of Swann on the Combray stage, the Verdurin stage, and the Guermantes stage: "Quand Arlequin quitta la scène bergamasque pour la française, de balourd il devint bel esprit. C'est ainsi que dans certaines sociétés Liduvina passe pour une femme supérieure et Girolamo pour un homme d'esprit" (p. 97). And in this Pirandellan world of masks and faces, some faces will not fit or accept any mask: "Il faut ajouter aussi que parfois un homme se présente pour qui la société ne possède pas de caractère tout fait ou au moins de caractère disponible, un autre tenant l'emploi. Elle lui en donne d'abord qui ne lui vont pas. Si c'est vraiment un homme original et qu'aucun ne soit à sa taille, incapable de se résigner à essayer de le comprendre et faute de caractère à mesure, elle l'exclut; à moins qu'il puisse jouer avec grâce les jeunes premiers, dont on manque toujours" (p. 97). Beyond this, Proust does not go, leaving the comparison of society and theater unplumbed, naming only the obvious points of resemblance which make society "theatrical"—its conformity, falsity, and play-acting. The much subtler and more complexly developed treatment in *A la recherche* begins where this leaves off.

The satirical description of the theater which appears in the Bouvard-Pécuchet section of *Les Plaisirs* offers some slight hint that Proust is prepared to present the world of Berma and of Saint-Loup's Rachel:

Le monde des théâtres est à peine distinct de ce dernier [le monde des arts]; on n'y pratique à aucun degré la vie de famille, on y est fantasque et inépuisablement généreux. Les artistes, quoique vaniteux et jaloux, rendent sans cesse service à leurs camarades, applaudissent à leurs succès, adoptent les enfants des actrices poitrinaires ou malheureuses, sont précieux dans le monde, bien que, n'ayant pas reçu d'instruction, ils soient souvent dévots et toujours superstitieux. Ceux des théâtres subventionnés sont à part, entièrement dignes de notre admiration, mériteraient d'être placés à table avant un général ou un prince, ont dans l'âme les sentiments exprimés dans les chefs-d'œuvre qu'ils représentent sur nos grandes scènes. Leur mémoire est prodigieuse et leur tenue parfaite. (p. 107)

A casual application of the terms of Bouvard and Pécuchet to Saint-Loup's mistress shows the direction of Proust's satire of this conventionalized summary. Rachel's fantastic and inexhaustible "generosity" is made evident in her cruel triumph over the dying Berma; her readiness to help her comrades and support their successes is made abundantly clear in the scene in which a young actress is hissed off the stage. Not even the soul of Berma seems filled with the sentiments of the masterpieces she performs, and there is even less evidence for such sublime sentiments in the souls of Léa or Rachel. But here Proust's attention is directed more at the speaker than at the subject, and he requires little subtlety or analysis. His point is made in isolation, for its own sake.

In "Sentiments filiaux d'un parricide," an account of an actual crime included in *Pastiches et mélanges*, Proust makes a number of comparisons to classical tragedy. He recalls the blinded Oedipus, Lear embracing the corpse of Cordelia, and Edgar speaking of Lear. He himself offers his reason for equating a sordid crime with great tragedies: "Si j'ai répété avec insistance ces grands noms tragiques, surtout ceux d'Ajax et d'Œdipe, le lecteur doit comprendre pourquoi. . . . J'ai voulu aérer la chambre du crime d'un souffle qui vînt du ciel, montrer que ce fait divers était exactement un de ces drames grecs dont la représentation était presque une cérémonie religieuse" (pp. 220–21). This latter comment underlines another familiar enough assumption about the relationship between life and art. In *A la recherche* Proust was to explore in greater depth the way in which art captures the essence of life, cleansing it of its mundanity and irrelevant everyday details.

In one of the parodies in "L'Affaire Lemoine," which also appeared in *Pastiches et mélanges* and which treated this scandal in the styles of various writers, Proust combined specific satire with a somewhat playful treatment of the improbability of the actual. Walter A. Strauss writes of "Dans un feuilleton dramatique de M. Émile Faguet": "The pastiche is reminiscent of one of Faguet's *Propos de théâtre* (Faguet is supposed to be reviewing *L'Affaire Lemoine,* a drama by Henri Bernstein), with all its gravity, with its rather irritating insistence on adopting the spectator's viewpoint, and with its chatty witticisms. Jean Mouton suggests with considerable plausibility that Proust was getting some preliminary practice in the reproduction of the language of university professor Brichot in *A la recherche.*"[23] Proust presents the imaginary criticism of the imaginary play in the following fashion:

L'auteur de *le Détour* et de *le Marché*—c'est à savoir M. Henri Bernstein—vient de faire représenter par les comédiens du Gymnase un drame, ou plutôt un ambigu de tragédie et de vaudeville, qui n'est peut-être pas son *Athalie* ou son *Andromaque,* son *l'Amour veille* ou son *les Sentiers de la vertu,* mais encore est quelque chose comme son *Nicomède.* . . . La pièce de M. Bernstein fourmille d'invraisemblances, mais sur un fonds de vérité. . . . Donc, l'escroc Lemoine, voulant faire une dupe avec sa prétendue découverte de la fabrication du diamant, s'adresse ... au plus grand propriétaire de mines de diamants du monde. Comme invraisemblance, vous m'avouerez que c'est une assez forte invraisemblance. . . . Notez que ce secret, qui n'est naturellement qu'une poudre de prelimpinpin insignifiante, Lemoine ne lui en fait pas cadeau. Il le lui vend deux millions et encore lui fait comprendre que c'est donné. . . .

Ce qui ne change pas grand'chose, à tout prendre, à l'invraisemblance n° 1, mais ne laisse pas d'aggraver considérablement l'invraisemblance n° 2. . . . Patatras! voilà les bijoutiers qui reconnaissent dans les diamants de Lemoine des pierres qu'ils lui ont vendues et qui viennent *précisément de la mine de Werner.* Un peu gros, cela. . . . Et chaque fois que le juge aimable et versatile lui répète qu'il a escroqué Werner, Lemoine répond: "Laissons ce discours et voyons ma balade." A quoi le juge pour lui donner la réplique: "La balade, à mon goût, est une chose fade." Personne de plus versé dans le répertoire molièriste que ce juge.[24]

Assuming the accuracy of the Faguet pastiche and its slaps at pedantry and assumed omniscience, we may notice, without unduly stressing it, that the focus of the satire is still the familiar idea that life is more improbable than art. The Lemoine affair was one of Aristotle's improbable possibles, unfit for artistic representation. "Faguet's" objections are all valid, except that the thing happened, and life does sometimes imitate art. The ironic contrasts between life and art, here used casually and spoofingly, become basic in *A la recherche*, which was begun at about the same time these pieces appeared.[25]

Marcel uses plays to clarify situations, characters, settings, moods, so that all aspects of his subject ironically take on a theatrical tone. A building by moonlight, by recalling "un décor de l'opérette *Orphé aux Enfers*" offers "pour la première fois une impression de beauté" (I, 489); the varied personalities of Gilberte offer "une ressemblance comme celle qui fait le fond des *Ménechmes*" (I, 566). A Racine anecdote is used to illustrate a delayed reaction: "Quand Racine . . . fit allusion à Scarron devant Louis XIV, le plus puissant roi du monde ne dit rien le soir même au poète. Et c'est le lendemain que celui-ci tomba en disgrâce" (I, 563). Another mention by Marcel of Racine occurs at the beginning of the famous passage on street cries: "Aussi, d'habitude (sans prévoir, hélas! le drame de tels réveils tardifs et mes lois draconiennes et persanes d'Assuérus racinien devaient bientôt amener pour moi) je m'efforçais de m'éveiller de bonne heure pour ne rien perdre de ces cris" (III, 126). These passages have in common the air of slightly belittling the circumstances which have called the allusion to mind, an effect which Proust produces also in his theatrical metaphors and in the application of many of his dramatic quotations. The effect is somewhat comparable to that involved in characterizing speakers by showing their own inferiority to those whom they discuss.

This sort of irony is not lessened by the fact that the august references apply at all levels of society, in the same way that they appear in the mouths of all sorts of people, or as quotations from the greatest tragedies are transposed to fit the most ordinary circumstances. The phrasing of Corneille is attributed, in one detail at least, to the earthy, practical Françoise, who "avait pu dépérir . . . à un mal qu'elle appelait elle-même l'ennui, l'ennui dans ce sens énergique qu'il a chez Corneille" (II, 19). This is comparable to the lift-boy who "disait volontiers en s'apitoyant sur sa propre classe 'chez l'ouvrier' ou 'chez le petit,' se servant du même singulier que Racine quand il dit: 'le pauvre ... '" (I, 800). The great names do not elevate Proust's characters to their ranks, but offer a standard of time past to which they seem inferior. Even a young footman is acquainted with literature, including the dramatists, as Marcel discovers from reading his letter, on the rather ingenuous excuse that since it was open, it seemed to offer itself: "Aussi c'est avec plaisir que jenverrai les livres de Racine, de Victor Hugo, de Pages choisies de Chenedollé, d'Alfred de Musset, car je voudrais guérir le pays qui ma donner le jour de l'ignorance qui mène fatalement jusquau crime" (II, 567).

One of the most unexpected allusions is to one of the best-known plays in English, and comes from Françoise's daughter: "La fille de Françoise . . . parlait . . . l'argot parisien et ne manquait aucune des plaisanteries adjointes. Françoise lui ayant dit que je venais de chez une princesse: 'Ah! sans doute une princesse à la noix de coco'" (II, 728). *Charley's Aunt*, in a version by Maurice Ordonneau and Brandon Thomas, "enjoyed a great run in 1894," [26] a fact which is important, as will appear, for the chronology of the novel, although otherwise unremarkable. Old Morel is impressed that Marcel's uncle thinks of him as an incipient dramatist. "J'étais plus en faveur," he reports, "parce que mon oncle disait tous les jours à son valet de chambre que je serais une espèce de Racine, de Vaulabelle . . . " (II, 265). A maid makes a similar comparison about him: "Ah! sac à ficelles, ah! douceur, ah! perfidie! rusé entre les rusés, rosse des rosses! Ah! Molière!" (II, 847).

Speaking of his astonishment at the inner aspects of the Duchesse's life, Marcel feels "le même étonnement qu'un voyageur, après avoir tenu compte, pour imaginer la singularité des mœurs dans un vallon sauvage de l'Amérique Centrale ou de l'Afrique du Nord . . . éprouve à découvrir . . . des habitants qui (parfois même devant les ruines d'un théâtre romain et d'une colonne dédiée à Vénus) sont en train de lire *Mérope* ou *Alzire*" (II, 525). Voltaire in the jungle—the irony is complete, and completes the attitude of the more mature Marcel toward the Guermantes. The relationship between Charlus and Saint-Loup, and the odd notion that one may inherit traits from an uncle are expressed by a reference to a translation by Schiller of François Louis Picard's *Locore des Menechnnes* (1791): " . . . Robert, dans son rancune, parlait de M. de Charlus avec trop de légèreté. On n'est pas toujours impunément le neveu de quelqu'un. C'est très souvent par son intermédiaire qu'une habitude héréditaire est transmise tôt ou tard. On pourrait faire ainsi toute une galerie de portraits, ayant le titre de la comédie allemande *Oncle et Neveu*, où l'on verrait l'oncle veillant jalousement, bien qu'involontairement, à ce que son neveu finisse par lui ressembler" (II, 695). The ironic equation with comedy is heightened by the fact that Robert, at this point, was mistaken about his uncle, whom he supposed to be an admirer of women, and that ultimately uncle and nephew come to show a resemblance in their homosexuality. It is not inappropriate, whether or not so intended, that the "German comedy" was actually French. The note of irony common to almost all these metaphors again expresses the feeling that the characters are somehow inferior to various creations of the theater.

The leveling method of applying allusions to varied characters and situations is most evident with Molière allusions. Molière is the dramatist to whom other characters, like Marcel himself, most frequently refer (except for the complex of allusions associated with Racine and *Phèdre*). M. de Norpois brings Molière into a discussion of Swann: "On plaisante beaucoup la manière dont Swann parle de sa femme, on en fait même des gorges chaudes. On ne demandait certes pas que, plus ou moins conscient d'être ... (vous savez le mot de Molière), il allât le proclamer *urbi et orbi*; n'empêche qu'on le trouve exagéré quand il dit que sa femme est une excellente épouse" (I, 467). Even a member of the Verdurin circle alludes to Molière; Brichot refers to a character from *Le Malade imaginaire*: "L'éminent professeur . . . s'exprime . . . dans un français aussi mêlé de latin et de grec qu'eut pu le faire M. Purgon lui-même, de moliéresque mémoire" (II, 891).

Molière appears most often in Marcel's remarks, first in an analysis of the effect of time on judgments of art: "Sans doute, il est aisé de s'imaginer . . . que toutes les révolutions qui ont eu lieu jusqu'ici dans la peinture ou la musique respectaient tout de même certaines règles et que ce qui est immédiatement devant nous . . . diffère outrageusement de ce qui a précédé. C'est que ce qui a précédé, on le considère . . . somme toute homogène, où Hugo voisine avec Molière" (I, 532). Time past in the arts offers the same contrast to time present, with the extremes of oversimplification and relativism, as time past does to time present in social and personal life. In a less significant context he writes of "le patois moliéresque" of M. de Charlus' old nurse (II, 289), and of the Baron's "contre-de-quarte qui rappelaient Molière" (II, 1070). Professor E——, who did little to save Marcel's grandmother, uses the term "hyperthermie," leading Marcel to observe (to himself), "C'est que la médicine a fait quelques petits progrès dans ses connaissances depuis Molière, mais aucun dans son vocabulaire" (II, 641). Another Molière reference comes to Marcel's mind when Cottard is coy: "Vous avez, dit Cottard une veine de ... turlututu, mot qu'il répétait volontiers pour esquiver celui de Molière" (II, 964).

These and the other allusions to Molière almost all tend to maintain a focus not only on the theatricality of society but also on the comedy which society performs, often in deadly earnest. A meeting between Marcel's grandmother and Mme de Villeparisis is presented as an artificial performance, "comme dans certaines scènes de Molière où deux acteurs monologuant depuis longtemps chacun de son côté à quelques pas l'un de l'autre, sont censés ne pas s'être vus encore, et tout à coup s'aperçoivent, n'en peuvent croire leurs yeux, entrecoupent leurs propos, finalement parlent ensemble, le chœur ayant suivi le dialogue, et se jettent dans les bras l'un de l'autre" (I, 694). A social discussion results in "ce bruit confus, produit dans les comédies de Molière par plusieurs personnes qui disent ensemble des choses différentes" (II, 639); and the relationship between Odette and the Duke is glanced at in the remark, "Et à un certain âge c'est en un personnage de Molière—non pas même en l'olympien amant d'Alcmène mais en un risible Géronte—que se change inévitablement Jupiter" (III, 1020).

The ironic tone created by these references is substantiated throughout *A la recherche* by other methods of using similar materials. What Proust accomplishes with specific allusions he also achieves, in more complex patterns, with the other theater elements in the novel. With quotations from drama by Marcel and others, with action involving actresses, and with his careful pattern of metaphors, he supports his milieu and verisimilitude, enriches characterization, provides standards of comparison between art and life, and creates the ironic ambiance which invites the reader to be his willing accomplice. How quotation, action, and patterned metaphor interweave and how they are controlled are the subjects of later chapters. How theater metaphors and allusions serve as chronological markers and how they are manipulated are the subject of the next chapter.

Proust's Manipulation of Chronology

CERTAIN of Proust's allusions to play titles or to theatrical events, such as the Paris performances of the Russian ballet, serve to establish the effect of the passage of time and the chronology of particular events in *A la recherche du temps perdu*. For this purpose, play titles operate in the same fashion as do song titles or phrases from popular songs in many contemporary novels. These allusions, in Marcel's text or in the dialogue, are only occasionally chronologically precise, unless we are to assume that Proust retained, and expected his readers to possess, an exact knowledge of the dates when plays were revived at the Comédie Française or elsewhere. But enough of the references are sufficiently exact to underline the passage of time. The period of Marcel's childhood is made to seem remote by the fact that the first set of plays mentioned, early in the "Combray" chapter, is made up of plays which had first been produced before Proust's own birth. The playbills for the *Testament de César Girodot* (Belto and Villetard, 1859), *Œdipe-Roi*, *Diamants de la couronne* (a comic opera by Scribe and Auber, 1841), and *Le Domino noir* (another comic opera by the same authors, 1837), all strike the young Marcel as strange and mysterious, partly because he must choose between revivals of the latter two for his first visit to the theater (I, 73–74).

A revival is also mentioned when the young Gilberte announces that she is going to the theater (I, 408). She is to see *Michel Strogoff* (Verne and Dennery, 1880); as will appear, the reference cannot possibly be to the original production. But Sacha Guitry tells us, "It was revived year after year, every Christmas." [1] The choice of revivals in these references not only makes the childhood seem remote, but, as will be seen, this vagueness about which particular production may be meant also seems both deliberate and functional, as Marcel indulges (or Proust has him indulge) in a kind of chronological sleight of hand.

Perhaps the simplest way to pursue Proust's chronological markers is to take them seriatim as they appear in the progress of the whole novel, omitting for the present such allusions in the "Amour de Swann" section, which, as a flash back, presents its own special problems. After *Du côté de chez Swann*, the first such allusion (which has been radically altered in the English translation) presents a slight anachronism. Bloch, during the action at Balbec, uses the catch-phrase, "Après tout, c'est pas mon père!" (I, 770), which, Jacques Nathan points out, is a celebrated line from Georges Feydeau's comedy *La Dame de chez Maxim's,* produced in 1899.[2] Bloch, according to the chronology of the novel, is using this remark the year before it became celebrated, as the action in this section seems to be of 1898. The section begins with the sentence, "J'étais arrivé à une presque complète indifférence à l'égard de Gilberte, quand deux ans plus tard je partis avec ma grand'mère pour Balbec" (I, 642). The material of two years earlier has included a reference to the Tsar Nicholas' visit to the Invalides (I, 543), which was in 1896.

Curiously enough, on the same page as the "deux ans plus tard" reference appears the phrase, "notre vie étant si peu chronologique, interférant tant d'anachronismes dans la suite des jours." Whether or not Proust intended that this be applied directly, it may be taken as a warning, conscious or not, that chronological references are not to be taken entirely literally. The chronological effects intended are psychological ones, and Bloch's catch-phrase recalls a general period rather than a specific date, just as "Twenty-three skiddoo" suggests yester-year to the contemporary reader without specifying an exact date. Bloch's catch-phrase establishes the action in the late nineties, contrasted with the playbills of Marcel's childhood, a much more remote time.

The action of *Le Côté de Guermantes* is also shown to be of the nineties, in part by the conversation about Maeterlinck's *Les Sept Princesses*, from which Saint-Loup's mistress has recited in the Guermantes drawing room (II, 223–30, 249–50). This play, an early work—Maeterlinck began his career as a writer in 1889—was published in Brussels in 1891, followed by *Pelléas et Mélisande* in 1893. The conversation indicates that to the fashionable speakers the play is an obscure work by an obscure author, although Marcel finds "une sorte d'âpre satisfaction à constater sa complète incompréhension de Maeterlinck" (II, 229). Again, without precision in dates, Proust has established the period: when Maeterlinck was a comparative unknown, as a contemporary might indicate a period when Maxwell Anderson and Noel Coward were just

73

getting started. Maeterlinck could hardly have been an obscure figure, even to Oriane, after *Pelléas et Mélisande* became an opera, which was in 1902.

The early part of *Sodome et Gomorrhe* would appear to be still in the nineties, but a number of references to plays moves us into the first decade of the twentieth century, and then to the last years of the decade. Françoise's daughter uses a catchphrase from *Charley's Aunt*: "Ah! sans doute une princesse à la noix de coco." The reference is underlined by a pun: "Voyant que j'attendais une visite, elle fit semblant de croire que je m'appelais Charles. Je lui répondis naïvement que non, ce qui lui permit de placer: 'Ah! je croyais! Et je me disais Charles attend (charlatan)" (II, 728). *Charley's Aunt* was produced in Paris in 1894, establishing the early events of Marcel's affair with Albertine in the nineties, but only fifteen pages further on, Marcel is looking forward to the time when Mme Verdurin is "discovered" by society with the Russian ballet (II, 743). The first season of the Russian ballet in Paris was in 1909, and the time when Mme Verdurin is a kind of patron goddess of the troupe, entertaining them at supper parties, is not reached in the novel until much later, on page 237 of *La Prisonnière*, thus enclosing most of *Sodome et Gomorrhe* and more than half of *La Prisonnière* approximately between 1894 and 1909.

Some chronological effect is established in the Verdurin conversation about Porel (director of the Odéon from 1884 to 1891), Antoine (who directed it later), and the dire possibility of Tolstoy plays at the Odéon: "D'ailleurs, la satrapie de Porel étant maintenant occupée par un fonctionnaire [Antoine] qui est un tolstoïsant de rigoureuse observance, il se pourrait que nous vissions *Anna Karénine* ou *Résurrection* sous l'architrave odéonienne" (II, 935). As was noted earlier, the chronology of this passage is in itself somewhat muddy, since although Antoine became director of the Odéon in 1906, the speakers assert the dreadful possibility of seeing Tolstoy plays there, whereas *Résurrection* had already appeared at the Odéon in 1902, although *Anna Karénine* did not appear until 1907. However, if we think of this confused set of references as indicating a general time, instead of a historical series of particular events, we have clearly moved into the twentieth century, somewhere apparently within its first five or six years. Again the reader is given the sense of a period as it appears in memory—a psychological marker of chronology.

We are kept in the early twentieth century with Charlus' remark, "Voir Sarah Bernhardt dans *l'Aiglon*, qu'est-ce que c'est? du caca" (II, 1070). This performance was in 1900. A few pages further on we are given two references to 1902, in remarks about *La Châtelaine,* and Périer in the opera *Pelléas et Mélisande* (II, 1086–87). The latter reference clearly marks the progress from the time when Maeterlinck was the obscure author of *Les Sept Princesses.* The final theatrical chronological marker in the novel is the already mentioned involvement of Mme Verdurin with the Russian ballet.

When we turn again to the "Amour de Swann" flash back, we find the period rather clearly indicated by similar theatrical allusions, although the chronology of this section also presents some inconsistencies. More confusing, however, are the inconsistencies or actual impossibilities which result when these allusions are set beside the allusions in Marcel's narrative about his own life. Germaine Brée states what has usually appeared to be the case when she writes: "Le narrateur en est définitivement localisé dans le temps. Dans

75

l'ensemble, et malgré quelques interférences de dates, le roman en bloc avance lentement et chronologiquement." But in adding for her example the "Amour de Swann" flash back, she correctly dates the flash back without noting the very real difficulty of fitting it into the novel as a whole:

L'histoire de l'amour de Swann pour Odette, nous pouvons au besoin en désigner assez précisément l'époque: celle où le "Francillon" d'Alexandre Dumas est une nouveauté. . . . Nous sommes de toute évidence dans la décade de 1880. Puis Odette, qui avait été "l'incarnation de l'Exposition universelle de 1878," incarne pour le narrateur "l'Allée des Acacias de 1892." . . . L'abondance et la précision de ces points de repère constituent une véritable "marche du Temp," dont Proust veut évidement nous donner la sensation directe.[3]

The "Amour de Swann" section certainly includes its contradictions of dates, but the discrepancy between this section and the novel as a whole is rather more startling.

The allusions noted by Professor Brée are, indeed, of the eighties, but they appear in the novel with several anachronisms. *Francillon* was a novelty in 1887, but appears in a discussion which seems to make *le Maître des forges*, of 1883, equally novel. Jules Grévy was president of France from 1879 to 1887, dates which are almost entirely of the eighties, but which hardly constitute a "precise" time reference; Gambetta died on December 31, 1882; the second page of "Un Amour de Swann" does indicate the general period with a reference to Wagner: "Si le pianiste voulait jouer la chevauchée de la *Walkyrie* ou le prélude de *Tristan*, Mme Verdurin protestait, non que cette musique lui déplût, mais au contraire parce qu'elle lui causait trop d'impression" (I, 189), but the fashion for Wagner can hardly be pinned to a particular year.

When the allusions to plays are examined seriatim, therefore, several inconsistencies appear. The first play mentioned is *Les Danicheff* (Alexandre Dumas fils and Pierre de Corvin-Krovkowski, under the pseudonym "P. Newski"), first presented in 1876; but since Swann is promising Mme Verdurin a lobby permit "pour la reprise des *Danicheff*" (I, 216), there is no anachronism. However, a useful chronological conclusion can be drawn from the fact that Swann proposes to get this permit from the prefect of police at a luncheon at the Elysée, where M. Grévy is to be the host. Also, Mme Verdurin has complained at the lack of such a permit on the day of Gambetta's funeral, apparently recent, a fact which would place this action early in 1883. The affair between Swann and Odette, on this evidence, can hardly have begun earlier than late 1882, since the conversation seems to take place during one of Swann's earliest visits at the Verdurins'. This cluster of references which places the beginning of the affair in 1882-83 is fairly precise, and provides the basis, as will be shown, for several discrepancies between the flash back and the main narrative.

Not long afterward, Odette is in a happy mood because she is going to see *Reine Topaze* (I, 245), necessarily a revival, since this comic opera was originally presented in 1856. On the next page, however, Swann is described as going again to see *Serge Panine* because Odette liked it. This play, by Georges Ohnet, appeared in 1881, a date not too far out of chronology. But the second allusion to this play, a few pages later, involves us in sleight of hand. Mme Cottard speaks of "cette fameuse *Francillon* dont tout le monde parle" (p. 256), goes on to remark that it is probably not as good as "*Serge Panine*, l'idole de Mme de Crécy" (p. 257), and wonders

77

whether Swann admires *le Maître des forges*. The reference to the latter might be taken as moving us forward just a year. It was a novel of 1882, adapted for the stage by its author, Georges Ohnet, in 1883. *Francillon*, however, did not appear until 1887. Aside from the obvious contradictions created by treating all three plays as comparatively recent, although produced over a period of six years, another complication results, as will be shown, from the fact that the love affair still continues apparently as late as 1887.

A minor inconsistency seems to result from the fact that after the quarrel between Swann and the Verdurins, Odette attends a production of 1885, after the *Francillon* production has already been discussed:

Alors ce salon qui avait réuni Swann et Odette devint un obstacle à leurs rendezvous. . . . "Nous ne pourrons pas nous voir demain soir, il y a un souper chez les Verdurin." Ou bien les Verdurin devaient l'emmener à l'Opéra-Comique voir *Une Nuit de Cléopâtre*. . . . "Vois-tu, *Une Nuit de Cléopâtre* (quel titre!) n'est rien dans la circonstance. . . . Evidemment j'aurais mieux aimé te demander comme une chose sans importance de renoncer à *Une Nuit de Cléopâtre* . . . dans l'espoir que tu irais cependant." (I, 289–91)

Even if *Francillon* was introduced early anachronistically, this discussion still has the affair continuing at mid-decade, as indeed it would have to do, if it is to take up years of Swann's life and still have begun in 1882. In "Un Amour de Swann," no additional plays or theatrical events serve as chronological markers. A reference to Swann's being moved by an advertisement for *Les Filles de marbre*, by Théodore Barrière, does not affect the issue, since this was a play of 1853, obviously revived during the eighties (I, 360). Thus, it is at some time after the presentations of *Une Nuit de Cléopâtre* (1885) or *Francillon* (1887) that Swann cries out, "Dire que j'ai gâché des années de ma vie, que j'ai voulu mourir, que j'ai eu mon plus grand amour, pour une femme qui ne me plaisait pas, qui n'était pas mon genre!" (I, 382).

The first difficulty in fitting these events of the eighties into Marcel's own narrative arises from a direct contradiction between two statements about the flash back. It is first described as

ce que, bien des années après avoir quitté cette petite ville, j'avais appris au sujet d'un amour que Swann avait eu avant ma naissance, avec cette précision dans les détails plus facile à obtenir quelquefois pour la vie de personnes mortes il y a des siècles que pour celle de nos meilleurs amis. . . . Tous ces souvenirs . . . ne formaient plus qu'une masse . . . entre les plus anciens, et ceux plus récents, nés d'un parfum, puis ceux qui n'étaient que les souvenirs d'une autre personne de qui je les avais appris. . . . (I, 186)

This certainly sounds as if the affair—"que Swann avait eu avant ma naissance"—ended before Marcel's birth. Within the flash back, however, Marcel remarks, "C'est vers l'époque de ma naissance que commença la grande liaison de Swann" (I, 194). If we follow the earlier assertion, Marcel would have been born either after 1885 or after 1887. From this, some curious results would follow, not the least being an almost psychopathic precocity. He would have been nine or eleven at the time of the first Dreyfus trial, and well established in society before he was thirteen or fifteen. He would also have arrived at puberty at the age of seven or nine, as the wrestling sequence with Gilberte takes place in 1894, when Gilberte is "une jeune personne de quatorze à quinze ans" (I, 476).

(Even Gilberte's age requires chronological testing, as will be seen.) If we choose to follow the later assertion, and assume Marcel's birth and the beginning of the affair as about 1882, we gain three to five years. Thus Marcel would be thirteen at the first Dreyfus trial, in society by the time he was eighteen, and the wrestling sequence would occur when he was twelve. This chronology clearly makes better sense, not only for these sample episodes, but for a number of others, and as the novel progresses, Marcel's precise adult age matters less and less.

Jacques Nathan has considered the difficulties of establishing the narrator's age:

De même, il est difficile de donner au narrateur un âge qui explique son rôle d'un bout à l'autre du roman. En effet, l'épisode "Un amour de Swann" se passe en 1887 (allusion à la première représentation de *Francillon*). Si nous laissons un temps raisonable pour les événements qui précèdent le mariage de Swann et d'Odette, ce mariage, et la naissance de Gilberte, ne peuvent guère avoir lieu avant 1890. Or par ailleurs, Gilberte est présentée comme la compagne de jeux du narrateur. En accordant au narrateur l'âge de Proust lui-même, il est difficile de le faire jouer avec elle aux Champs-Elysées, car il devient son aîné de dix-neuf ans; si au contraire nous en faisons un contemporain de Gilberte, il a trente ans à peine au moment de la dernière réception Guermantes au cours de laquelle il se dépeint comme un vieillard. Nous pensons qu'il est inutile de chercher une solution à ce problème qui n'en comporte pas. Quelques-fois, nous l'avons vu, Proust brouille les dates pour rester enfant le plus longtemps possible, mais cette explication ne vaut pas quand il s'agit des autres personnages. Dans les deux cas que nous avons cités, et dans plusieurs autres aussi clairs, il n'a voulu qu'échapper au temps.[4]

A complete solution is, as Nathan suggests, impossible, but some light can be cast. What seems to have happened is that for purposes of the novel, Proust has subtracted ten or eleven years from his own age—for to assume 1871, when Proust was born, as Marcel's birth date is quite impossible, since the events of Swann's love affair would then run from Marcel's eleventh to fourteenth or sixteenth years. Having made this subtraction in creating Marcel as narrator, Proust seems nonetheless to have used the public events of his own adolescence as the background for the Swann flash back, running the risk of the actual overlapping of the two times. The risk seems to have been justified, as the discrepancy seems seldom to be pointed out, although numerous critics are, of course, aware that there are anachronisms.[5]

Albert Feuillerat indicates, after a careful examination of the differing versions:

Mais le thème qui a subi la plus sérieuse dislocation est celui du Temps. Dans la première forme, la succession des événements ne prêtait à aucune confusion. . . . Si, dans la forme définitive, il y a maintenant conflit entre quelques-unes de ces dates, s'il est parfois impossible de situer les événements dans le déroulement de l'action, si le narrateur est en même temps jeune, inexpérimenté et au terme d'une existence lourde d'expérience, c'est uniquement parce que l'auteur, perdu dans le monde dont il étendait indéfiniment les limites, atteint de troubles de la mémoire, ne se rendait plus compte du désordre qu'il créait par ses innombrables additions, ou en rapprochant brusquement des événements qui appartenaient quelquefois à des périodes très différentes de sa vie. Si Proust avait pu exécuter son œuvre comme il l'entendait, on peut être sûr qu'il aurait persisté dans son dessein de rendre sensible cet écoulement du temps, sans lequel son livre n'a plus de sens.[6]

Although there is no doubt that further revisions of the text would have resolved some of the conflicts between dates, the

fact that *Du côté de chez Swann* appeared in the most satis-
factorily revised form would seem to indicate that while Proust
might still have adjusted minor anachronisms within the
periods (such as Bloch's quoting from a play that had not yet
appeared), he might very well have left the relative times of
the flash back and the main action untouched.

It is not enough to say that the present ordering works for
the rather simple reason that most readers are unlikely to
notice the difference. Proust's arrangement works better, not
in spite of, but because of the deliberate discrepancy. It has
already been shown how Proust, by alluding to plays earlier
than his own childhood, makes Marcel's early childhood,
before "Un Amour de Swann," seem extremely remote. The
word *seem* is a deliberate choice here, as we are dealing, it
must always be noted, with psychological time, although the
allusions are necessarily in chronological time. To the reader
of 1913, events of the eighties, more than a quarter of a century earlier, would have seemed sufficiently remote to fit
Proust's purpose, especially as exactness is blurred by the
ambiguity over whether Swann's affair was beginning, or
continuing, or completed when Marcel was born. Few readers
can have very precise orderings of public events during a
period of from five years before to five years after their dates
of birth, and it is just in this period that Proust has rested his
chronological ambiguities. Whether he deliberately or consciously planned to do this; or whether he was aware of the
literal contradictions but decided not to revise them away;
or whether, as Feuillerat suggests, he had weaknesses of
memory on which he did not trouble to check, the resulting
effect is the same. The chronology seems to be intentionally
confused in order to preserve a psychological ambiguity which

causes the reader to relive the past in general, not historical, terms.

Since the material of the flash back, whether we take it as before or just after Marcel's birth, is material actually within Proust's own lifetime (from his eleventh to sixteenth years), it gains a psychological strength and validity that it might very well not have had as a result of research. If Proust had made Marcel his own age, the "Amour de Swann" section would have become secondhand. As it stands, the novel presents Proust's memories, in this one section observed differently, but not different in quality. All the memories are, as Marcel writes, "une masse" (I, 186), an effect less likely to have come about had Proust combined memory with research. (A minor advantage arises from not having to account for the Franco-Prussian War in the flash back, nor to show its effect on society in the main narrative. By beginning in the eighties, Proust was able to work with a stable society uninterrupted by major historical crises. The importance of this for his theme hardly requires discussion.)

If we accept the view that Marcel was born about 1882, at the beginning of Swann's affair, we are still left with two chronological problems, the age of Gilberte and the time of the episode when Marcel met Odette at his Uncle Adolphe's. The greater number of applicable references indicates that Gilberte and Marcel are about the same age. In the early part of "Combray," when Marcel's family receives visits from Swann without his wife, Marcel's mother speaks of Gilberte as of a young child: "'Voyons, monsieur Swann,' lui dit-elle, 'parlez-moi un peu de votre fille; je suis sûre qu'elle a déjà le goût des belles œuvres comme son papa'" (I, 24). When Marcel sees her in the garden with Odette and Charlus, he

83

sees "une fillette d'un blond roux" (I, 140), and later, when he meets her in the Bois, she is still "une fillette à cheveux roux" (I, 394). The period when Gilberte and Marcel used to meet in the park can be fairly precisely dated by juxtaposing two rather widely separated passages. The first is the description (I, 417–21) of Marcel's watching Gilberte's mother walking in the Allée des Acacias. This was before Odette knew Marcel, and hinges on a theater metaphor: " . . . J'étais pour elle . . . un des personnages secondaires, familiers, anonymes, aussi dénués de caractères individuels qu'un 'emploi de théâtre,' de ses promenades au bois" (p. 421). Years later, almost at the end of the novel, remembering this period, Marcel observes, "... Elle ne semblait pas dire: 'Je suis l'Exposition de 1878,' mais plutôt: 'Je suis l'Allée des Acacias de 1892!'" (III, 950). The 1892 date for their childhood meetings would make Marcel about ten, and the "little girl" presumably about the same age.

Another indication of their approximate age may be drawn from the episode in which they wrestle in the park (I, 494). The physiological details here make it sufficiently clear that the narrative has reached a stage at which the epithets "little boy" and "little girl" no longer seem applicable. This episode occurs apparently in 1895, the year before the visit of the Tsar Nicholas (I, 543). Seemingly, at this time the two children would have been about twelve or thirteen years old, an age which can be accepted for the episode. Another reference, however, to Gilberte in the same year seems to make her two or three years older, as M. de Norpois says of her, "Oui, une jeune personne de quatorze à quinze ans?" (I, 476). We seem, if we hold to 1882 as Marcel's birth year, to have a Gilberte who is a year or two older than Marcel, a possibility which is acceptable so far as their own relationships are concerned, but which immediately gives rise to some obviously peculiar implications.[7]

If Gilberte is as little as two years older than Marcel, she would have had to have been born before her parents had met. Even if she is the same age as Marcel, she would have to have been born at the time when her parents met. The only direct indication that the novel gives of when Gilberte was born is somewhat vague: "Il y a eu, il est vrai, dans les années qui précédèrent le mariage, d'assez vilaines manœuvres de chantage de la part de la femme; elle privait Swann de sa fille chaque fois qu'il lui refusait quelque chose. Le pauvre Swann, aussi naïf qu'il est pourtant raffiné, croyait chaque fois que l'enlèvement de sa fille était une coïncidence et ne voulait pas voir la réalité" (I, 466–67). The final version of the novel casts no further light on the circumstances of the marriage, and the account of Swann's affair includes no mention of the child, and, consequently, none of Odette's blackmailing. Feuillerat indicates that the original plan was more explicit, and that the existence of Gilberte was one reason for the marriage: "Odette, impatiente de sortir de sa situation irrégulière, surtout à cause de sa fille, avait tourné à la méchanceté."[8] This, then, is the explanation, clearly implicit but never defined in the novel as it stands, of why Swann married a woman who did not please him, who was not in his style. But in incorporating this story, or building the novel around this story, Proust never made the necessary chronological adjustments, either to clarify Marcel's age or that of Gilberte, his contemporary.

The adjustment for Gilberte has to be made in a fashion similar to Proust's telescoping of his own life to provide the chronology for Marcel's. Gilberte must be slightly younger than Marcel if we take it that her parents' affair began about the time of Marcel's birth; she could be his age or somewhat older if we take it that the affair was merely continuing when he was born. As the former chronology works best for Marcel, it seems preferable to attach Gilberte to it. Thus, although she could have been born in 1883, she has gained two or three years by 1895, by Norpois' account. As the two children grow older, the discrepancies one way or another matter less and less, the difference between twelve and fourteen being greater than that between twenty-two and twenty-four.

To recapitulate, although Proust has used some of his own memories of the eighties for the background of Swann's affair, Marcel seems to have been born about 1882, simultaneously with the beginning of Swann's affair; Gilberte to have been born possibly a year later; the affair to have ended by 1885 or 1887; and the marriage to have taken place soon after 1885 or 1887. The "little girl" at Combray could be any age from five to eight, when Marcel would be between six and nine; the "little girl" in the park, in 1892, would be about nine, Marcel about ten; and the wrestling episode, two or three years later, would involve a boy of twelve or thirteen and a girl of twelve—or, if she has caught up with M. de Norpois, of fourteen or fifteen. In any event, the transitions from childhood to puberty and adolescence are clear and acceptable, even if the precise years or months are not.

In each of these childhoods there remains, however, one episode almost impossible to draw into the chronologies. Gilberte's friendship with Bergotte seems to take place when she is improbably young, whether we start from 1883 or go back from 1894. Swann mentions this friendship before Marcel has seen the "little girl": "C'est le grand ami de ma fille. Ils vont ensemble visiter les vieilles villes, les cathédrales, les châteaux" (I, 99). Even if we accept M. de Norpois' "fifteen" in 1894 or 1895, Gilberte would have to have been between nine and twelve when she went about with Bergotte from cathedral to castle, from one town to another. One can just barely imagine the possibility of Bergotte's being interested in so young a girl, and the suitability of their traveling together, but it has echoes in *Lolita*, with Gilberte as an unlikely nymphet. The obvious unlikelihood of it is of the same sort as has often been pointed out in the episode of Albertine's living with Marcel while his family is away, and with neither family raising serious objections. While the Albertine episode rests on an incomplete transposition of sexes,[9] this episode rests on an incomplete transposition of chronology in working the Bergotte material into the lives of Marcel and Gilberte. It is mentioned, however, in a portion of the novel where the chronology is vague enough that the episode does not strike the reader as an obvious discrepancy. By the time it is again alluded to, it may be taken as having occurred merely in an undefined "past."

Marcel's first meeting with Odette, difficult or impossible to fit into the chronology of his life, is also more important retroactively than when it happens, with the episode and the recalling of it separated by more than a thousand pages. When it is first mentioned, it is as a flash back within the narration of Marcel's childhood days at Combray: "Mais depuis nombre d'années je n'entrais plus dans le cabinet de mon oncle Adolphe, ce dernier ne venant plus à Combray à cause d'une brouille qui était survenue entre lui et ma famille, par ma faute, dans les circonstances suivantes" (I, 72). As the account continues, however, the chronology becomes blurred. Marcel writes of a time when he used to visit his uncle, a time when his love of the theater, necessarily platonic since he was still too young to be allowed to attend, is expressed in admiration of playbills on the advertising boards; but the account moves on to his schooldays, when he wrote notes about the theater to his classmates. Then, "plus tard, quand [il fut] au collège," he made lists of actresses in order of their talent. These actresses and various cocottes are visitors at his Uncle Adolphe's (I, 72–75). In this introduction to the episode of his meeting Odette, there already appears a contradiction between the phrase "depuis nombre d'années je n'entrais plus dans le cabinet de mon oncle Adolphe" and the reference to much later schooldays, from which the episode apparently moves.

References within the episode make it clear, too, that Marcel is a schoolboy, although Odette is described as a young woman: " . . . En face de lui, en robe de soie rose avec un grand collier de perles au cou, était assise une jeune femme qui achevait de manger une mandarine" (p. 76). This young woman has met Marcel's father, and wonders if Marcel could not visit her, to which Uncle Adolphe replies, " . . . Il est très tenu; il travaille beaucoup. Il a tous les prix à son cours . . . " (p. 79). Marcel reports his visit to his parents, precipitating the family quarrel with Adolphe. The transition back to the main narrative is explicit: "Quelques jours après, croisant dehors mon oncle qui passait . . . je détournai la tête. Mon oncle pensa que je suivais en cela les ordres de mes parents, il ne leur pardonna pas, et il est mort bien des années après sans qu'aucun de nous l'ait jamais revu. Aussi je n'entrais plus dans le cabinet de repos, maintenant fermé, de mon oncle Adolphe . . . " (I, 80). Although Marcel knows Odette as Gilberte's mother in 1892, he does not discover for a number of years her identity as the young lady in pink, whom he met as a schoolboy at about the same time.

Before we examine the passage in which Marcel discovers her identity, it is necessary to introduce another thread of this chronological web. It is established during Marcel's first visit to the studio of Elstir, at Balbec, when he becomes curious about a watercolor sketch lying there: "Je me trouvai ainsi mettre au jour une aquarelle qui devait être d'un temps bien plus ancien de la vie d'Elstir . . . le portrait d'une jeune femme pas jolie, mais d'un type curieux. . . . C'était une jeune actrice d'autrefois en demi-travesti. . . . Au bas du portrait était écrit: *Miss Sacripant,* octobre 1872" (I, 847–49). After Marcel has identified the subject as Mme Swann before she was married, he remarks, during his thoughts about this remarkable circumstance: "Cette manière, la première manière d'Elstir, était l'extrait de naissance le plus accablant pour Odette . . . parce qu'il faisait de son portrait le contemporain d'un des nombreux portraits que Manet ou Whistler ont peints d'après tant de modèles disparus qui appartiennent déjà à l'oubli ou à l'histoire" (I, 863).

The emphasis, then, is on the remoteness of the period when Odette played Miss Sacripant, a remoteness clearly labeled "October, 1872." A reference late in the novel causes yet more chronological confusion, when Charlus says of Swann and his wife: "Mais, voyons, c'est par moi qu'il l'a connue. Je l'avais trouvée charmante dans son demi-travesti, un soir qu'elle jouait Miss Sacripant; . . . les mauvaises langues avaient prétendu . . . que j'avais couché avec Odette. Seulement, elle en avait profité pour venir m'embêter, et j'avais cru m'en débarrasser en la présentant à Swann" (III, 299–300). This observation throws the beginning of the affair back exactly ten years, and would therefore have it continuing for thirteen to fifteen or more years.

Another, more complicated explanation might be that Odette in 1882 either played Miss Sacripant again, or disguised herself in the costume at some sort of masquerade. No allusion, however, is made to either possibility, nor is there any evidence that she was still an actress when she met Swann. In fact, she is identified as "la demi-mondaine" (I, 190), and, although the meeting is at the theater, nothing suggests that she was performing: " . . . Un jour au théâtre il fut presenté à Odette de Crécy par un de ses amis d'autrefois qui lui avait parlé d'elle comme d'une femme ravissante avec qui il pourrait peut-être arriver à quelque chose . . . " (I, 195). This, except for the date, in part coincides with Charlus' account, but omits any suggestion of acting, or of Miss Sacripant.

What seems to have happened is that Proust has forgotten the telescoping of his own life, and has moved the start of Swann's affair back to the period of his, rather than Marcel's birth. In any event, his realization of the identity of the lady in pink is combined with the identification of the portrait with Odette, and includes Odette among the actresses (and cocottes) with whom his uncle had had "friendships."

Marcel's realization that he had met Odette before he knew her as Swann's wife and Gilberte's mother comes some time after the adolescent love affair with Gilberte is over, and Marcel has found a regular place in the Guermantes circle. Charles Morel, the son of Uncle Adolphe's valet, brings Marcel a collection of photographs of actresses and cocottes, friends of Adolphe who had died the year before (II, 264). Looking over these photographs and recognizing one of Miss

Sacripant, Marcel is troubled, oddly enough, by a question of chronology, concerning, not himself, but his uncle:

Comme j'avais été très étonné de trouver parmi les photograpnies que m'envoyait son père une du portrait de miss Sacripant (c'est-à-dire Odette) par Elstir, je dis à Charles Morel, en l'accompagnant jusqu'à la porte cochère: " . . . Est-ce que mon oncle connaissait beaucoup cette dame? Je ne vois pas à quelle époque de la vie de mon oncle je peux la situer; et cela m'intéresse à cause de M. Swann ... —. . . En effet, cette demi-mondaine déjeunait chez votre oncle le dernier jour que vous l'avez vu. (II, 266–67)

If Marcel cannot see to what stage in his uncle's life he can assign Odette exactly, the reader's problem is to see to what stage in Marcel's life he can assign the meeting exactly.

It is, in fact, impossible to fit this episode into the established chronology of the novel, either of "Un Amour de Swann" in the eighties, or of Marcel's life, beginning in 1882. Inexplicable inconsistencies result from Marcel's having seen, as "a little boy," Gilberte as "a little girl," when she came to Combray with her mother, whom Marcel had seen, according to an earlier passage, "some years" earlier. Additional inconsistencies result from the association of the lady in pink with Miss Sacripant as a figure of the seventies, on the basis of the 1872 date of the Miss Sacripant portrait and of the association of this portrait with those of Manet, who died in 1883. Psychologically, the effect is similar to that of making the playbills of Marcel's childhood refer to plays older than Proust. Practically, Proust again seems to be using his own birth date, ignoring the fact that Marcel is a decade younger. The mention of Marcel's puzzlement over his uncle's chronology seems to partake of the same chronological sleight

91

of hand as is used with the playbills, switching the reader's attention from the true puzzle to a false one. The technique of distraction here is of the same quality as the seemingly disingenuous remark on the first page of the "Noms de pays: le pays" section: "notre vie étant si peu chronologique, inter-férant tant d'anachronismes dans la suite des jours" (I, 642).

There is no way, of course, to know how aware Proust may have been of all the chronological contradictions, or whether the conjuror's tricks to conceal them were entirely deliberate. Samuel Beckett assumes that Proust was consciously cavalier: "He will write as he has lived—in Time. . . . He raises him-self artificially out of Time in order to give relief to his chro-nology and causality to his development." [10] More revisions might have removed all the contradictions, but the fact re-mains that many of them were not removed after the numer-ous revisions which Proust did make, especially in *Du côté de chez Swann*. (In point of fact, as Feuillerat indicates, it was revision which introduced some of the contradictions.) None-theless, it does not seem certain that Proust would have wished to remove all chronological contradictions if this meant the sacrifice of psychological and artistic effects.

The chronological outlines might have been clearer, but at the expense of unity of tone and of psychological effective-ness. The consideration of this handling of chronology under-lines the fact that Proust was engaged in writing a novel, a work of art, not a disguised memoir or a minor piece of history. Just as no one should be distracted by the fact that accord-ing to the literal chronology of *Othello* Desdemona simply had no opportunity for the unfaithfulness for which Othello slays her, the reader of Proust need not be distracted by literal chronological facts. As in Shakespeare, we find an operation of "double time," in which the effect or appearance of time is more powerful than the facts of time. What is important is that chronological references should seem clear in their contexts, and that their progression should seem psychologically valid. These criteria Marcel's narrative meets, making his childhood sufficiently remote, and the progress from period to period convincing as he looks back over various strata of time.

Three months before he died, Proust suggested that Einstein might help to resolve some of the apparent contradictions. Benjamin Crémieux had written to Proust about the question: "Dans une autre lettre, j'avais adressé au grand roman de Proust le reproche de dérouter le lecteur sur sa chronologie. 'Vous parlez, lui disais-je à peu près, d'automobiles ou de ballets russes, alors qu'on s'imagine être en 1890.'" To this, Proust replied, on August 6, 1922: "Je crois que les anachronismes dont vous avez la bonne grâce de me féliciter ne sont pas dans mon livre. Je ne le jure pas et cela m'ennuierait trop d'ouvrir cet assomant ouvrage pour vous répondre avec certitude. Mais enfin, autant que je me souviens, entre la soirée Guermantes et le deuxième séjour à Balbec, il y a un grand intervalle de temps. Einsteinisons-le si vous voulez pour plus de commodité." [11] Proust has artistic justice on his side. Although certain discrepancies may simply be the result of errors of memory, a greater number of discrepancies seem less important than the valid effects which they create. While details may be confused, as in combining plays of several seasons into one reference, the general periods are clearly presented. Precise ages of characters may be ill-defined, but the progress from one stage of life to another is kept clear. Although Marcel's memories and Swann's may overlap with Proust's, their vividness is unimpaired. Although the telescoping of the chronologies of Marcel and Gilberte may result in unlikely episodes, such as Gilberte's early friendship with Bergotte— or even impossible ones, such as Marcel's apparently meeting Odette in the seventies—the relationship between Marcel and Gilberte is kept convincing and credible. Remote events seem remote, even when they are made more so than is literally possible. When events are recalled—and such an episode as the meeting with the lady in pink is important only when recalled—they fit without difficulty into what has been established as an indefinite past. If they seem inconsistent, it is as memories seem inconsistent; and if remote, as memories are remote. The standard used is the standard of the human mind, not that of the calendar, the engagement book, the journal, or the memoir. The effect is more important than the fact, psychological truth more important than literal fact. Conforming to the requirements of a work of art and the demands of fiction, Proust does not carelessly confuse chronology: he deliberately manipulates it.

4

Quotations from Drama in "A la recherche du temps perdu"

PROUST'S use of quotations from drama shows most clearly his direct and indirect use of autobiographical material in the novel, and the development of a practice that is common in his conversation and correspondence into an organic artistic device, employed with great rigor and complexity. He uses direct quotations from drama in much the same way that he does other theatrical allusions: characters quote from plays, as characters in Marcel's milieu naturally would, and in their choices characterize themselves. Marcel, for example, quotes in metaphors and comparisons, and he uses four clusters of quotations from Racine, two of them to sustain a continuing and central ironic equation of society with theater. All kinds of characters quote, just as all kinds of characters make other allusions, and the theater in quotations continues as a unifying and leveling process throughout the novel.

Marcel indicates very early in the novel that quotation is a family habit by having his grandfather quote a favorite line of Marcel's mother, one of the two quotations from Corneille in the novel: "Et mon grand-père . . . disait à voix basse à maman: 'Rappelle-moi donc le vers que tu m'as appris et qui me soulage tant dans ces moments-là. Ah! oui: "Seigneur, que de vertus vous nous faites haïr!" Ah! comme c'est bien!'" (I, 27). As is often true when Proust cites, the quotation has been slightly altered,[1] making the line somewhat less formal, and bringing the quotation closer to the family context, whether because Proust remembers it that way, or deliberately has his character alter it. Proust's very casualness with quotations— their tangential applications, their rewordings to suit his contexts—underlines the naturalness with which quotations and allusions came to him. Marcel describes himself as "habitué dès [son] enfance à prêter, même à ce qui est muet, le langage des classiques" (II, 665), and notes that Albertine "avait pris notre habitude familiale des citations" (III, 18). The methods by which Proust transmutes this family habit into fiction are of both biographical and aesthetic interest.

Both Proust and his mother carry into their correspondence the family habit of conversational allusions and quotations, including many examples from drama. This habit was, in any event, more common in both the writing and speaking, public and private, of Proust's time than it is in ours, as Jacques Nathan points out. But Proust's family was particularly given to the habit. "Il a transposé," Nathan writes, "dans ses romans, avec amour, une sorte de langage conventionnel de sa famille, pratiqué notamment par sa mère et sa grand'mère, et bientôt adopté par un enfant aussi précoce";[2] Maurois, whom Nathan cites, writes on the same point, "Both his grandmother and his mother were highly educated women, and unwearying readers of the classic authors. Quotations from Racine and

Madame de Sévigné adorned and enriched their conversation." [3] One of Proust's friends makes it clear that the habit of quotation was not confined to family conversation: "Racine, Hugo, Musset, Lamartine, Baudelaire chantaient déjà dans sa prodigieuse mémoire poétique. . . . " [4]

Mme Proust writes as apparently she talked. She ends a letter of April 28, 1890, with a line from Racine's *Esther* (Act I, scene 1), "Ah que ce temps est long à mon impatience." [5] She remarks in another letter, "On aurait vu comme dans *Macbeth* la forêt d'Auteuil marcher vers la forêt d'Orléans." [6] Another Shakespeare allusion occurs in a letter of 1894:

Je reçois ta lettre; et me casse la tête pour savoir ce que j'ai pu t'écrire de "spirituel"? N'importe

> Since I am crept in favour with myself
> I will maintain it with some little cost. [7]

She alludes also to Molière, in a letter of 1896: "Entendre la *voix* du pauvre loup [Marcel]—le pauvre loup entendre la mienne! Rien que ton hallo! 'Cet hallo est admirable et j'aime mieux avoir cet hallo qu'un poème épique.'" [8] And to Marivaux: "Mais quant à conclure parce qu'elle ne t'aurait pas réussi à les abandonner toutes—c'est comme le renoncement aux femmes de Lelio dans Marivaux à cause de la trahison de la Marquise." [9] It is clear that the Proust family's interest in drama did not begin with Marcel.

Among French playwrights, Proust alludes to and quotes Corneille, Racine, and Molière; but for some reason—or possibly none at all—most of the Corneille quotations are found in his correspondence with Montesquiou. He twice equates the latter with Corneille, in praising two lines from *Laus noctis*,[10] and, again, in a personal application.[11] He twice quotes from *Le Cid*, explicitly labeling his source.[12] From the tone of the allusions, one would suspect that Montesquiou, not Proust, admired Corneille, a suspicion which is confirmed by the fact that only two Corneille quotations appear in all of *A la recherche*.

Proust's allusions to Racine are less restricted in their purposes. In a letter to Mme Straus, he uses Racine as a standard from which contemporary literature has declined:

Hélas les plus beaux vers de Racine

> *Je t'aimais inconstant, qu'eusse fait fidèle!*
> *Pourquoi l'assassiner? Qu'a-t-il fait? A quel titre?*
> *Qui te l'a dit?*

n'auraient jamais passé, même de nos jours dans une revue.[13]

He writes to Robert Dreyfus, "J'aurais pu dire comme *Phèdre*: 'Mes yeux sont éblouis du jour que je revois et mes genoux tremblants se dérobent sous moi.'" [14] He also quotes *Phèdre* to the Comtesse de Noailles: "Je n'ose plus penser à vous à cause de heurts que cela me donne: 'J'ai même défendu par une expresse loi qu'on osât prononcer votre nom devant moi.'" [15]

Considering Proust's knowledge of Molière and the number of Molière allusions in *A la recherche,* those in the correspondence seem most infrequent, and somewhat self-conscious. This passage, with its double reference, seems designedly "literary," for the benefit of Mme Straus: "Mais je voudrais réunir autant de médecins et de sommités que dans l'*Amour médecin.* . . . Et je n'hésiterais pas à demander comme dans le *Médecin malgré lui*: 'La matière, est-elle louable?'" [16] Molière references in letters to Montesquiou are similar to the Corneille references: they seem to be somewhat forced, and one of them is carefully labeled, as though Montesquiou might not be trusted to notice Proust's accomplishment.[17]

In a letter to Dreyfus, dated in June, 1906, Proust refers to Montesquiou in an allusion to Harpagon that he credits to Plautus, but which could be as easily taken from Molière. In this passage, Proust comes close to some of the effects of theater allusions in *A la recherche*:

Je connais un exemple bien différent auprès de nous d'orgueil encore plus excessif qui donne à rire, mais celui-là exprès. Ou du moins, comme Baron a peut-être naturellement sa voix comique, mais l'a remarqué et s'en sert exprès, M. de Montesquiou (c'est lui) fait œuvre d'art avec son ridicule et l'a merveilleusement stylisé. Ah! X*** n'en est pas à le styliser: il l'ignore! Je ne sais par quelle convention, comme au théâtre, il n'entend pas les rires autour de lui ou si vagues qu'il demanderait comme Harpagon dans Plaute entendant rire la salle (c'est-à-dire des gens irréels pour lui): "Qu'ont donc à rire tous ces gens-là?" [18]

Without attempting to guess whether there is a private train of association, one may note that the sole reference to Harpagon in *A la recherche* occurs in a passage about Charlus: "[L'inverti] est obligé, comme Harpagon, de veiller sur son trésor et se relève la nuit pour voir si on ne le lui prend pas" (II, 921).

Marcel frequently quotes from plays in *A la recherche*, showing that he has acquired the family habit. He twice alludes to the particular speech in *Phèdre* which he wishes to hear Berma repeat:

J'aurais le même ravissement que le jour où une gondole m'emmènerait au pied du Titien des Frari . . . si jamais j'entendais réciter par la Berma les vers:

> On dit qu'un prompt départ vous éloigne de nous,
> Seigneur, etc. (I, 440–41)

Only two pages later, the line from Phèdre's declaration to Hippolyte is mentioned again, almost as if it had not just been referred to:

J'implorais mes parents, qui, depuis la visite du médecin, ne voulaient plus me permettre d'aller à *Phèdre*. Je me récitais sans cesse la tirade:

On dit qu'un prompt départ vous éloigne de nous ...

cherchant toutes les intonations qu'on pouvait y mettre, afin de mieux mesurer l'inattendu de celle que la Berma trouverait. (I, 443)

This quotation, although it plays its part in the action of the novel and provides a reference point for later use, need hardly be regarded at this point as significant in itself. Here it seems no more remarkable than would be an English schoolboy reciting the "To be or not to be" soliloquy before his first viewing of *Hamlet*.

After Albertine has left him, Marcel applies words from *Manon* to his situation, quoting two short passages (III, 452). The handling of these quotations is remarkable only for its unusual explicitness and directness of application. Equally bald is the quotation from *La Belle Hélène* (libretto by Meilhac and Halévy, music by Offenbach): " . . . Partageant en un mot l'opinion de ce personnage d'opérette qui déclare: 'Mon nom me dispense, je pense, d'en dire plus long,' [Gilberte] se mit à afficher son mépris pour ce qu'elle avait tant désiré . . . " (III, 669). The fact that the original speaker was Agamemnon casts little light on Gilberte, nor is she behaving in a comic-opera fashion. The line seems simply to have come to mind, the words are included solely for their content, and the implied comparison is not enlightening.

The wide range covered by the habit of quoting is shown in quotations from plays in the dialogue of Françoise's daughter, who uses the catch phrase from *Charley's Aunt* (II, 728), and of Oriane, who says, " . . . Tandis que la demoiselle de Robert, je vous assure qu'elle est à mourir de rire. Je sais bien qu'on m'objectera cette vieille rengaine d'Augier: 'Qu'importe le flacon pourvu qu'on ait l'ivresse!' Hé bien, Robert a peut-être l'ivresse, mais il n'a vraiment pas fait preuve de goût dans le choix du flacon!" (II, 229). Proust seems to have introduced this quotation not so much for its relevance as to allow it to make a comment on Oriane, who attributes to the fashionable Augier a line by Alfred de Musset.[19] Whether this would be evident to most readers or if Proust was enjoying a semi-private joke, it is an indication of his method of characterizing speakers through their choice of quotations. The fact that this example occurs in the midst of Oriane's attack on Rachel's performance of *Les Sept Princesses* makes it seem less likely that the faulty attribution is accidental, since it provides a grace note to her snobbish dramatic criticism.

Bloch's character is clearly indicated by his excursions into dramatic quotation and its misattribution. His use of the catch phrase from the *Dame de chez Maxim's* (I, 770) is accurate, although hardly indicative of critical penetration. (Bloch cannot be blamed for Proust's anachronistic use of the phrase.) His jejune air of superiority is expressed by his patronizing approval of Racine's "'La blanche Oloossone et la blanche Camyre,' et 'La fille de Minos et de Pasiphaé'" (I, 90). The previous quotation shows Bloch's attitude at an age when sophomoric iconoclasm is excusable, but he is still shown later as airily incorrect in saying:

Selon les deux ridicules alexandrins du sieur Arouet, je dirai
à Saint-Loup, pour charmer son cléricalisme:

Apprends que mon devoir ne dépend pas du sien;
Qu'il y manque, s'il veut; je dois faire le mien. (I, 880)

Nathan indicates that the lines are really Corneille's (*Polyeucte*, Act III, scene 2, 795–96), and that the error is evidently
voluntary on Proust's part.[20] As is true of other kinds of
theatrical allusions, the intention of the quotations is not
decorative, but functional.

Oddly enough, considering the Proust family conversation
and letters, it was not until *Contre Sainte-Beuve*—that strange
medley of autobiography, fiction, and criticism on which
Proust was working late in the first decade of the century—
that he made use of quotations to characterize speakers,[21] as
he was to do more rigorously in *A la recherche*. In *Les Plaisirs
et les jours* he made one use of quotations from drama that
he did not follow elsewhere, in the choice of four epigraphs
for stories, or sections of stories, from *Macbeth*, *Hamlet*,
Phèdre, and Beaumont and Fletcher, of which perhaps only
the last choice is at all surprising. It is not surprising that
Pastiches et mélanges does not employ quotations from drama,
since the selections consist either of parody or of exposition.
But their lack in the characterization in *Les Plaisirs et les
jours* and *Jean Santeuil* is somewhat more remarkable. When
he does use them, in *Contre Sainte-Beuve*, it is not only the
habit which he follows, but actual family quotations in actual
family situations. In *A la recherche* he uses some of the same
quotations, but transposes them.

A striking example of Proust's fictional use of real-life quotations is given in Jacques Nathan's account of the allusions

made by Marcel's grandmother after her mild stroke, and the allusions made by Proust's dying mother.[22] In identifying the biographical source, Nathan refers to "les cahiers intimes de Proust,"[23] but the passage is found in only slightly different form, and with the addition of a further quotation, in *Contre Sainte-Beuve*:

> Maman avait quelquefois bien du chagrin mais on ne le savait jamais, car elle ne parlait jamais qu'avec douceur et esprit. Elle est morte en me faisant un citation de Molière et une citation de Labiche: "Son départ ne pouvait plus à propos se faire." [Molière, *Le Misanthrope*] "Que ce petit-là n'ait pas peur, sa Maman ne le quittera pas. Il ferait beau voir que je sois à Etampes et mon orthographie à Arpajon!" [Labiche, *La Grammaire*] Et puis elle n'a plus pu parler. Une fois seulement elle vit que je me retenais pour ne pas pleurer, et elle fronça les sourcils et fit la moue en souriant et je distinguai dans sa parole déjà si embrouillée:

> Si vous n'êtes Romain, soyez digne de l'être. [Corneille, *Horace*][24]

Oddly, the reference to Molière, here attributed to his mother, was one that Proust had made use of in one of his letters to Montesquiou, complaining that the absence of his father had left him as "gardien de maman."[25]

In using this deathbed material in *A la recherche*, Proust altered the circumstances from deathbed to onset of illness, and used a different Molière allusion, and a citation from Mme de Sévigné instead of from Labiche. He transposes his mother's deathbed remarks into the episode when Marcel's grandmother has had the first attack of her fatal illness, and emerges from the pavilion that encloses the public toilets in the park. Fearful of alarming her grandson, the old lady makes a brave attempt to maintain a "natural" conversation, commenting sharply on the overheard remarks of the pavilion attendant:

—J'ai entendu toute la conversation entre la "marquise" et le garde, me dit-elle. C'était on ne peut plus Guermantes et petit noyau Verdurin. Dieu! qu'en termes galants ces choses-là étaient mises.[26] Et elle ajouta encore, avec application, ceci de sa marquise à elle, Mme de Sévigné: "En les écoutant je pensais qu'ils me préparaient les délices d'un adieu." [27]

Voilà le propos qu'elle me tint et où elle avait mis toute sa finesse, son goût des citations, sa mémoire des classiques, un peu plus même qu'elle n'eût fait d'habitude et comme pour montrer qu'elle gardait bien tout cela en sa possession. (II, 312)

The effect of this in characterizing the grandmother, and its identification with the family habit of quotation, surely requires no further discussion. It is typical of the relationship between the two works that what in *Contre Sainte-Beuve* is presented as illustrative anecdote, in *A la recherche* is altered and integrated into the action and characterization. *Contre Sainte-Beuve* lies halfway between fact and fiction. This use of his mother's dying words, directly in *Contre Sainte-Beuve* and indirectly in *A la recherche*, illustrates most clearly just how natural quotation was to the Prousts, and how directly Proust transposes the actual into his fiction. The method is, nonetheless, in *A la recherche*, one of transposition, not of transferral; and the controlling principle is one of art, not of fact.

Four clusters of quotations from Racine mentioned earlier are presented by Marcel as threads of the narrative and with a cumulative effect. The quotations and allusions referring to *Phèdre* are so interconnected with the material about Berma, and lead to so explicit an analysis of the resemblances between

Marcel and the characters of the play (III, 458–60) that they
become part of the major action of the novel and need separate treatment. Although the three other clusters of Racinian
quotation and allusion, from *Athalie* and *Esther*, fulfil some
of the same functions as the *Phèdre* cluster, their force is
more emphatically ironic. The quotations from these two
plays are the most extensive in the novel, and are applied
to four main subjects: the Guermantes family, Marcel and
Albertine, homosexuals in smart society, and the page-boys
and waiters at the hotel in Balbec. The last two groups begin
to intertwine as the quotations and accompanying comparisons
proceed, with a perceptible increase in the ironies. To these
passages of Racinian comparison, Léon Pierre-Quint applies
the concept of "transpositions":

Souvent Proust développe une scène à l'aide d'éléments em-
pruntés à une autre scène, qui n'a aucun rapport logique avec
la première. Elles se trouvent simplement l'une et l'autre fondues
dans sa conscience. C'est ainsi qu'il cite des vers de Racine tirés
du rôle d'un roi, et, les détournant de leur sens naturel et les
interprétant selon sa pensée du moment, il les applique à un
valet ou à une cuisinière dont il parle dans son roman. Ces
rapprochements du ton grave et du ton vulgaire dégagent des
effets d'un irrésistible comique.[28]

Later in the volume, he returns to this idea:

Souvent Proust opère en transposant, dans une page écrite en
style familier, les vers solennels de la tragédie classique, sans
d'ailleurs changer le texte original. La portée de son comique
va cette fois plus loin: il veut nous prouver, par exemple, que
la manière dont Joad, grand prêtre, enseigne la méfiance à la
reine ne diffère pas profondément de celle dont une humble
femme de chambre parlera à sa maîtresse.[29]

The terms of this latter comparison ought to be reversed, for the effect is not that great figures speak like chambermaids, but that chambermaids (and duchesses) speak like tragic figures. By a kind of literary mathematics, things comparable to the same thing become comparable to each other.

The tragic figures and situations are the unchanging terms in the equations in which the characters and situations of the novel continually change their value. Sometimes, as J. M. Cocking suggests, "Racine is quoted in contexts where the prestige of his verse clashes amusingly with the trivial incident which brings it to Proust's mind." [30] But these juxtapositions of the grave and the vulgar, or of the solemn and the familiar, may be regarded as comic only if one isolates the tone from the content and examines the examples separately. As soon as one moves to the terms of the comparisons and examines them in related groups, the logical connections which Pierre-Quint denies them become apparent. The connections have meaningful, aesthetic, and ironic logic.

Not only has Proust chosen classical tragedies as his vehicle; he has also doubled the impressiveness of his choice by selecting tragedies on Old Testament subjects. Hence it cannot be accidental that the first connection between Esther and the Guermantes refers to the biblical (not the dramatic) Esther, and is introduced into the description of the Combray church at the period when the Guermantes are to Marcel glamorous figures from another world: "Deux tapisseries de haute lice représentaient le couronnement d'Esther (la tradition voulait qu'on eût donné à Assuérus les traits d'un roi de France et à Esther ceux d'une dame de Guermantes dont il était amoureux), auxquelles leurs couleurs, en fondant,

avaient ajouté une expression, un relief, un éclairage . . . "
(I, 60–61). Nothing in this association of the Guermantes
with the story of Esther is ironic or metaphorical, although
it is clearly symbolic of the "historic" position of the Guermantes, and the boy Marcel's feeling about them. When he
returns to this tapestry, in describing his Combray walks, his
attitude toward the Guermantes remains the same, but a note
of metaphor has come into the expression of it: "Je savais
que là résidaient des châtelains, le duc et la duchesse de
Guermantes, je savais qu'ils étaient des personnages réels
et actuellement existants, mais chaque fois que je pensais
à eux, je me les représentais tantôt en tapisserie, comme
était la comtesse de Guermantes, dans le "Couronnement
d'Esther" de notre église, . . . " (I, 171). When next Marcel
alludes to the connection between the Guermantes and the
story of Esther, he alludes to the biblical book, but, omitting
the historical link of the tapestry, turns the comparison to
Racine's play.

In the shift, within a few lines, from Old Testament to
drama can be seen the change in Marcel's attitude toward
Oriane. Where the biblical Esther had added glamor to the
name of Guermantes, the dramatic Esther makes the actual
Guermantes seem trivial:

Peut-être parfois, quand, à l'imitation des princes persans qui, au
dire du *Livre d'Esther,* se faisaient lire les registres où étaient
inscrits les noms de ceux de leurs sujets qui leur avaient témoigne
du zèle, Mme de Guermantes consultait la liste des gens bien
intentionnés, elle s'était dit de moi: "Un à qui nous demanderons
de venir diner." Mais d'autres pensées l'avaient distraite

(De soins tumultueux un prince environné
Vers de nouveaux objets est sans cesse entrainé)

jusqu'au moment où elle m'avait aperçu seul comme Mardochée à la porte du palais; et ma vue ayant refraîchi sa mémoire, elle voulait, tel Assuérus, me combler de ses dons. (II, 378)

When Oriane was admired from afar, the story of Esther had added luster to Marcel's association. Now that he has come close enough to be invited to dine, she is compared not to Esther, but to the exotic and tyrannical Ahasuerus, ("Assuérus") and the comparison has her exercise her royal power on questions of dinner invitations. The terms of comparison are the same, but the values of the terms have been interchanged. The ironic development is complete. In brief form, this example shows Proust's method of inverting the theatrical and dramatic metaphors over the whole progress of the novel. What is first a convenient term of reference becomes a standard against which living characters are tested and found wanting, until the living are ultimately shown as less alive than the characters of art, literature, and drama. The present example, less than halfway through the novel, does not carry the process to its end, but stops at the penultimate step, where Oriane is now shown as inferior to a dramatic character.

The impressiveness of comparing Oriane to Esther has also been reduced by associating such comparisons with lesser characters in the novel. Even Françoise is associated, by use of quotation, with Racine, if not *Esther*: "'. . . Le bon Dieu les punit tout par un beau jour,' disait-elle, avec le regard latéral et l'insinuation de Joas pensant exclusivement à Athalie quand il dit: 'Le bonheur des méchants comme un torrent s'écoule'" (I, 108). The comparison of Françoise with Joas works immediately as ironic, with no development from direct to ironic comparison, whereas Oriane finally works down to the level from which Françoise starts. Another ironic comparison with a minor character helps to underline Oriane's decline to the implied level of a "bâtonnier . . . ivre de l'honneur d'avoir le gentilhomme à sa table," (I, 686), of whom Marcel writes, "Je vous aurais présenté! dit-il en corrigeant par une légère ironie l'énormité de cette proposition, comme Assuérus quand il dit à Esther: 'Faut-il de mes Etats vous donner la moitié?' " (I, 687). The method of applying the quotation is the same for Françoise, the minor character, and the Duchesse; and when Oriane is ironically compared in the same way to a Racinian character, she is also ironically equated with the other two subjects of comparison.

Marcel himself and Albertine also become enmeshed in the same way with the characters in *Esther*, at a point in the novel when homosexuals in the best society and among the servants at the Balbec hotel have also been equated with characters in that play and in *Athalie*. Albertine, when she has become Marcel's "prisoner," first makes the comparison:

La défense d'entrer chez moi avant que j'eusse sonné, l'amusait beaucoup. . . . Elle me comparait toujours à Assuérus:

Et la mort est le prix de tout audacieux
Qui sans être appelé se présente à ses yeux.

Rien ne met à l'abri de cet ordre fatal,
Ni le rang, ni le sexe, et le crime est égal.

Moi-même ...
Je suis à cette loi comme une autre soumise,
Et sans le prévenir il faut pour lui parler
Qu'il me cherche ou du moins qu'il me fasse appeler. (III, 18)

Marcel accepts the validity of the comparison. Françoise, he writes, "eût voulu qu'Albertine-Esther fût bannie" (III, 99).

When Albertine laughingly quotes from the play, Marcel goes along with her:

"J'espère que je n'ai pas eu tort, ajouta-t-elle. Je craignais que vous ne me disiez:

> Quel mortel insolent vient chercher le trépas?

Et elle rit de ce rire qui me troublait tant. Je lui répondis sur le même ton de plaisanterie:

> Est-ce pour vous qu'est fait cet ordre si sévère?

Et de peur qu'elle l'enfreignît jamais j'ajoutai: "Quoique je serais furieux que vous me réveilliez. — Je sais, je sais, n'ayez pas peur," me dit Albertine. Et pour adoucir j'ajoutai, en continuant à jouer avec elle la scène d'*Esther,* tandis que dans la rue continuaient les cris rendus tout à fait confus par notre conversation:

> Je ne trouve qu'en vous je ne sais quelle grâce
> Qui me charme toujours et jamais ne me lasse.

(et à part moi je pensais: "Si, elle me lasse bien souvent.") (III, 120)

Several of these quotations were used in a similar way in *Contre Sainte-Beuve*, where the application was to Proust and his mother, who was perhaps fortunate not to have seen this fictional application of the material.

The longest passage of dialogue and action including dramatic quotation in *Contre Sainte-Beuve* begins and ends with quotations from Molière's *Amphitryon*, but its main point and development are carried by a series of quotations from Racine's *Esther*:

> Les ordres sont donnés, tout nous paraît tranquille.
> Point d'ordre, point de bruit sur la ville. [*Amphitryon*]

110

Et tâché de dormir le plus tard possible, on ne te fera pas l'ombre de bruit jusqu'à cinq heures, six heures si tu veux, on te fera durer ta nuit aussi tard que tu voudras.

> Eh là là! Madame la Nuit
> Un peu doucement, je vous prie,
> Que vos chevaux, aux petits pas réduits,
> De cette nuit délicieuse
> Fassent la plus longue des nuits.[31]

Et c'est mon Loup qui finira pas trouver qu'elle est trop longue et qui demandera du bruit. C'est toi qui diras:

Cette nuit en longeur me semble sans pareille. [*Amphitryon*]

.   .   .   .

—Mais n'oublie pas de dire qu'on ne laisse entrer personne. . . . Peut-être ferais-tu bien de laisser un petit mot à Robert . . . qu'il n'entre directement chez moi. — Entrer directement chez toi!

> Peut-il donc ignorer quelle sévère loi
> Aux timides mortels cache ici notre roi,
> Que la mort est le prix de tout audacieux
> Qui sans être appelé se présente à ses yeux [*Esther*].[32]

Et Maman, pensant à cette *Esther* qu'elle préfère à tout, fredonne timidement . . . la mélodie divine qu'elle sent près d'elle: "Il s'apaise, il pardonne," ces chœurs divins que Reynaldo Hahn a écrits pour *Esther.* . . . Maman essayait timidement un air de chœur. . . . Et les belles lignes de son visage juif, tout empreint de douceur chrétienne et de courage janséniste, en faisaient Esther elle-même. . . .

After a time, his mother says:

—Je te dirai que j'avais peur de m'être trompée et que mon Loup me dise:

> C'est vous Esther qui sans être attendue ...
> Sans mon ordre on porte ici ses pas.
> Quel mortel insolent vient chercher le trépas.[33]

—Mais non, ma petite Maman.

> Que craigniez-vous, suis-je pas votre frère?
> Est-ce pour vous qu'on fit un ordre si sévère?

— . . . Est-ce que je peux dire à Félicie d'apporter l'électricité?
—Non, non; je ne pourrai plus m'endormir.
   Maman en riant:
—C'est toujour du Molière.

> Défendez, chère Alcmène, aux flambeaux d'approcher.
> (pp. 126–29)

This comparison of himself with the biblical king is one which evidently appealed to Proust. In a letter to Montesquiou, he wrote of having "avec Assuérus cette seule ressemblance qu'on n'entre pas dans ma chambre sans y être appelé,"[34] and in *A la recherche* he makes and alludes to this comparison several times.

From the account involving his mother in *Contre Sainte-Beuve*, Proust carries three parts of quotations over into *A la recherche*: " . . . La mort est le prix de tout audacieux/ Qui sans être appelé se present à ses yeux" (III, 18), "Quel mortel insolent vient chercher le trépas," and "Est-ce pour vous qu'est fait cet ordre si sévère?" (III, 120). But this is no mere coincidence of minor quotations. In both books, Proust uses extensive quotations from *Esther*; but what in *Contre Sainte-Beuve* has illustrated family conversation in some rather charming scenes becomes in *A la recherche* part of a larger complex illustrating the relationship between Marcel and Albertine, and tying in that relationship with the illicit and homosexual atmosphere of Balbec. By switching the references of the quotations, Mme Proust is transmuted, with an ease which might bemuse the Freudian, into Marcel's mistress. It has been suggested that the writing of *A la recherche* had to await the death of Proust's mother, who would have been appalled at her son's revelations of his putative homosexuality. Some of these transpositions of intimate family matters, baldly sketched in the posthumous *Contre Sainte-Beuve*, and manipulated in *A la recherche*, might have been almost as offensive. But aside from the biographical interest of the episode as presented in *Contre Sainte-Beuve*, of much more interest is the greater development, subtlety, and sea-change of the materials as they were later employed. As in the case of the deathbed quotations, anecdote is transformed into art.

Marcel applies the comparison to Assuérus indirectly to himself in a passage which does not directly bear on Albertine: "Aussi, d'habitude (sans prévoir, hélas! le drame que de tels réveils tardifs et mes lois draconiennes et persanes d'Assuérus racinien devaient bientôt amener pour moi) je m'efforçais de m'éveiller de bonne heure pour ne rien perdre de ces cris" (III, 126). He returns to the same terms of comparison, earlier applied by Albertine, just before she breaks out of her captivity:

. . . Je me rappelai qu'Albertine m'avait dit une fois combien elle me trouvait l'air terrible quand j'étais en colère, et m'avait appliqué les vers d'*Esther*:

> Jugez combien ce front irrité contre moi
> Dans mon âme troublée a dû jeter d'émoi ...
> Hélas! sans frissoner quel cœur audacieux
> Soutiendrait les éclairs qui partent de vos yeux?

J'eus honte de ma violence. (III, 395–96)[35]

113

This speech is from the same scene of *Esther* (Act II, scene 7) which Marcel and Albertine "acted" together against a chorus of street cries, and serves to close the Racinian circle around their whole affair. The first quotation was ten pages after the beginning of *La Prisonnière*, the above quotation is only twenty pages from the end, and another brief quotation only three pages from the end provides the final underlining:

. . . Je me félicitais de la "sévère loi" qui faisait que . . .
aucun "timide mortel" . . . ne s'aviserait de venir me troubler
"au fond de ce palais" où
Une majesté terrible
Affecte à mes sujets de me rendre invisible. (III, 413)

Here Proust has selected from a speech by Esther and has altered the pronouns. Like Caesar, constant as the northern star just before he is to be struck down, Marcel finally congratulates himself on being Assuérus, adapting the quotation to make it come from him instead of being applied to him, just before he is to discover that Albertine has defied His Majesty and left.

Even when considered in isolation, this complex of quotations relating Marcel and Albertine with Assuérus and Esther constitutes an ironic structure far beyond the comic effects of juxtaposing classical tragedy with latter-day events. Biographically and psychologically, the transposition of the material originally attached to Proust and his mother adds its very curious overtones and ambiguities. But as this cycle of *Esther* quotations in the novel follows the Guermantes cycle of *Esther* quotations, and Oriane and Marcel are both compared to Assuérus, it is impossible to ignore the parallel by which both characters are elevated in order to sustain an ironic tragicomic fall. Proust's equivalent for the Greek "Call no man happy until he is dead" might be "Take no elevating comparison seriously until it has been completed." As the Greek audience knew how to interpret expressions of joy or pride in the mouth of a tragic hero, Proust's reader may well hold his breath, or withhold his judgment, when Racine's tragedies provide terms of reference.

The most complicated of these interwoven clusters of quotations begins in *A l'ombre des jeunes filles en fleurs* and is not completed until late in *Sodome et Gomorrhe*. The first reference to the Balbec page boys in a Racinian context does not include quotations: "Mais l'après-midi ils restaient là seulement commes des choristes qui, même quand ils ne servent à rien, demeurent en scène pour ajouter à la figuration. . . . Du moins, . . . remplissaient-ils le vide de l'action, comme des élèves de Mme de Maintenon qui, sous le costume de jeunes israélites, font intermède chaque fois qu'Esther ou Joad s'en vont" (I, 706). Before Marcel returns to his chorus of pages, who have here been defined only in their public functions, a different cluster of comparisons and quotations casts its lurid light on the metaphor, which he then continues.

Comparisons and quotations from Racine, and specifically from *Esther*, are used to amplify Charlus' "revelations" about homosexuality in high places:

Mais ces révélations rapides, pareilles à celles qui dans les tragédies de Racine apprennent à Athalie et à Abner que Joas est de la race de David, qu'Esther "dans la pourpre assise" a des parents "youpins," changeant l'aspect de la légation de X ... ou tel service du ministère des Affaires étrangères, rendaient rétrospectivement ces palais aussi mystérieux que le temple de Jérusalem ou la salle du trône de Suse. Pour cette ambassade dont le jeune personnel vint tout entier serrer la main de M. de

115

Charlus, M. de Vaugoubert prit l'air émerveillé d'Elise s'écriant dans *Esther*:

> Ciel! quel nombreux essaim d'innocentes beautés
> S'offre à mes yeux en foule et sort de tous côtés!
> Quelle aimable pudeur sur leur visage est peinte!

. . . Habitué dès mon enfance à prêter, même à ce qui est muet, le langage des classiques, je faisais dire aux yeux de M. de Vaugoubert les vers par lesquels Esther explique à Elise que Mardochée a tenu, par zèle pour sa religion, à ne placer auprès de la Reine que des filles qui y appartinssent.

> Cependant son amour pour notre nation
> A peuplé ce palais de filles de Sion,
> Jeunes et tendres fleurs par le sort agitées,
> Sous un ciel étranger comme moi transplantées.
> Dans un lieu séparé de profanes témoins,
> Il (*l'excellent ambassadeur*) met à les former son
>   étude et ses soins.

Enfin M. de Vaugoubert parla, autrement que par ses regards. "Qui sait, dit-il avec mélancolie, si, dans le pays où je réside, la même chose n'existe pas? — C'est probable, répondit M. de Charlus, à commencer par le roi Théodose, bien que je ne sache rien de positif sur lui. . . . " Paroles que j'entendis, car j'étais peu éloigné, et qui firent que je me récitai mentalement:

Le Roi jusqu'à ce jour ignore qui je suis,
Et ce secret toujours tient ma langage enchaînée. (II, 665–66)[36]

These descriptions by Charlus are to be combined with still others.

For this, and for similar passages yet to be examined, Nathan offers a biographical explanation which also partly explains their ironic effect:

Signalons encore une sorte très particulière de citation, c'est celle qui consiste à faire des allusions aux chœurs d'*Esther* et aux jeunes filles qui les chantent et les dansent, pour caractériser les ébats de jeunes garçons très admirés par certains personnages du roman. . . . S'il n'avait voulu qu'amuser son lecteur, ou l' étonner par une association d'idées imprévue, Proust n'aurait pas recommencé sa plaisanterie aussi souvent. Nous pensons qu'une fois de plus il se torture à dessein en profanant ce qu'il aime, et en faisant servir les citations favorites de sa mère pour peindre l'inversion sexuelle qu'elle détestait, de même que dans le roman, le narrateur donne les meubles hérités de sa tante Léonie pour orner une maison de passe.[37]

Thus Nathan explains the double irony of each of such citations in each of its own contexts, but in attributing the repetitions merely to Proust's own perversity, he misses the further ironies by which various characters are reduced to the same level by being placed against the same backgrounds of comparison. He points out that this complex of quotations involves both Vaugoubert and the embassy attachés, and Nissim Bernard, Charlus, and the grooms at the Balbec hotel, but does not treat this fact as a growing equation.

Proust combines the two earlier passages—one comparing the hotel pages to a tragedy chorus, the other comparing homosexuals to characters in *Esther*—in a passage in *Sodome et Gomorrhe* which begins as the expression of a theatrical metaphor. The general artificiality and staginess with which the passage begins narrows down to a more specific falseness and play acting:

En bas, c'était l'élément masculin qui dominait et faisait de cet hôtel, à cause de l'extrême et oisive jeunesse des serviteurs, comme une sorte de tragédie judéo-chrétienne ayant pris corps et perpétuellement représentée. Aussi ne pouvais-je m'empêcher de me dire à moi-même, en les voyant, non certes les vers de Racine qui m'étaient venus à l'esprit chez la princesse de Guermantes

117

tandis que M. de Vaugoubert regardait de jeunes secrétaires d'ambassade saluant M. de Charlus, mais d'autres vers de Racine, cette fois-ci non plus d'*Esther*, mais d'*Athalie*: car dès le hall, ce qu'au XVIIe siècle on appelait les portiques, "un peuple florissant"[38] de jeunes chasseurs se tenait, surtout à l'heure du goûter, comme les jeunes Israélites des chœurs de Racine. Mais je ne crois pas qu'un seul eût pu fournir même la vague réponse que Joas trouve pour Athalie quand celle-ci demande au prince enfant: "Quel est donc votre emploi?" cars ils n'en avaient aucun.[39] Tout au plus, si l'on avait demandé à n'importe lequel d'entre eux, comme la vieille Reine:

> "Mais tout ce peuple enfermé dans ce lieu,
> A quoi s'occupe-t-il?"

aurait-il pu dire:

> "Je vois l'ordre pompeux de ces cérémonies

et j'y contribue." Parfois un des jeunes figurants allait vers quelque personnage plus important, puis cette jeune beauté rentrait dans le chœur. . . . Ils menaient la même existence ecclésiastique que les lévites dans *Athalie*, et devant cette "troupe jeune et fidèle"[40] . . . je pouvais me demander si je pénétrais dans le grand hôtel de Balbec ou dans le temple de Salomon. (II, 774–75)

Thus in creating this interplay between the two choruses, Proust enables Marcel to move from observations on the public activities of the hotel pages to speculations on their private ones. Germaine Brée finds in this process a characterization of the narrator (and presumably of Proust himself): "Le narrateur cède facilement à l'éblouissement devant les garçons de café ou grooms, au point de leur appliquer, parfois par un personnage interposé qui sert d'excuse, les vers des chœurs de Racine qui lui permettent de célébrer ainsi leurs 'jeunes beautés.'"[41] But more is at issue than any fascination felt by Marcel: such a fascination does not explain the structural, ironic use of the quotations.

Having equated the servants with the homosexual attachés, Proust next makes use of this complex of quotations to characterize the activities of an individual, Nissim Bernard, whom he also denigrates with other theatrical comparisons:

C'est qu'il entretenait, comme d'autres un rat d'opéra, un "commis," assez pareil à ces chasseurs dont nous avons parlé, et qui nous faisaient penser aux jeunes israélites d'*Esther* et d'*Athalie*. . . . Mais, comme le dit Racine avec tant de sagesse dans les mêmes chœurs:

> Mon Dieu, qu'une vertu naissante,
> Parmi tant de périls marche à pas incertains!
> Qu'une âme qui te cherche et veut être innocente,
> Trouve d'obstacle à ses desseins![42]

Le jeune commis avait eu beau être "loin du monde élevé,"[43] dans le Temple-Palace de Balbec, il n'avait pas suivi le conseil de Joad:

> Sur la richesse et l'or ne mets point ton appui.[44]

Il s'était peut-être fait une raison en disant: "Les pécheurs couvrent la terre." [45] Quoi qu'il en fût, et bien que M. Nissim Bernard n'espérât pas un délai aussi court, dès le premier jour,

> Et soit frayeur encore, ou pour le caresser
> De ses bras innocents il se sentit presser.[46]

Et dès le deuxième jour, M. Nissim Bernard promenant le commis, "l'abord contagieux altérait son innocence." Dès lors la vie du jeune enfant avait changé. Il avait beau porter le pain et le sel, comme son chef de rang le lui commandait, tout son visage chantait:

> De fleurs en fleurs, de plaisirs en plaisirs
> Promenons nos désirs ...

119

De nos ans passagers le nombre est incertain
Hâtons-nous aujourd'hui de jouir de la vie! ...
    L'honneur et les emplois
Sont le prix d'une aveugle et douce obéissance.
    Pour la triste innocence
    Qui voudrait élever la voix?[47]

Depuis ce jour-là, M. Nissim Bernard n'avait jamais manqué de venir occuper sa place au déjeuner. . . . Il se plaisait singulièrement, qu'elle fût juive ou catholique, à la cérémonie racinienne. Si elle eût une véritable représentation d'*Esther* ou d'*Athalie* M. Bernard eût regretté que la différence des siècles ne lui eût pas permis de connaître l'auteur, Jean Racine, afin d'obtenir pour son protégé un rôle plus considérable. (II, 842–44)

In such a passage as this complex represents, Proust focuses all the ironies inherent in the associations he makes between actual life and tragic life, figures in contemporary society and great figures of classical tragedy.

So well-established is the principle and the intention, that Proust provides merely a reminder when he applies the same technique, finally, to Charlus:

Même les jeunes chasseurs, les "lévites" qui descendaient en foule les degrés du temple à ce moment . . . ne firent pas attention aux deux arrivants, dont l'un, M. de Charlus, tenait, en baissant les yeux, à montrer qu'il leur en accordait très peu. . . . "Prospérez, cher espoir d'une nation sainte," dit-il en se rappelant des vers de Racine, cités dans un tout autre sens. . . . Mais, ayant continué les vers de Josabeth: "Venez, venez, mes filles," il se sentit dégoûté et n'ajouta pas, comme elle: "il faut les appeler," car ces jeunes enfants n'avaient pas encore atteint l'âge où le sexe est entièrement formé et qui plaisait à M. de Charlus. (II, 986–87)

Thus the quotations from Racine's plays and others provide their standard, either of permanence or of superiority, against which Proust places the materials of his novel. What is presented indirectly and analogically with quotations is presented directly and explicitly with the contrasts in the action between theatrical and non-theatrical characters, all of it sustained by the implications of recurrent specific allusions and the pattern of metaphor leading to the grand *coup de théâtre*, in which all the threads find their completed pattern.

Theater in the Action of
"A la recherche du temps perdu"

F. C. GREEN'S assertion that "Marcel, in his small way, also collects actresses"[1] concerns the young Marcel's "hierarchies" of actors and actresses mentioned in connection with the episode when the schoolboy Marcel sees Odette de Crécy at the apartment of his uncle Adolphe. But Marcel and Proust "collect" actresses throughout *A la recherche du temps perdu*: Berma, Rachel, Léa, a young actress at Balbec, an old actress in the audience the second time Marcel sees Berma perform, and others. Odette was once, however briefly, some kind of actress "dans une stupide petite opérette" (I, 860), in which Charlus found her charming (III, 299). Even Albertine had acted, if only in plays at her convent school (III, 18); this fact has more adumbrations than a first glance might suggest, since it bears on associations of Albertine with the Lesbian Léa.[2]

Berma and Rachel, of course, play the most important parts as actresses in the novel. Berma begins in the novel as a legend, and ends as a pathetic and neglected figure. Rachel begins in the novel as a pathetic prostitute, and ends well on her way to becoming the legend that will replace Berma. Their careers cross during the point of denouement of the whole novel, the *coup de théâtre* of the last Guermantes reception. Although the two women never meet in the action, each helps to establish the importance and significance of the other, and the replacement of Berma by Rachel is one of Time's greater ironies.

BERMA

The material about Berma falls into four clusters, the first three widely separated from the last. The young Marcel's glamorous image of Berma is described in *Du côté de chez Swann*. His disappointment the first time he sees her is taken up in *A l'ombre des jeunes filles en fleurs*, and his realization of her genius in *Le Côté de Guermantes*. *Sodome et Gomorrhe* includes only one casual reference to his first disappointment, while *La Prisonnière* and *La Fugitive* include no references to Berma. The last cluster of Berma material begins less than two hundred pages from the end of *Le Temps retrouvé*, leaving more than eighteen hundred pages between the third and fourth cluster. Once the legend and status of Berma have been established, time can be left to work its reversals.

The importance of Rachel's replacement of Berma is solidified by the fact that Berma has been set up as a standard of comparison in three different ways: aesthetic, social, and personal. First, she is one of the touchstones for Marcel's views about art, particularly to demonstrate the immortality of art as compared with the evanescence of life. Berma is something

124

of an exception to Milton Hindus' description of Proust's attitude toward interpretive artists:

The interpreters of artistic works rank far below the creative artists in the realm of art. . . . When the narrator went to the theatre to see the famous actress Berma for the first time, he was aware of the talents of everybody in the cast except herself—not because she didn't possess any talent but because she had identified herself so completely with the part of Phèdre which she was playing that to an untrained eye she could no longer be distinguished from it. But most interpreters in Proust are very shallow-minded.[3]

But Berma as an interpretive artist rises among the clouds of immortality surrounding the peaks of art.

The novel illustrates the change in Berma's personal fortunes and reputation, but it has also caught in the crystal of art her achievement as an artist, which is ultimately more important than her personal life. Georges Piroué presents Proust's view thus: "To the extent to which they are creators, they avoid the common destiny of their fellow-men. . . . If the artists have thus the power to endure, the reason is that they are blessed with the gift of transposing life into a series of equivalents. For the ordinary man dreams are drowned in reality."[4] It is in this sense that Berma is established as one of Marcel's standards of comparison.

The second way in which Berma establishes a standard of comparison is in the contrast with Rachel which is designed to show the greater importance of artistic achievement over position in worldly society. In a fashion similar to that in which Rachel replaces Berma, the conclusion of the novel interchanges the values of society and the values of the theater. In the early part of the novel the theater is subservient to society. Piroué describes it as a satellite:

The theatre is the temple of an aristocracy which, like the Jewish people, has lost its home. . . . Performances proceed in obedience to a law of double ceremonial, one on the stage, the other in the auditorium. The latter resembles a vast submarine grotto. . . . Meanwhile, behind the footlights, Berma goes through her part, the high-priestess of a cult of which the narrator, though at first disappointed, later becomes an initiate.[5]

The curious double way in which Proust uses the theater as a standard (of which Berma is one example) is illustrated in two observations by Milton Hindus. On the one hand, society comes "down" to the level of actresses: "The character of the Duchesse as it finally emerges in Proust's work is that of one who desperately seeks for notoriety rather than for wisdom. She finds her true intellectual level at the end of the book in the company of actresses." [6] But on the other hand, actresses maintain values which the Duchesse knows not at all. Hindus writes of Rachel, but his observation, without the negative qualifications, would apply as well to Berma: "Rachel's reputation as an actress is more important to her than all the wealth and social rank offered by her aristocratic lover, Saint-Loup. . . . It is this standard of values which, in spite of all her viciousness, cruelty, and prostitution, raises her in Proust's pages far above the fine but vapid society women who fancy themselves her superiors. It is Rachel who reveals the genius of Maeterlinck from the stage, not they." [7] It is Berma's family, not she herself, that truckles to society at the end, and society is shown as unworthy in neglecting her. Marcel, however, is clearly pleased to be able to mention Berma among his "anciens amis" (III, 856) who remember him after his long absence at the sanatorium.

The third way in which Berma serves as a steady standard in a changing world appears in passages where various characters reveal themselves by what they have to say about the actress. These passages do not present "a cloud of witnesses" about Berma, since her genius is given as the accepted fact against which observations and comments are tested. When Norpois talks nonsense about her, and Bergotte talks wisdom, it is not Berma whom we are to judge. When Rachel is patronizing of Berma in conversation (II, 167) and action (III, 1013–15), it is not Berma who is being characterized, any more than Bernhardt is characterized by the observations of Marcel, Cottard, or Charlus.

The identification that most readers will make of Berma as Sarah Bernhardt helps to establish Berma as reigning queen of the theater. Bernhardt is herself mentioned six or seven times in the novel, just enough to make the disingenuous suggestion that Berma is not she; but in one cross reference, Proust all but establishes that she is. Berma and Bernhardt are each first mentioned in Marcel's boyish hierarchy of actresses, in which Berma is the sole fictional actress (I, 75). The next mention of Bernhardt is a minor bit of action characterizing Cottard: when Mme Verdurin utters conventional thanks for his coming to a theater party, he agrees that he is doing her something of a favor, saying, "En effet on est beaucoup trop près et on commence à être fatigué de Sarah Bernhardt" (I, 201). The next reference to Bernhardt, more than eighteen hundred pages later, has Charlus sneering at the actress: "Voir Sarah Bernhardt dans *l'Aiglon*, qu'est-ce que c'est? du caca" (II, 1070). Charlus is still sneering almost nine hundred pages after that: "Je me demande jusqu'à quel point *Madame* Sarah Bernhardt est qualifiée pour parler au nom de la France" (III, 825–26). Her name is used in two metaphors (III, 234, 959); but the oddest use of her name, twice repeated, occurs when Marcel says (after the discussions of twice having seen Berma as Phèdre) that he has never seen "Rome, Venise, Sienne, le Prado, le musée de Dresde, les Indes, Sarah dans *Phèdre*" (II, 1084). This identification of Phèdre as the supreme role for Bernhardt and for Berma clinches the obvious parallel, which, in any event, seems never to have been doubted.

George B. Painter mentions "two originals of 'Berma,' Réjane and Sarah Bernhardt."[8] Réjane is mentioned twice in Proust's novel, once in a comparison with Jeanne Granier (II, 495), and again as a rival of Berma's (III, 997). Réjane, however, cannot provide much of the basis for Berma's artistic life, since she specialized in comedy and undertook none of the classic roles. Berma's identification with Phèdre seems to throw the weight of identification and association on Bernhardt. In any case, Berma's status as a dramatic artist is one of the few unchanging assumptions in *A la recherche du temps perdu.*

The "Combray" section of *Du côté de chez Swann* shows Marcel's passion for the theater and for Berma developing in the same way as others of his passions. His first admiration is, as he says, platonic, based on an ideal growing from a name and a reputation—an ideal almost certainly doomed to disappointment. His platonic passion for the theater and his enormous admiration of the work of Bergotte are the begetters of his glamorizing of Berma before he has ever set foot in a theater or seen an actress on a stage. The art of the actor is for him *the* art before he has ever seen a performance, when his conception of what a theater is like is vague and incorrect —including the idea that "chaque spectateur regardait comme dans un stéréoscope un décor qui n'était que pour lui . . . "

(I, 73). He goes on to describe his morning inspections of the posters for plays he knows only by name, his schoolboy discussions of the reputation and talents of actors he has never seen, and his lists of hierarchies. Bergotte causes Marcel to interchange his first two names in the hierarchy of actresses, putting Berma first.

Before he has seen Berma, names of plays act upon the young Marcel in the same romantic fashion as the names of Guermantes and other people and places. He writes of the "images inséparables des mots qui en composaient le titre et aussi de la couleur des affiches" (I, 73). The magic of names creates the ideal against which the reality of life cannot but be a disappointment. Marcel's involvement with the theater and then with Berma is an epitome of his involvements with the Guermantes, with Gilberte, and with Albertine—just as Swann's involvement with Odette is a pattern of Marcel's affairs. The pattern of glamorizing, disillusionment, and adjustment repeats from Marcel's mental and artistic experience to his passional experience.

In the atmosphere of Marcel's platonic love of the theater, the idea implanted by Bergotte's preference for Berma develops rapidly, one admiration leading easily to another. Just as his first hearing of Berma is clouded by too much expectation, so his first reading of Bergotte, although sympathetic, does not reveal the qualities that he later finds so admirable:

Les premiers jours . . . ce que je devais tant aimer dans son style ne m'apparut pas. . . . Un de ces passages de Bergotte, le troisième ou le quatrième que j'eusse isolé du reste, me donna une joie incomparable à celle que j'avais trouvé au premier. . . .

Je n'étais pas tout à fait le seul admirateur de Bergotte; il était aussi l'écrivain préféré d'une amie de ma mère qui était très lettrée. (I, 93–94)

129

The need to feel that his admiration is shared is common to both the initial experience of reading Bergotte and that of hearing Berma. To anticipate the latter, in order to make the parallel clear, Marcel reports, "Enfin éclata mon premier sentiment d'admiration: il fut provoqué par les applaudissements frénétiques des spectateurs" (I, 450).

So uncertain is the young Marcel of his standards that he feels a need to have his discoveries shared, and is astonished that an admired author should have had thoughts similar to his own:

Chaque fois qu'il parlait de quelque chose dont la beauté m'était restée jusque-là cachée . . . d'*Athalie* ou de *Phèdre*, il faisait dans une image exploser cette beauté jusqu'à moi. . . . Quand par hasard il m'arriva d'en rencontrer, dans tel de ses livres, une [pensée] que j'avais déjà eue moi-même, mon cœur se gonflait comme si un dieu dans sa bonté me l'avait rendue, l'avait déclarée légitime et belle. (I, 95–96)

The tinder is set for the spark that Proust lights in the conversation which directly follows, when Marcel discovers that the Swanns, who are illuminated in his mind by the magical coincidence, count Bergotte among their friends. He is fascinated that Swann can tell him that Bergotte's favorite actress is Berma and can pass on Marcel's questions to Bergotte, who visits the Swanns weekly (I, 97–99). The anticipation created by this, and by Gilberte's having given him Bergotte's pamphlet on Racine, is defeated by Marcel's sudden illness and the doctor's stern commands: "Et hélas, il défendit aussi d'une façon absolue qu'on me laissait aller au théâtre entendre la Berma: l'artiste sublime, à laquelle Bergotte trouvait du génie . . . " (I, 393). And there, having established Marcel's image of Berma and its importance for him, *Du côté de chez Swann* leaves the subject.

The defeat of all Marcel's expectations forms the first important episode in *A l'ombre des jeunes filles en fleurs,* interconnected with the visit of M. de Norpois. Since the accomplishment of Marcel's dearest wish is an unqualified disappointment—"Hélas! cette première matinée fut une grande déception" (I, 445)—which occurs at the precise moment of Berma's entrance, and since this episode is representative of Marcel's many inevitable disappointments, it seems worthwhile to examine rather carefully the causes of the carefully planned anticlimax. The total cause may be summed up in the apt phrase "l'image inconcevable" (I, 443) which Marcel uses in speaking of Berma, and the implications of the phrase may be separated into three related causes of letdown: excessive anticipation, false assumptions, and overanalysis.

Above and beyond these psychological and philosophical causes of disappointment is the problem of pure practical ignorance. Throughout the description of this first visit to the theater (I, 438–51) runs a pattern of naïve misconceptions corrected by plain fact. First, there is the discovery that, contrary to his earlier misconception, the theater has but one stage (p. 446). Second, there is Marcel's failure to recognize actors as actors, even after the curtain has risen and "deux hommes entrèrent sur la scène, bien en colère, puisqu'ils parlaient assez fort pour que dans cette salle où il y avait plus de mille personnes on distinguât toutes leurs paroles . . . mais dans le même instant, étonné de voir que le public les entendait sans protester . . . je compris que ces insolents étaient les acteurs et que la petite pièce, dit lever de rideau, venait de commencer" (p. 447). Third, he mistakenly "recognizes" Berma twice before she actually appears:

. . . Une actrice entra par le fond, qui avait la figure et la voix qu'on m'avait dit être celles de la Berma. . . . Mais une autre actrice donna la réplique à la première. J'avais dû me tromper en prenant celle-là pour la Berma, car la seconde lui ressemblait davantage encore et, plus que l'autre, avait sa diction. . . . Mais tout d'un coup, dans l'écartement du rideau rouge du sanctuaire, comme dans un cadre, une femme parut et aussitôt . . . je compris que les deux actrices que j'admirais depuis quelques minutes n'avaient aucune ressemblance avec celle que j'étais venu entendre. (pp. 448–49)

The last corrected misconception is more subtle, and is qualified by a gentle irony which leaves in doubt whether Marcel at the time really noticed what he had been missing: "La déclaration à Hippolyte . . . elle passa au rabot d'une mélopée toute la tirade où se trouvèrent confondues ensembles des oppositions pourtant si tranchées qu'une tragédienne à peine intelligente, même des élèves de lycée, n'en eussent pas négligé l'effet [!]; d'ailleurs, elle la débita tellement vite que ce fut seulement quand elle fut arrivée au dernier vers que mon esprit prit conscience de la monotonie voulue qu'elle avait imposée aux premiers" (pp. 449–50). This description of *Phèdre* is clearly that of a precocious schoolboy, ironically viewed by the mature psychological novelist. Despite the importance of some of the issues in Marcel's future development and experience, part of the episode is designedly comic, a facet of the portrait of the artist as a very young man.

The inconceivable image which Marcel has created of Berma is itself an important reason why he cannot appreciate the real Berma. What he demands of a single theatrical performance is one of the supreme summits of art: "La Berma dans *Andromaque,* dans *Les Caprices de Marianne,* dans *Phèdre,* c'était de ces choses fameuses que mon imagination avait tant désirées" (I, 440). He attaches to the experience the already familiar mystique of magic names. He writes of "deux actes de *Phèdre* avec Mme Berma, et aux matinées suivantes *Le Demi-Monde, Les Caprices de Marianne,* noms qui, comme celui de *Phèdre,* étaient pour moi transparents, remplis seulement de clarté, tant l'œuvre m'était connue, illuminés jusqu'au fond d'un sourire d'art" (p. 442). He plays with the terms which Bergotte has applied to *Phèdre:* "noblesse plastique, cilice chrétien, pâleur janséniste, princesse de Trézène et de Clèves, drame mycénien, symbole delphique, mythe solaire" (p. 443); and, on seeing the complete bill of the performance posted, balances these magic terms with the magic terms of a particular performance: " . . . Je ne fis qu'un bond jusqu'à la maison, cinglé que j'étais par ces mots magiques qui avaient remplacé dans ma pensée 'pâleur janséniste' et 'mythe solaire': 'Les dames ne seront pas reçues à l'orchestre en chapeau, les portes seront fermées à deux heures'" (p. 445). His excitement recalls my own boyish misconception that "No one seated during the first scene" meant that this first scene was so compelling as to lift the entire audience to its feet, like royalty at Handel's *Messiah.*

Marcel's experience at the theater is not his first disappointment with the magic of names. Late in the "Combray" chapter he has already described one, when, at a wedding, he notices that a Duchesse may have so common an ailment as a pimple on her nose:

133

. . . Un mouvement que fit le suisse en se déplaçant me permit de voir assise dans une chapelle une dame blonde avec un grand nez, des veux bleus et perçants, une cravate bouffante en soie mauve, lisse, neuve et brillante, et un petit bouton au coin du nez. . . . Ma déception était grande. Elle provenait de ce que je n'avais jamais pris garde, quand je pensais à Mme de Guermantes, que je me la représentais avec les couleurs d'une tapisserie ou d'un vitrail, dans un autre siècle, d'une autre matière que le reste des personnes vivantes. Jamais je ne m'étais avisé qu'elle pouvait avoir figure rouge, une cravate mauve comme Mme Sazerat. . . . (I, 174–75)

When Marcel gets permission to go to the theater through the casual good offices of M. de Norpois, he momentarily fears that Berma might have the equivalent of the Duchesse's pimple, for he begins to weigh the reasons for not going.

He wonders whether his parents have given their permission against their better judgment, and whether his having won it will hurt their feelings. (When his mother assures him that he must not let such doubts spoil their pleasure in having him go, he feels an onerous obligation to enjoy himself.) He also wonders if his going might not bring on an illness that would prevent his meeting Gilberte in the Champs-Elysées. But when he sees the announcement of the performance on a billboard, it restores all his anticipation which lasts through his arrival in the square in front of the theater, his passage through the lobby, and his entrance into the theater itself. As any theatergoer knows, the moment when the lights dim and the curtain starts to rise is sometimes the best moment of the evening. Marcel even enjoys the backstage noises before this, which remind him of the sounds from inside an eggshell just before the chick bursts forth. His anticipation survives the ordinary setting and the quarrelsome actors of the curtain-raiser, and even the early scenes of *Phèdre*, but with Berma's entrance the pretty magic bubble bursts, as always it must when it is over-inflated.

Besides the psychological difficulties of excessive anticipation, Marcel's experience of Berma is beclouded at this stage by some aesthetic misconceptions—false assumptions about the art of the theater and of acting. One of these, of which he later makes a point, is his failure to separate the artistic responsibility of the actress from that of the dramatist. For this reason he overestimates the importance of seeing the actress in a classic role in order to understand the qualities of her genius: " . . . Si j'avais été voir . . . la Berma dans quelque pièce dont je n'aurais jamais entendu parler, je n'aurais plus éprouvé le même étonnement délicieux d'avoir enfin les yeux ouverts devant l'objet inconcevable et unique de tant de milliers de mes rêves" (I, 441). In Berma's acting he looks for strangeness, surprises, some gesture or intonation that he himself could never have imagined. His reactions and judgments are those of Partridge at the play in *Tom Jones*: "The king for my money; he speaks all his words distinctly, half as loud again as the other. Anybody may see he is an actor." In the "Nouveaux mélanges" of *Contre Sainte-Beuve*, Proust had described the purity of acting that was precisely of the kind which made it difficult for the young Marcel to appreciate Berma's playing, and therefore caused him disappointment: "Le jeu d'un grand acteur est plus nu et donne ainsi moins de prise à l'admiration de la foule que le jeu d'un acteur habile. Car son geste et sa voix sont si parfaitement décantés de toutes parcelles d'or ou scories qui le troublaient, qu'il semble que c'est seulement l'eau claire, comme un vitrage qui laisse seulement voir l'objet naturel qui est au-delà" (p. 330).

Marcel's difficulty is precisely that he cannot see that Berma is an actress; he is thinking in terms of "acteurs venus pour réciter" (I, 447). He is looking for truths beyond the real world: " . . . —Ce que je demandais à cette matinée, c'était tout autre chose qu'un plaisir: des vérités appartenant à un monde plus réel que celui où je vivais . . . " (I, 442). He prepares himself for strangeness by studying to eliminate the likely: "Je me récitais sans cesse la tirade: On dit qu'un prompt départ vous éloigne de nous ... cherchant toutes les intonations qu'on pouvait y mettre, afin de mieux mesurer l'innattendu de celle que la Berma trouverait" (I, 443). He is impressed by the other actresses because this is what they offer him: "Toutes deux d'ailleurs ajoutaient à leur rôle de noble gestes—que je distinguais clairement et dont je comprenais la relation avec le texte, tandis qu'elles soulevaient leurs beaux péplums—et aussi des intonations ingénieuses, tantôt passionées, tantôt ironiques, qui me faisaient comprendre la signification d'un vers que j'avais lu chez moi sans apporter assez d'attention à ce qu'il voulait dire" (I, 448).

This strangeness is what he misses in Berma's performance: "Quant à la déclaration à Hippolyte, j'avais compté sur ce morceau où . . . elle aurait certainement des intonations plus surprenantes que celles que chez moi, en lisant, j'avais tâché d'imaginer" (I, 449–50). At the precise moment of his disappointment, Marcel sounds most like Partridge, and underlines his naïveté with deliberate irony:

Mais en même temps tout mon plaisir avait cessé; j'avais beau tendre vers la Berma mes yeux, mes oreilles, mon esprit, pour ne pas laisser échapper une miette des raisons qu'elle me donnerait de l'admirer, je ne parvenais pas à en recueillir une seule. Je ne pouvais même pas, comme pour ses camarades, distinguer dans sa diction et dans son jeu des intonations intelligentes, de beaux gestes. Je l'écoutais comme j'aurais lu *Phèdre*, ou comme si Phèdre elle-même avait dit en ce moment les choses que j'entendais, sans que le talent de la Berma semblât leur avoir rien ajouté. (p. 449)

The episode is exemplary of Marcel's unending penchant for creating his own disappointments by looking in the wrong way for the wrong things—in art, in love, and in life—until the realization at the last Guermantes reception that gives him a new perspective on what it all meant, and makes possible the transmutation of raw experience into art.

The episode is exemplary, too, of the peril of overanalysis which makes it impossible for him to take experience as it comes, and in the fashion proper to it. Marcel goes to the theater to study Berma rather than to hear and observe her; he destroys empathy by trying to anticipate, and by wishing he could stop the action to analyze it. His analytical approach is one reason he does not wish to see her in an unfamiliar play: "Les œuvres anciennes que je savais par cœur, m'apparaissaient comme de vastes espaces réservés et tout prêts où je pourrais apprécier en pleine liberté les inventions dont la Berma les couvrirait, comme à fresque, des perpétuelles trouvailles de son inspiration" (p. 441). Having carefully studied the text of the play, and having looked for all that might reasonably be done with it, he wishes above all that he could destroy the essential nature of the drama, the progress of its action, catching the intonations and gestures to turn them appreciatively about and admire all their facets:

J'aurais voulu—pour pouvoir l'approfondir, pour tâcher d'y découvrir ce qu'elle avait de beau—arrêter, immobiliser longtemps devant moi chaque intonation de l'artiste, chaque expression de sa physionomie; du moins, je tâchais, à force d'agilité mentale, en ayant avant un vers mon attention tout installée et mise au point, de ne pas distraire en préparatifs une parcelle de la durée de chaque mot, de chaque geste. . . . Mais que cette durée était brève! A peine un son était-il reçu dans mon oreille qu'il était remplacé par un autre. Dans une scène où la Berma reste immobile un instant, le bras levé à la hauteur du visage, baignée grâce à un artifice d'éclairage dans une lumière verdâtre, devant le décor qui représenta la mer, la salle éclata en applaudissements, mais déjà l'actrice avait changé de place et le tableau que j'aurais voulu étudier n'existait plus. (p. 449)

Proust in this episode has given us several pages for a primer on how not to see a play, or how to lose the forest in the trees. The whole thing is a deftly and ironically contrived demonstration of trying to crack a pecan with a sledgehammer, of putting the violet in the crucible.

No wonder Marcel goes on to another aesthetic error, that of trying to borrow his opinions from others, and absorbing their wrong reasons along with the right ones that he fails to understand. Finally, having failed to go along with the performance, he allows himself to go along with the enthusiasm, both well and ill founded, of the audience:

Enfin éclata mon premier sentiment d'admiration: il fut provoqué par les applaudissements frénétiques des spectateurs. . . . Ce qui est du reste curieux, c'est que le moment où se déchaîna cet enthousiasme du public fut, je l'ai su depuis, celui où la Berma a une de ses plus belles trouvailles. . . . On découvre un trait génial du jeu de la Berma huit jours après l'avoir entendue, par la critique, ou sur le coup, par les acclamations du parterre. . . . Je partageai avec ivresse le vin grossier de cet enthousiasme populaire. Je n'en sentis pas moins, le rideau tombé, un désappointement que ce plaisir que j'avais tant désiré n'eût pas été plus grand. . . . (pp. 450–51)

This final experience in the theater, of trying to force enthusiasm for what he ought to like, and of seeking understanding through the reactions of other people, is echoed throughout
several discussions of the performance in the course of the
first part ("Autour de Mme Swann") of *A l'ombre des jeunes
filles en fleurs.* The significance of the episode as an exemplar
of his loves appears on the fifth page of the second part
("Noms de pays: Le Pays"). The episode is then left, and
Berma is not mentioned again until Marcel sees her a second
time, early in *Le Côté de Guermantes.*

The brief discussion of the performance which Marcel has
with Norpois on the same evening establishes the basic pattern
of his looking to other people's opinions, and trying to follow
them even when they are contradictory. The pattern is the
more forcefully established by the vapidity of Norpois' remarks, when he and Marcel's father are both surprised to
hear that Marcel has been disappointed. When Marcel admits
that Berma was no doubt very good, Norpois pontificates,
"Une des choses qui contribuent certainement au succès de
Mme Berma . . . c'est le goût parfait qu'elle apporte dans
le choix de ses rôles et qui lui vaut toujours un franc succès,
et de bon aloi. Elle joue rarement des médiocrités. Voyez, elle
s'est attaqué au rôle de Phèdre." In this, Norpois is unfor-
tunately confirming one of Marcel's own misconceptions about
the nature of acting, but he goes on to greater nonsense:

D'ailleurs, ce goût elle l'apporte dans ses toilettes, dans son jeu.
. . . Jamais de couleurs trop voyantes, de cris exagérés. Et puis
cette voix admirable qui la sert si bien et dont elle joue à ravir,
je serais presque tenté de dire en musicienne!

Mon intérêt pour le jeu de la Berma n'avait cessé de grandir
depuis que la représentation était finie. . . . "C'est vrai, me

disais-je, quelle belle voix, quelle absence de cris, quels costumes simples, quelle intelligence d'avoir été choisir *Phèdre*! Non, je n'ai pas été deçu." (I, 457–58)

The irony of Norpois' vapidities is triple-edged. There is the double irony of Marcel's misconception of the man and the value of his opinions, and the man's misconception of himself. There is the third irony that this is the man who persuades Marcel's father, as casually as he did in gaining permission for the boy to see Berma in *Phèdre,* of the suitability of allowing the boy to engage in a literary career. The characterization of Norpois, and the resultant ironies, depend in part on the reader's assumption of the talents of Berma, missed at this point both by Marcel and by Norpois.

Having already had Marcel declare that "on découvre un trait génial du jeu de la Berma huit jours après l'avoir entendue, par la critique," Proust allows us to see this happening somewhat sooner:

Or mon père me passa le journal en me désignant un entrefilet conçu en ces termes: "La représentation de *Phèdre* qui a été donnée devant une salle enthousiaste où on remarquait les principales notabilités du monde des arts et de la critique a été pour Mme Berma, qui jouait le rôle de Phèdre, l'occasion d'un triomphe comme elle en a rarement connu de plus éclatant au cours de sa prestigieuse carrière." . . . Dès que mon esprit eut conçu cette idée nouvelle de "la plus pure et haute manifestation d'art," celle-ci se rapprocha du plaisir imparfait que j'avais éprouvé au théâtre, lui ajouta un peu de ce qui lui manquait et leur réunion forma quelque chose de si exaltant que je m'écriai: "Quelle grande artiste!" (I, 480–81)

That the need to strengthen our ideas with those of others does not operate only in the aesthetic realm, nor only with

140

the naïve or inexperienced, and that Marcel's experience with Berma is typical of his passional experience, Proust lets us see when Marcel's preoccupations with Berma turn away from her identity as an artist.

When Marcel buys a photograph of Berma, it is not because he finds it beautiful, but as a reflection of the attitudes of others: "Ce visage, d'ailleurs, ne m'eût pas à lui semblé beau, mais il me donnait l'idée et par conséquent l'envie, de l'embrasser à cause de tous les baisers qu'il avait dû supporter et que, du fond de la 'carte-album,' il semblait appeler encore par ce regard coquettement tendre et ce sourire artificieusement ingénu" (I, 487). In this attitude, Marcel might again be said to be going along with the audience in order vicariously to deepen his own inadequate experience. In the next paragraph but one, he introduces his usual association of actresses with the passional life, and his usual emotional catalyst in the realm of love: jealousy. It cannot be by accident that as he lies awake the train of association leads to Gilberte:

Je pensais à tous les gens qui finiraient leur nuit dans les plaisirs, à l'amant, à la troupe de débauchés peut-être, qui avaient dû aller chercher la Berma à la fin de cette représentation que j'avais vue annoncée pour le soir. . . . A la pensée qu'il était sans doute en ce moment caressé par ces hommes que je ne pouvais empêcher de donner à la Berma, et de recevoir d'elle, des joies surhumaines et vagues, j'éprouvais un émoi plus cruel qu'il n'était voluptueux. . . . A ce moment-là, un mot de Gilberte n'eût peut-être pas été ce qu'il m'eût fallu. (I, 488–89)

With these boyish reactions to Berma the actress and Berma the imagined woman, and with Swann's affair behind us, the outlines of Marcel's affairs and their psychological bases are predictable. They mutter of what is to come as persistently as any Greek chorus.

The two remaining discussions of the *Phèdre* performance in *A l'ombre des jeunes filles en fleurs,* with Bergotte and with Swann about seventy pages further on, return to aesthetic matters. The first part of the discussion with Bergotte concerns Marcel's continued impatience with the rapid progress of dramatic action, and his belief in the necessity of knowing everything in advance:

[Bergotte] me dit que dans la scène où [Berma] reste le bras levé à la hauteur de l'épaule—précisément une des scènes où on avait tant applaudi—elle avait su évoquer avec un art très noble des chefs-d'œuvre qu'elle n'avait peut-être d'ailleurs jamais vus, une Hespéride qui fait ce geste sur une métope d'Olympie, et aussi les belles vierges de l'ancien Eréchthéion. . . . Je parlais des Koraï de l'ancien Eréchthéion, et je reconnais qu'il n'y a peut-être rien qui soit aussi loin de l'art de Racine, mais il y a déjà tant de choses dans *Phèdre.* . . .

. . . Les paroles qu'il prononçait en ce moment étaient fort claires pour moi et me donnaient une nouvelle raison de m'intéresser au jeu de la Berma. Je tâchais de la revoir dans mon souvenir, telle qu'elle avait été dans cette scène où je me rappelais qu'elle avait élevé le bras à hauteur de l'épaule. . . . Mais pour que ces pensées pussent m'embellir le geste de la Berma, il aurait fallu que Bergotte me les eût fournies avant la représentation. . . . Mais de la Berma dans cette scène, ce que je gardais c'était un souvenir qui n'était plus modifiable, . . . une image à laquelle on ne peut imposer rétroactivement une interprétation qui ne serait plus susceptible de vérification, de sanction objective. (I, 560–61)

Bergotte seems to confirm Marcel's idea that there is one truth, of which art—all the arts—are a reflection, and also Marcel's attempts to establish wider and wider circles of association to strengthen any single idea. He unintentionally confirms, too, Marcel's penchant for overanalysis, and his failure to realize that the dramatic arts properly function, like music, in moving time rather than in extended space.

Bergotte's second group of remarks, although it corrects some of Marcel's views, serves mostly to establish the contrast between Bergotte and Norpois, underlining the latter's glibness with surface acquaintance as against Bergotte's modest and tactful presentation of direct and backstage knowledge:

> Je me laissai aller à raconter mes impressions. Souvent Bergotte ne les trouvait pas justes, mais il me laissait parler. Je lui dis que j'avais aimé cet éclairage vert qu'il y a au moment où Phèdre léve le bras. "Ah! vous feriez très plaisir au décorateur qui est un grand artiste, je le lui raconterai parce qu'il est très fier de cette lumière-là. Moi, je dois dire que je ne l'aime pas beaucoup, ça baigne tout dans une espèce de machine glauque, la petite Phèdre là dedans fait trop branche de corail au fond d'un aquarium." . . . Et quand l'avis de Bergotte était ainsi contraire au mien, il ne me réduisait nullement au silence, à l'impossibilité de rien répondre, comme eût fait celui de M. de Norpois. . . . Les arguments de M. de Norpois (en matière d'art) étaient sans réplique parce qu'ils étaient sans réalité. (I, 561–62)

Despite the discrepancy between the opinions of Bergotte and Norpois, Marcel still shows his willingness to look to others for the expression of proper reactions to his own experience when Swann makes a pronouncement about Berma.

Marcel also still persists in one of his false expectations:

> [Swann] me fit remarquer . . . avec quelle intelligence, quelle justesse imprévue l'actrice disait à Œnone: "Tu le savais!" Il avait raison: cette intonation-là, du moins, avait une valeur vraiment intelligible et aurait dû par là satisfaire à mon désir de trouver des raisons irréfutables d'admirer la Berma. . . .

L'intonation était si ingénieuse, d'une intention, d'un sens si définis, qu'elle semblait exister en elle-même et que toute artiste intelligente eût pu l'acquérir. . . . Il restait à la Berma qu'elle l'avait trouvé, mais peut-on employer ce mot de "trouver," quand il s'agit de quelque chose qui ne serait pas différent si on l'avait reçu, quelque chose qui ne tient pas essentiellement à votre être, puisqu'un autre peut ensuite le reproduire? (I, 567)

With this last reference to Marcel's aesthetic problems before he sees Berma for the second time and "discovers" her, the emphasis is left for almost four hundred pages on the fact that in hearing Berma and seeking to "appreciate" her, Marcel puts his strongest focus on trying to qualify some trait or talent that shall be strange, unlooked-for, special, and unique. In the sentence in which he describes Berma as the type of his loves, between the two views of her, he reiterates the importance of this fact: "Pour moi, j'avais déjà appris, et même bien avant d'aller entendre la Berma, que, quelle que fût la chose que j'aimerais, elle ne serait jamais placée qu'au terme d'une poursuite douloureuse, au cours de laquelle il me faudrait d'abord sacrifier mon plaisir à ce bien suprême, au lieu de l'y chercher" (I, 646). This sentence summarizes the pursuit of and disappointment in the achievement of Berma that runs through *Du côté de chez Swann* and the first half of *A l'ombre des jeunes filles en fleurs*. The discovery that aesthetic appreciation, like happiness, comes as an unexpected by-product instead of as the goal of an unremitting determined search is given some years later in *Le Côté de Guermantes*.

Whereas the pursuit and disappointment episodes run through some twenty-five pages, separated into about a dozen passages of varying lengths, Marcel's second experience with Berma appears within a single block of some seventeen pages

(II, 36–52), after which Berma disappears from the action (although she is once discussed) until *Le Temps retrouvé.* Marcel's pursuit and disappointment are long drawn out, but the "miracle" of realization comes as a sudden revelation. Within the passage, the parallels with Marcel's other involvements are maintained. Specific parallels with Gilberte are presented, and at the same moment that his understanding of Berma is clarified, he renews his "poursuite douloureuse" of his ideal of the Duchesse. The motive of his pursuit may be summed up simply by one of his later sentences: "Nous sommes attirés par toute vie qui nous représente quelque chose d'inconnu, par une dernière illusion à détruire" (II, 567). The cycle of pursuit, disappointment, and adjustment is almost endlessly repeated until all the cycles are subsumed under the great adjustment that leads to the writing of the novel itself.

In presenting the "miracle," Marcel explicitly analyzes the contrasts between his second and first experiences of Berma, showing how the causes of his earlier disappointment—excessive anticipation, overanalysis, and misconceptions of the nature of dramatic art—have been changed by the years between. In the first instance, he has lost his boyhood naïveté: "Si je n'avais pas eu de plaisir la première fois que j'avais entendu la Berma, c'est que, comme jadis quand je retrouvais Gilberte aux Champs-Elysées, je venais à elle avec un trop grand désir" (II, 49). This time, the contrast is complete:

A vrai dire je n'attachais aucun prix à cette possibilité d'entendre la Berma qui, quelques années auparavant, m'avait causé tant d'agitation. . . . Ce n'est pas que fût moins passionné qu'alors mon désir de pouvoir contempler de près les parcelles précieuses de réalité qu'entrevoyait mon imagination. Mais celle-ci ne les

145

situait plus maintenant dans la diction d'une grande actrice. . . . Ma foi, mon désir ne venant plus rendre à la diction et aux attitudes de la Berma un culte incessant, le "double" que je possédais d'eux, dans mon cœur, avait dépéri peu à peu. . . . Cet art était devenu mince et minable. (II, 36–37)

The change is regrettable, but unavoidable, as Marcel now knows too much and has experienced too much for the old expectations of fine careless rapture:

Je ne pus constater sans mélancolie qu'il ne me restait rien de mes dispositions d'autrefois à l'égard de l'art dramatique et de la Berma quand, pour ne rien perdre du phénomène extraordinaire que j'aurais été contempler au bout du monde . . . quand je tremblais que quelque nuage (mauvaise disposition de l'artiste, incident dans le public) empêchât le spectacle de se produire dans son maximum d'intensité. . . . Tout cela avait quitté le monde de l'absolu et n'était plus qu'une chose pareille aux autres, dont je prenais connaissance parce que je me trouvais là, les artistes étaient des gens de même essence que ceux que je connaissais, tâchant de dire le mieux possible ces vers de *Phèdre*. . . . (II, 44–45)

Proust seems to be preparing us for an account of polite boredom, a threnody for the lost pleasures of enthusiastic youth. It is all in the mood of regret; nothing in the description of the leading social figures present gives warning of an aesthetic revelation to come.

As if to underline the contrast, just before the "miracle" is announced, Marcel writes of a subject not at all touched upon in the account of the first performance when he shows knowledge of the personal life of Berma, her debts and her extravagances: "A défaut de frais plus considérables, et moins voluptueuse que Cléopâtre, elle aurait trouvé le moyen de manger en pneumatiques et en voitures de l'Urbaine des provinces et des royaumes" (II, 47). The ordinary humanity of actresses is also sketched in with the vivid portrait of the jealous old actress who views Berma with rage:

Cependant mes regards furent détournés . . . par une petite femme mal vêtue, laide, les yeux en feu, qui vint, suivie de deux jeunes gens, s'asseoir à quelques places de moi.

. . . .

. . . La petite dame qui était près de moi s'écria:
—Pas un applaudissement! Et comme elle est ficelée! Mais elle est trop vieille, elle ne peut plus, on renonce dans ces cas-là.

Devant les "chut" des voisins, les deux jeunes gens qui étaient avec elle tâchèrent de la faire tenir tranquille, et sa fureur ne se déchaînait plus que dans ses yeux. Cette fureur ne pouvait d'ailleurs s'adresser qu'au succès, à la gloire [de la Berma]. . . . La petite dame était une actrice qui n'avait pas eu de chance et avait voué une haine mortelle à la Berma. (II, 44–47)

Here is such an "incident dans le public" as might have completely distracted the younger Marcel. It appears here precisely as if to demonstrate that it made no difference. The old lady is still enraged at the end, sitting stiffly, with rigid face and arms crossed over her breast to show that she protests the resounding applause (p. 50). That her activities are not entirely unnoticed underlines the fact that even Marcel's close observation of his neighbors does not prevent, as he would have expected at the earlier performance, his participation in what happens on the stage.

Having emphasized his indifference to the performance, Marcel makes it clear that mere indifference is not the appropriate attitude for developing aesthetic understanding. He makes the point just before the celebrated description of the fashionable audience in terms of underwater life. (The submarine grotto oddly recalls Bergotte's sardonic objection to the green lighting which made Berma resemble a branch of coral, and the action appear like the love affairs of sea urchins in Neptune's court.) Describing the audience, or part of it, Marcel clearly implies the difference between detachment and indifference, leading his description to a careful and emphatic anticlimax:

Un étudiant génial qui a pris un fauteuil pour entendre la Berma, ne pense qu'à ne pas salir ses gants, à ne pas gêner, à se concilier le voisin que le hasard lui a donné. . . . Au contraire, c'était parce que les gens du monde étaient dans leurs loges . . . c'est parce qu'ils posaient une main indifférente sur les fûts dorés des colonnes qui soutenaient ce temple de l'art lyrique,—c'est parce qu'ils n'étaient pas émus des honneurs excessifs . . . que seuls ils auraient eu l'esprit libre pour écouter la pièce si seulement ils avaient eu de l'esprit. (II, 39)

Marcel has come to this second Berma performance with two of the prerequisites for appreciating it: he is not expecting too much, but he has the mind to appreciate what does appear.

Since he is not in an attitude of tremendous anticipation, he is not prepared to be analytical, but to take the experience as it comes. He has not studied the text, and does not have the lines of the play at his ready command; in fact, he presents at some length his struggle to recall to mind one half-remembered line (II, 38). He is explicit about the difficulties created by too much awareness, too much exercise of the critical sense:

[Notre esprit attentif] entend un son aigu, une intonation bizarrement interrogative. Il se demande: "Est-ce beau? ce que j'éprouve, est-ce de l'admiration? est-ce cela la richesse de coloris, la noblesse, la puissance?" . . . Aucun espace vide n'est laissé pour la "largeur de l'interprétation." . . .

. . . Je n'avais pas eu de plaisir à entendre la Berma (pas plus que je n'en avais, quand je l'aimais, à voir Gilberte). Je m'étais dit:

"Je ne l'admire donc pas." Mais cependant je ne songeais alors qu'à approfondir le jeu de l'actrice, je n'étais préoccupé que de cela, je tâchais d'ouvrir ma pensée le plus largement possible pour recevoir tout ce qu'il contenait: je comprenais maintenant que c'était justement cela, admirer. (II, 49–50)

When Marcel finally understands, on this second occasion, the real nature of dramatic pleasure, he loses his desire to isolate lines and gestures and his wish that the performance might be fragmented into static moments:

Je comprenais que mon désir ancien était plus exigeant que la volonté du poète, de la tragédienne, du grand artiste décorateur qu'était son metteur en scène, et que ce charme répandu au vol sur un vers, ces gestes instables perpétuellement transformés, ces tableaux successifs, c'était le résultat fugitif, le but momentané, le mobile chef-d'œuvre que l'art théâtral se proposait et que détruirait en voulant le fixer l'attention d'un auditeur trop épris. (II, 52)

Marcel, then, has learned not to overanticipate and not to over-analyze, leaving himself free to participate in the performance. To apply this to love takes him longer. He has also, as the last passage shows, lost some of his misconceptions about the nature of dramatic art—and not only the boyish ones.

Ce génie dont l'interprétation de la Berma n'était seulement que la révélation, était-ce bien uniquement le génie de Racine?
Je le crus d'abord. Je devais être détrompé, une fois l'acte de *Phèdre* fini. . . . La pièce suivante était une des nouveautés qui jadis me semblaient, à cause du défaut de célébrité, devoir paraître minces, particulières. . . . Ce rôle figurerait un jour dans la liste de ses plus beaux, auprès de celui de *Phèdre*. Non qu'en lui-même il ne fut dénué de toute valeur littéraire; mais la Berma y était aussi sublime que dans *Phèdre*. Je compris alors que l'œuvre de l'écrivain n'était pour la tragédienne qu'une matière, à peu près indifférente en soi-même, pour la création de son chef-d'œuvre

d'interprétation. . . . Ainsi dans les phrases du dramaturge moderne commes dans les vers de Racine, la Berma savait introduire ces vastes images de douleur, de noblesse, de passion, qui étaient ses chefs-d'œuvre à elle. (II, 50–52)

Marcel, in brief, has made the not very surprising discovery that the art of the actress is the art of acting, and that Norpois was not discussing art at all.

Marcel has also broken away from the Partridge error of supposing that the best actress is the one most obviously an actress, that she adds to a role something strange, wonderful, and totally unforeseen:

Je n'eus plus la même indulgence qu'autrefois pour les justes intentions de tendresse ou de colère que j'avais remarquées alors dans le débit et le jeu d'Aricie, d'Ismène et d'Hippolyte. Ce n'est pas que ces artistes—c'étaient les mêmes—ne cherchassent toujours avec la même intelligence à donner ici à leur voix une inflexion caressante ou une ambiguïté calculée, là à leurs gestes une ampleur tragique ou une douceur suppliante. Leurs intonations commandaient à cette voix: " . . . Fais-toi furieuse," et alors se précipitaient sur elle pour tâcher de l'emporter dans leur frénésie. Mais elle, rebelle, extérieure à leur diction, restait irréductiblement leur voix naturelle, avec ses défauts ou ses charmes matériels, sa vulgarité ou son affectation quotidiennes, et étalait ainsi un ensemble de phénomènes acoustiques ou sociaux que n'avait pas altéré le sentiment des vers récités.

De même le geste de ces artistes disait à leurs bras, à leur péplum: "Soyez majestueux." Mais les membres insoumis laissaient se pavaner entre l'épaule et le coude un biceps qui ne savait rien du rôle; ils continuaient à exprimer l'insignifiance de la vie de tous les jours et à mettre en lumière, au lieu des nuances raciniennes, des connexités musculaires. . . . (II, 46)

Free from his misconceptions Marcel is now, without having struggled for it, ready for the revelation for which as a boy he had struggled so much.

150

The revelation, when it comes, is sudden and complete, like Marcel's other intuitive revelations during the course of the novel:

Et alors, ô miracle . . . le talent de la Berma qui m'avait fui quand je cherchais si avidement à en saisir l'essence, maintenant, après ces années d'oubli, dans cette heure d'indifférence, s'imposait avec la force de l'évidence à mon admiration. Autrefois, pour tâcher d'isoler ce talent, je défalquais en quelque sort de ce que j'entendais le rôle lui-même, le rôle, partie commune à toutes les actrices qui jouaient *Phèdre* et que j'avais étudié d'avance pour que je fusse capable de le soustraire, de ne recueillir comme résidu que le talent de Mme Berma. Mais ce talent que je cherchais à apercevoir en dehors du rôle, il ne faisait qu'un avec lui. (p. 47)

Marcel continues, showing that just as he has reversed his opinion of the other actors to their detriment, he has reversed his opinion of Berma as far in the other direction:

. . . Mon esprit n'avait pas réussi à arracher à la diction et aux attitudes, à appréhender dans l'avare simplicité de leurs surfaces unies, ces trouvailles, ces effets qui n'en dépassaient pas, tant ils s'y étaient profondément résorbés. La voix de la Berma, en laquelle ne subsistait plus un seul déchet de matière inerte et réfractaire à l'esprit, ne laissait pas discerner autour d'elle cet excédent de larmes qu'on voyait couler, parce qu'elles n'avaient pu s'y imbiber, sur la voix de marbre d'Aricie ou d'Ismène, mais avait été délicatement assouplie en ses moindres cellules. . . . Les bras de la Berma que les vers eux-mêmes, de la même émission par laquelle ils faisaient sortir sa voix de ses lèvres, semblaient soulever sur sa poitrine. . . . Tout cela, voix, attitudes, gestes, voiles, n'était, autour de ce corps d'une idée qu'est un vers . . . que des enveloppes supplémentaires qui, au lieu de la cacher, rendaient plus splendidement l'âme qui se les était assimilées et s'y était répandue. . . . Telle l'interprétation de la Berma était, autour de l'œuvre, une second œuvre vivifiée aussi par le génie. (pp. 48–49)

Thus Marcel defines the genius of the interpretive artist. Just as he finds the appreciation that he seeks only when he gives himself completely to the work, so the interpretative artist "n'est plus qu'une fenêtre qui donne sur un chef-d'œuvre" (II, 47). The interpretive artist should not by consciousness of self make the spectator self-conscious; both together must participate in the artistic experience.

The real significance of this experience in the theater appears in the analysis with which Marcel follows his moment of discovery. Here he describes the conflict between the universal and the particular, the world in which we think, analyze, and expect, and the world in which we live and feel—or to put it crudely, the world of ideals and the world of reality. For Marcel, the reality seems likely always to define the ideal, in his cycles of anticipation, disappointment, and usually painful adjustment. His analysis is explicit, in itself and in applying his conclusions beyond the aesthetic realm:

> Mon impression, à vrai dire, plus agréable que celle d'autrefois, n'était pas différente. Seulement je ne la confrontais plus à une idée préalable, abstraite et fausse, du génie dramatique, et je comprenais que le génie dramatique, c'était justement cela. . . . Nous avons apporté avec nous les idées de "beauté," "largeur de style," "pathétique," que nous pourrions à la rigeur avoir l'illusion de reconnaître dans la banalité d'un talent, d'un visage corrects. . . . Ce sont les œuvres vraiment belles, si elles sont sincèrement écoutées, qui doivent le plus nous décevoir, parce que, dans la collection de nos idées, il n'y en a aucune qui réponde à une impression individuelle.
>
> C'était précisément ce que me montrait le jeu de la Berma. C'était bien cela, la noblesse, l'intelligence de la diction. Maintenant je me rendais compte des mérites d'une interprétation large, poétique, puissante. . . . Nous sentons dans un monde, nous pensons, nous nommons dans un autre, nous pouvons entre les deux établir une concordance mais non combler l'intervalle. . . .

Et la différence qu'il y a entre une personne, une œuvre forte-
ment individuelle et l'idée de beauté existe aussi grande entre ce
qu'elles nous font ressentir et les idées d'amour, d'admiration. (II,
49–50)

Twice within this context (in passages already cited) Marcel
explicitly makes comparisons between this experience and
his experience with Gilberte.

Marcel's comparison with such episodes as the clash between the name of Guermantes and the pimple near the
Duchesse's nose is evident enough. The discrepancy between
the absolute and the individual in the attitudes of Swann
toward Odette, and Marcel toward Gilberte and Albertine is
equally evident. With Berma, Marcel has made the necessary
adjustment in the aesthetic realm, when the novel is less than
a third over; but again and again he will have the same problem to deal with in life and love. At a crucial point in the
action, Marcel returns to the declaration scene in *Phèdre,*
which now becomes the subject of an analysis that clarifies for
Marcel and the reader his relationships with Gilberte and
Albertine, now that both have left him. J. M. Cocking has
shown the development of varied *Phèdre* themes into this
sequence:

Gradually when Bergotte's name is mentioned, his pamphlet on
Racine is brought into the foreground. . . . It is Bergotte who
will reveal to Marcel the beauty of Berma's acting. But *Phèdre*
also provides overtones to Marcel's passion, first for Gilberte, then
for Albertine.[9]

Cocking also shows how this *Phèdre* thread is intertwined
with another theme leading to the same end:

And the last stage in the development of the hawthorn theme is
a half-suggestive, half-ironic reference to *Phèdre*: Marcel, on the
eve of his departure for Paris, is found by his mother embracing

the hawthorns as he would have liked to embrace the lilies, trampling his new hat and tearing his new coat as Phèdre tore off her *vains ornements*. The Phèdre suggestions move forward into the rest of the novel with the story of Marcel's passion for Gilberte and Albertine; the theme is wound up in *Albertine disparue* with an overt and detailed analogy between Phèdre and Marcel in which Proust interprets Racine's psychology in his own terms.[10]

Proust almost always does interpret his quotations and analyses in his own terms, not only by using quotations, but by reacting to them at the same time.

The passage on the declaration scene from *Phèdre* is so excellent an example of Proust's method of combining themes —here, his own love affairs, Swann's affair, and Phèdre and Hippolyte—that it is worth quoting at length:

Alors je me souvins des deux façons différentes dont j'avais écouté *Phèdre*, et ce fut maintenant d'une troisième que je pensai à la scène de la déclaration. . . . C'était l'énonce des lois que je devais expérimenter dans ma vie. Il y a dans notre âme des choses auxquelles nous ne savons pas combien nous tenons. Ou bien si nous vivons sans elles, c'est parce que nous remettons de jour en jour, par peur d'échouer, ou de souffrir, d'entrer en leur possession. C'est ce qui m'était arrivé pour Gilberte, quand j'avais cru renoncer à elle. Qu'avant le moment où nous sommes tout à fait détachés de ces choses . . . nous sommes fous. . . . Ou bien, si la chose est en notre possession, nous croyons qu'elle nous est à charge, que nous nous en déferions volontiers; c'est ce qui m'était arrivé pour Albertine. Mais que, par un départ, l'être indifférent nous soit retiré, et nous ne pouvons plus vivre. Or l'"argument" de *Phèdre* ne réunissait-il pas ces deux cas? Hippolyte va partir. Phèdre qui jusque-là a pris soin de s'offrir à son inimitié . . . n'y tient plus. Elle vient lui avouer son amour. . . . Sans doute cette raison du départ d'Hippolyte est accessoire, peut-on penser, à côté de celle de la mort de Thésée. Et de même

154

quand . . . Phèdre fait un instant semblant d'avoir été mal comprise:

> ... Aurais-je perdu tout le soin de ma gloire,

on peut croire que c'est parce qu'Hippolyte a repoussé sa déclaration:

> Madame, oubliez-vous
> Que Thésée est mon père, et qu'il est votre époux?

Mais il n'aurait pas eu cette indignation, que, devant le bonheur atteint, Phèdre aurait pu avoir le même sentiment qu'il valait peu de chose. Mais dès qu'elle voit qu'il n'est pas atteint, qu'Hippolyte croit avoir mal compris et s'excuse, alors, comme moi . . . , elle veut que le refus vienne de lui, elle veut pousser jusqu'au bout sa chance:

> Ah! cruel, tu m'as trop entendue.

Et il n'y a pas jusqu'aux duretés qu'on m'avait racontées de Swann envers Odette, ou de moi à l'égard d'Albertine . . . qui ne se trouvent aussi dans cette scène:

> Tu me haïssais plus, je ne t'aimais pas moins.
> Tes malheurs te prêtaient encor de nouveaux charmes.

La preuve que le "soin de sa gloire" n'est pas ce à quoi tient le plus Phèdre, c'est qu'elle pardonnerait à Hippolyte et s'arracherait aux conseils d'Œnone, si elle n'apprenait à ce moment qu'Hippolyte aime Aricie. . . . C'est du moins ainsi, en réduisant la part de tous les scrupules "jansénistes," comme eût dit Bergotte, que Racine a donnés à Phèdre pour la faire paraître moins coupable, que m'apparaissait cette scène, sorte de prophétie des épisodes amoureux de ma propre existence. (III, 458–60)

This is not the last time—nor the most important one— when Proust will resolve multiple themes by intertwining them with theater material and quotations.

Marcel continues to use the declaration scene in the curious episode when a garbled telegram makes him mistakenly believe that Albertine is mysteriously alive again: "Est-ce pour cette fille que je revoyais en ce moment si bouffie et qui avait certainement vieilli, . . . est-ce pour elle qu'il fallait renoncer à l'éclatante fille qui était mon souvenir d'hier, . . . renoncer à cette 'Albertine nouvelle,' 'non point telle que l'ont vue les Enfers,' 'mais fidèle, mais fière et même un peu farouche'?" (III, 644). As Nathan points out, these are the ambiguous words with which Phèdre, thus describing her "love" for Thésée, hints at her real love for Hippolyte.[11] Nathan also indicates another use of the *Phèdre* material, with Marcel this time implying a different comparison:

On sait qu'Albertine va mourir d'une chute de cheval. Quelques phrases, insérées dans le texte de façon assez maladroite et peut-être tardive, rendent le narrateur indirectement responsable de cet accident. . . . La parole de mauvais augure prononcée à la légère, le cheval, il est difficile de ne pas penser à la mort d'Hippolyte, et nul doute que Proust ne se soit identifié au personnage coupable de Thésée. Coïncidence curieuse: il est précisément question de Thésée et d'Hippolyte dans un passage voisin qui a trait aussi à Albertine mais pour des raisons absolument différentes. De pareils jeux ne sont pas rares chez Proust.[12]

Nor is it rare that these *jeux* are, as in the present examples, tied in with theater and drama.

From the first citations of the declaration scene of *Phèdre* to the final application of the citations to the dead Albertine, Proust has made a typical progression from drama as part of the milieu of his characters to drama as an aesthetic standard to which life may be compared, with the usual implication that art is unchanging, while life is ever shifting. The differ-

156

ence between this particular set of comparisons and many of the others is that the element of irony is slight. In fact, probably only the unsympathetic reader would consider Marcel's love affairs to be lowered in the comparison. More is involved, however, than a point-for-point comparative analysis, even though the analysis is valid, both for the points it makes and for the characterization of Marcel which it provides. The fact that he is able to make such an analysis shows us how intellectual and subjective are his approaches to passions, and how memory organizes the past for him. The affairs, now over, have acquired the impersonal status of aesthetic experience. These episodes of his passional life have been altered by habit and memory into a form that his understanding can control. He is no longer the victim of constantly changing circumstances, but has become their intellectual master.

The overtones of the *Phèdre* comparisons are not ironic, but rather serve to underline Marcel's basic attitudes on the subject of love. In comparing himself to Phèdre, he treats of love as a matter of guilt, suffering, and jealousy. To use one of his own repeated metaphors, love is in the nature of a disease, which may be cured by time (and its accompanying active ingredients, habit and memory), or is otherwise likely to be fatal. On this, Clive Bell comments, "Proust understood love, could realize that it was love, only when the passion was thwarted and devastating. In this he inherits a peculiarity of the greatest of French masters, of him who of Frenchmen has best understood and most grandly expressed the miseries of the human heart, of Racine. For, as M. Mauriac has pointed out, when Racine is portraying happy lovers—Junie, Atalide—he is tepid and commonplace; it is Phèdre, Hermione, Roxane, who illuminate the eternal theme." [13] While Phèdre's love leads to a literal death, love in *A la recherche* leads to corrosion and destruction of personality.

The speech in *Phèdre* was, as Marcel says, the statement of laws that he had to experience in his own life. When assimilated in memory, art and life become one. This is the implication of Germaine Brée's statement that "il est certain que Proust a voulu délibérément démolir toutes les habitudes de pensée qui séparent soigneusement le domaine de l'art de celui de la vie ou de la nature." [14] But Marcel does not treat art and life as equally real in the self-conscious fashion of the Symbolists, who deliberately create *correspondances* between sense impressions and attribute colors to sounds or scents. Proust has Marcel go beyond metaphor, not artificially breaking down walls between unlike things, but accurately recognizing how memory transmutes his experience. As art and life are reflected in memory, they lose their separateness and differences. Comparisons between them are not analogies made between unlike things, but direct comparisons between what have become members of the same order of being. Life may be validly compared to drama, because memory is an artist making the actual past into an aesthetic structure and giving aesthetic experiences full reality. Only when *Phèdre* and Marcel's two love affairs are at last brought together do they finally, in the novel, make complete sense. Two halves of the same experience have been joined into one concept.

The completion of the Phèdre and Berma cycles will come in the *coup de théâtre* passage in *Le Temps retrouvé*, when Marcel's whole life will be turned to the world of art in the writing of the novel. By then, he will number Berma among his old friends (she and the Guermantes send him invitations for the same afternoon). Nothing in the novel shows the development of this friendship; we leave Berma as a public figure and take her up later as a friend. In reverse, nothing appears in the novel to show the development of the career of Rachel; we leave her as Saint-Loup's former mistress, and find her later as an eminent actress, and friend of the Duchesse.

RACHEL

Before considering the sequence in *Le Temps retrouvé* when the lives of the two actresses ironically cross, the earlier action in which Rachel figures should be clarified. Marcel sees her in *A l'ombre des jeunes filles en fleurs,* after he has first seen Berma, and discussed his disappointment. Rachel is more important than Berma as a character in the plot of the novel, but is not always important in her quality as actress. As mistress, she illustrates one set of themes; as actress, another. It is only in the outcome that the two aspects of her personality and the two sets of themes fall into place together. Until *Le Temps retrouvé,* the fact that she is an actress seems almost incidental, perhaps to underline society's reaction to the woman Saint-Loup has chosen.

The first movement in the presentation of Rachel as a character ranges from Marcel's seeing her as a young prostitute in a house of assignation to his discovery that Saint-Loup's mistress, of whom he has heard so much, is this same person —these two events being separated by more than five hundred pages. In the contrast between the "Rachel quand du Seigneur" of the brothel and the Rachel of Saint-Loup, Marcel presents one of the most striking illustrations of one of his key ideas, which he explicitly states late in the novel:

159

Je m'étais rendu compte que seule la perception grossière et erronée place tout dans l'objet, quand tout est dans l'esprit; . . . j'avais vu les personnes varier d'aspect selon l'idée que moi ou d'autres s'en faisaient, une seule être plusieurs selon les personnes qui la voyaient. . . . J'avais vu l'amour placer dans une personne ce qui n'est que dans la personne qui aime. Je m'en étais d'autant mieux rendu compte que j'avais fait s'étendre à l'extrême la distance entre la réalité objective et l'amour (Rachel pour Saint-Loup et pour moi, Albertine pour moi et Saint-Loup, Morel ou le conducteur d'omnibus pour Charlus ou d'autres personnes, et malgré cela tendresses de Charlus: vers de Musset, etc.). (III, 912)

Marcel analyzes the violent contrast immediately after he has recognized Rachel:

Voyant ces deux éléments dissociés (parce que j'avais connu "Rachel quand du Seigneur" dans une maison de passe), je comprenais que bien des femmes pour lesquelles des hommes vivent, souffrent, se tuent, peuvent être en elles-mêmes ou pour d'autres ce que Rachel était pour moi. . . .

. . . Sans doute c'était le même mince et étroit visage que nous voyions Robert et moi. Mais nous étions arrivés à lui par deux routes opposées qui ne communiqueraient jamais, et nous n'en verrions jamais la même face. . . . Les faveurs de Rachel, Saint-Loup pourtant avait réussi par chance à les avoir toutes. Certes, s'il avait su maintenant qu'elles avaient été proposées à tout le monde pour un louis, il eût sans doute terriblement souffert, mais n'eût pas moins donné ce million pour les conserver. . . . La regardant tous les deux, Robert et moi, nous ne la voyions pas du même côté du mystère.

Ce n'était pas "Rachel quand du Seigneur" qui me semblait peu de chose, c'était la puissance de l'imagination humaine, l'illusion sur laquelle reposaient les douleurs de l'amour, que je trouvais grandes. (II, 158–60)

The affair between Saint-Loup and Rachel is a case history for Marcel's views of love, which is a disease that creates illusions that will inevitably cause suffering, jealousy, and disappointment. Marcel himself indicates the parallels to Swann and himself in their loves. When the Duchesse denies the parallel between Saint-Loup and Swann (M. d'Argencourt having suggested it), the denial only calls the parallel to the reader's attention (II, 228). Like all of Proust's lovers, Saint-Loup is first of all in love with love, then—because his mistress is his own creation—in love with himself.

Proust makes the development of Marcel's knowledge of Rachel very gradual, through scraps of gossip. In the first meeting, when he sees her and hears her without her knowing it, he makes her memorable for the reader by attaching to her the odd nickname—"Rachel quand du Seigneur"—taken from a Halévy opera, while at the same time he explicitly fails to think of her as a person: "Et ces mots m'avaient empêché de voir en elle une personne, parce qu'ils me l'avaient fait classer immédiatement dans une catégorie générale de femmes dont l'habitude commune à toutes était de venir là le soir voir s'il n'y avait pas un louis ou deux à gagner" (I, 577). Before he knows the identity of Robert's mistress, Marcel has nonetheless heard of her as having a bad reputation. Mme de Villeparisis "laissa entendre à ma grand'mère qu'il était malheureusement tombé dans les griffes d'une mauvaise femme dont il était fou et qui ne le lâcherait pas . . . " (I, 728). The reported attitude of Robert's relatives and acquaintances not only blackens her reputation, but makes her connection with the theater seem ambiguous and dubious, the term "actress" seemingly a *nom de guerre*: " . . . L'attitude méprisante ou hostile qu'il y prenait augmentait encore chez tous ses proches parents le chagrin de sa liaison avec une femme 'de théâtre,' liaison qu'ils accusaient de lui être fatale et notamment d'avoir développé chez lui cet esprit de dénigrement, ce mauvais esprit, de l'avoir 'dévoyé,' en attendant qu'il se 'déclassât' complétement" (I, 780). As usual, Proust prepares his reader well for the coming surprise: all the necessary details are ready to fall into place when Marcel reaches the revelation. We know enough of both aspects of Rachel by the time of the revelation scene so that the surprise does not blunt the point of the contrast: the illusion which the lover has created to fit his love.

The second movement in the private career of Rachel proceeds from Marcel's recognition of her identity to the breaking off of the affair which sends Saint-Loup to Morocco, all within two hundred pages of *Le Côté de Guermantes*. In this section we see the quarrels, jealousies, and sufferings which result from Robert's illusions—the usual symptoms of the disease which is love. Their affair is compounded of jealous scenes and threats and fears of breaking off. Even before Marcel meets Rachel as Saint-Loup's mistress he is aware that Robert's curiosity about other women is paralyzed by his love for his mistress, and a kind of superstition that her faithfulness depends upon his (I, 807–8). Despite the importance which she holds in his life—more than his army career, his social position, or his family—he has no wish to marry her. The malady called love sometimes forces him to believe that she loves him, but he also knows that her love depends upon his money (II, 156). Marcel has heard of Robert's fears of a rupture of the affair several times before he meets Rachel. The opinions of Robert held by her actor and author friends persuade Rachel that Saint-Loup lacks intelligence, and that an uncrossable chasm lies between them (I, 782–83). When his presence in Paris exasperates her, she forces him to join his garrison at Balbec (I, 784). This fact is repeated: "Saint-Loup ne pouvait pas depuis longtemps venir à Paris, soit, comme il le disait, à cause des exigences de son métier, soit plutôt à cause de chagrins que lui causait sa maîtresse avec laquelle il avait déjà été deux fois sur le point de rompre" (II, 70).

In the sequence in which Marcel meets Rachel and spends most of the afternoon with her and Saint-Loup, he goes through two episodes of Saint-Loup's jealousy—of a waiter, and of a dancer. These are illustrative of the cycle of the relationship: "Car dès que Saint-Loup se trouvait avec sa maîtresse dans un endroit public, il s'imaginait qu'elle regardait tous les hommes présents, il devenait sombre, elle s'apercevait de sa mauvaise humeur qu'elle s'amusait peut-être à attiser, mais que, plus probablement, par amour-propre bête, elle ne voulait pas, blessée par son ton, avoir l'air de chercher à désarmer; elle faisait semblant de ne pas détacher ses yeux de tel ou tel homme, et d'ailleurs ce n'était pas toujours par pur jeu" (II, 164–65). In the restaurant, Robert takes umbrage at the way she looks at the waiter: "Ce maître d'hôtel est très intéressant, Zézette? . . . On dirait que tu veux faire une étude d'après lui" (p. 166), and they leave Marcel for the reconciliation with champagne in a private room of the restaurant (p. 171), but not before she has also "made eyes" at a young man at a nearby table (p. 168). Backstage at the theater, his jealousy of a young dancer leads Saint-Loup to make a scene which ends in his striking a bystanding journalist who refuses to put out his cigar. This time there is no reconciliation. A hundred pages later (p. 279), Robert is blaming himself for making her suffer, but she refuses to accept a gift from him (pp. 281–82). Suddenly (p. 347), the final break is said to have happened, and Robert to be in Morocco. For all practical purposes, Rachel disappears, except for some passing mention, until *Le Temps retrouvé*, when she enters as Rachel the actress.

Rachel as a person has some further importance in her lasting effect on Saint-Loup's character, and in Marcel's later memories of his friend. Robert several times tries to further a friendship between her and Marcel, on the ground that the latter will like her because she is "literary" (I, 868; II, 161). Marcel is surprised to find that she actually is (II, 164), although the Duchesse thinks Robert is deluded (II, 238). Rachel's influence over Robert extends from making him kinder to dumb animals to lessening his snobbery and breaking him away from society: "D'autre part, une actrice, . . . en lui faisant trouver ennuyeuse la société des femmes du monde et considérer comme une corvée l'obligation d'aller dans une soirée, l'avait préservé du snobisme et guéri de la frivolité. . . . Sa maîtresse avait ouvert son esprit à l'invisible, elle avait mis du sérieux dans sa vie, des délicatesses dans son cœur . . . " (I, 781–82). The attitude of his family, and particularly remarks made after Rachel has recited at his aunt's—a fiasco—freeze Robert's rejection of society: "Paroles qui avaient changé l'antipathie de Robert pour les gens du monde en une horreur autrement profonde et douloureuse et que lui inspiraient particulièrement ceux qui la méritaient le moins, des parents dévoués qui, délégués par la famille, avaient cherché à persuader l'amie de Saint-Loup de rompre avec lui, démarche qu'elle lui présentait comme inspirée par leur amour pour elle" (I, 785).

The most striking and pathetic instance of the continuing influence of Rachel on the life of Saint-Loup comes in Gilberte's later attempts to remind him of her—significantly, in the section "Nouvel aspect de Robert de Saint-Loup." Gilberte's discovery of photographs of her husband's former mistress is given in *Le Temps retrouvé* (III, 702). The pathos and irony of her attempted imitation appears a few pages earlier:

Mais si Robert trouvait quelque chose de Rachel à Charlie, Gilberte, elle, cherchait à avoir quelque chose de Rachel, afin de plaire à son mari, mettait comme elle des nœuds de soie ponceau, ou rose, ou jaune, dans ses cheveux, se coiffait de même, car elle croyait que son mari l'aimait encore et elle en était jalouse. . . . De cette générosité envers Rachel Gilberte n'eût pas souffert si elle avait su qu'elle était seulement l'accomplissement résigné d'une promesse à laquelle ne correspondait plus aucun amour. (III, 683)

Before Rachel appears as the great actress, Saint-Loup is dead, the affair long past, only a sad memory. Hearing of Robert's death, Marcel recalls him "au théâtre où il avait giflé un journaliste" (III, 847); and at the end of *La Fugitive,* his memories of Saint-Loup and Rachel bring him close to tears (III, 688). Three hundred pages later Rachel enters upon a different stage, in another character.

The artistic career of Rachel is presented in three episodes: the occasion on which Marcel first meets her with Saint-Loup and they go backstage, the fiasco of her Maeterlinck scene in the drawing room of the Duchessse, and her triumph at the last Guermantes reception. In the first two episodes, Proust uses sleight of hand to make the final surprise possible, since, although Marcel asserts that he is mistaken in thinking her an inferior actress, the impression is given that her acting does not amount to much. Harold March writes of the "double-cross": "Rachel in fact becomes a great actress, and at the end has taken the place of the incomparable Berma. The reader may well feel that he has been double-crossed; but if he has, it has been by the Marcel of the moment and other fallible observers, and not by the author, who has been careful not to commit himself." [15] In presenting Rachel's career and reputation, Proust does not rely, as he can with Berma, on the reader's recognition of the *clef* to the *roman*. The fact that Rachel's career was partly modelled on that of Louisa de Mornand is of little assistance to the reader, and, in any event, that parallel is broken in the outcome. One can only speculate on what associations are intended with the historical Rachel (1820–1858). George D. Painter would seem to indicate that no association is intended: "[Louisa de Mornand] specialized in light comedy, first in soubrette parts, later in leads; she was of Jewish birth, and had a maid, Rachel, from whom Proust took the name of Saint-Loup's mistress." [16] But in view of the indentification of Berma with Phèdre, it is at least worth noting that the fame of the actual actress Rachel rested on her genius in classical French tragedy, and that Phèdre was her greatest role. Unlike Bernhardt, the actual Rachel is never mentioned in the novel. It may be mere coincidence that her sister Lia's name is so similar to that of another of Marcel's actresses, the Lesbian Léa. But the public career of Proust's Rachel makes its own way in the novel, without any of the analysis given to the art of Berma. Marcel reports her success as a fact, not as a personal aesthetic experience.

Although the reader may be led to underestimate Rachel's abilities, Marcel is unequivocal in asserting her great talent, while admitting that it escaped him: " . . . La maîtresse de Saint-Loup parlait des artistes les plus connus sur un ton d'ironie et de supériorité qui m'irritait, parce que je croyais—faisant erreur en cela—que c'était elle qui leur était inférieure. Elle s'aperçut très bien que je devais la tenir pour une artiste médiocre. . . . Mais elle ne s'en froissa pas, parce qu'il y a dans le grand talent non reconnu encore . . . une certaine humilité" (II, 168). This assertion, so clearly made, is obscured by a mass of apparently contradictory evidence. Even her table manners are used to suggest that her association with the theater is meretricious: "Elle était, en mangeant, maladroite de ses mains à un degré qui laissait supposer qu'en jouant la comédie sur la scène, elle devait se montrer bien gauche" (II, 167). Her patronizing remarks about Berma, after Marcel's detailed appreciation of that great actress, make Rachel sound fatuous and spiteful:

> Je cessai de prendre part à la conversation quand on parla théâtre, car sur ce chapitre Rachel était trop malveillante. Elle prit, il est vrai, sur un ton de commisération . . . la défense de la Berma, en disant: "Oh! non, c'est une femme remarquable. Évidement ce qu'elle fait ne nous touche plus, cela ne corresponde plus tout à fait à ce que nous cherchons, mais il faut la placer au moment où elle est venue, on lui doit beacoup. Elle a fait des choses bien, tu sais. Et puis c'est une si brave femme, elle a un si grand cœur, elle n'aime pas naturellement les choses qui nous intéressent, mais elle a eu, avec un visage assez émouvant, une jolie qualité d'intelligence." (II, 167)

These remarks are the only passage in which the careers of Berma and Rachel cross until the denouement; the episodes about the two actresses are kept carefully separate until the end.

At the theater Rachel is again made malicious and unattractive in an episode which Marcel finds most painful, so that her possible real motive, preserving the standards of her profession, is obscured by Marcel's dismay and embarrassment:

> Un numéro du programme me fut extrêmement pénible. Une jeune femme que détestaient Rachel et plusieurs de ses amies devait y faire dans des chansons anciennes un début sur lequel elle avait fondé toutes ses espérances d'avenir et celles des siens. . . . Rachel avait aposté dans la salle un certain nombre d'amis et d'amies dont le rôle était de déconcontenancer par leurs sarcasmes la débutante, qu'on savait timide, de lui faire perdre la tête de façon qu'elle fît un fiasco complet après lequel le directeur ne conclurait pas d'engagement. . . . L'instinct d'imitation, le désir de se montrer spirituelles et braves, mirent de la partie de jolies actrices qui n'avaient pas été prévenues, mais qui lançaient aux autres des œillades de complicité méchante, se tordaient de rire, avec de violents éclats. . . . Rachel s'imaginait certainement que l'actrice qu'elle avait torturée était loin d'être intéressante, en tous cas qu'en la faisant huer, elle-même vengeait le bon goût et donnait une leçon à une mauvaise camarade. (II, 173–74)

Not only does this episode have its denigrating effect on the portrait of Rachel, but it also, in opposition to the material about Berma, makes the whole atmosphere of the theater distasteful. Whereas the Berma material has been kept on an aesthetic level, this put the theater on a backstage personal level on which the malice of so-called actresses is easily equated with the cheapness of jealous prostitutes. Except for Berma, all the actresses in the novel are associated with jealously or immorality, or both, a fact which makes Rachel's final apotheosis the more startling.

Even the description of Rachel's stage presence is backhanded, and thoroughly undermining. Marcel uses it as an example of Robert's illusions about his mistress:

Rachel avait un de ces visages que l'éloignement—et pas nécessairement celui de la scène, le monde n'étant qu'un plus grand théâtre—dessine et qui, vus de près, retombent en poussière. Placé à côté d'elle, on ne voyait qu'une nébuleuse, une voie lactée de taches de rousseur, de tout petits boutons, rien d'autre. A une distance convenable, tout cela cessait d'être visible et, des joues effacées, résorbées, se levait, comme un croissant de lune, un nez si fin, si pur, qu'on aurait voulu être l'objet de l'attention de Rachel, la revoir indéfiniment, la posséder auprès de soi, si jamais on ne l'avait vue autrement et de près. . . . Les portes d'or du monde des rêves s'étaient refermées sur Rachel avant que Saint-Loup l'eût vue sortir du théâtre. . . . (II, 174–75)

The illusory and false stage beauty is explicitly exposed in the backstage view which follows, in which Rachel's stage presence is removed with the scenery:

Les décors encores plantés entre lesquels je passais, vus ainsi de près et dépouillés de tout ce que leur ajoutent l'éloignement et l'éclairage . . . étaient misérables, et Rachel, quand je m'approchai d'elle, ne subit pas un moindre pouvoir de destruction. Les ailes de son nez charmant étaient restées dans la perspective, entre la salle et la scène, tout comme le relief des décors. . . . La forme, l'éclat de ce jeune astre si brillant tout à l'heure avaient disparu. (p. 177)

Except for the material concerning Berma, most of the theater discussion in the novel before *Le Temps retrouvé* easily assimilates this concept of falsity attached to Rachel, whose portrait here symbolizes the conventionally "theatrical" rather than the dramatic, literary, or aesthetic. It accords with the system of metaphors in which life, with its accidents, its misconceptions and hypocrisies, is made to seem artificial and inferior to drama.

The episode of Rachel's fiasco seems at first to show her as ridiculous, pretentious, and untalented, since society utterly rejects her as an actress; but in the final analysis, it turns out that it is society that is ridiculous, pretentious, and unappreciative, simply rejecting a novelty which it does not understand. But whatever the grounds, it marks Rachel at this juncture as a failure. The fiasco, briefly presented first in *A l'ombre des jeunes filles en fleurs,* is fully described in *Le Côté de Guermantes,* after the backstage episode. The first presentation occupies only a page:

Cette période dramatique de leur liaison . . . avait commencé un soir chez une tante de Saint-Loup, lequel avait obtenu d'elle que son amie viendrait pour de nombreux invités dire des fragments d'une pièce symboliste qu'elle avait jouée une fois sur une scène d'avant-garde. . . .

Mais quand elle était apparue, un grand lys à la main, dans un costume copié de l'"Ancilla Domini" et qu'elle avait persuadé à Robert être une véritable "vision d'art," son entrée avait été accueillie dans cette assemblée d'hommes de cercle et de duchesses par des sourires que le ton monotone de la psalmodie, la bizarrerie de certains mots, leur fréquente répétition avaient changés en fous rires, d'abord étouffés, puis si irrésistibles que la pauvre récitante n'avait pu continuer. (I, 784)

Although Marcel does not point to them, the parallels between Rachel's experience in this episode and the humiliation of the unfortunate singer whom she and her friends drove from the stage are clear enough. The deliberate conspiracy is lacking, but the common elements and several other details suggest that her failure, like the singer's, may be justified: the costume, which she has "persuaded" Saint-Loup is a veritable "vision of art," the smiles and laughter (rather than disgust or hooting), the fact that she is forced to break off her bizarre and monotonous performance.

Minor clues suggest that perhaps the audience is at fault (combining with the much earlier suggestion that society should make the perfect audience, if only it had a mind).

There are the words "symboliste" and "avant-garde," and the rather fatuous comments of an unidentified but well-known duke: "Cette petite demoiselle a évidemment cru étonner Paris. Mais Paris est plus difficile à étonner que cela" (p. 784). Rachel's own comment does not add to her stature: "Il n'y avait pas un, des hommes présents, qui ne m'eût fait de l'œil, du pied, et c'est parce que j'ai repoussé leurs avances qu'ils ont cherché à se venger" (pp. 784–85). The general effect of this first report of the episode fits in with the identification of Rachel as a *soi-disant* actress.

During the second discussion of Rachel's failure, her play is first identified as Maeterlinck's *Les Sept Princesses,* and the snobbish and uncomprehending conversation about Maeterlinck's work now makes it seem that Rachel, although she is still ridiculed, may not be either so pretentious or so fatuous as earlier seemed possible. Marcel is explicit about his irritation with the Duchesse's lack of comprehension:

—Ah! vous connaissez *Les Sept Princesses?* répondit la duchesse à M. d'Argencourt. Tous mes compliments! Moi je n'en connais qu'une, mais cela m'a ôté la curiosité de faire la connaissance des six autres. . . .

"Quelle buse!" pensais-je, irrité de l'accueil glacial qu'elle m'avait fait. Je trouvais une sorte d'âpre satisfaction à constater sa complète incompréhension de Maeterlinck. (II, 229)

The Duchesse and M. d'Argencourt are equally obtuse, although the latter is pleased to assert that the King of Belgium asked him to explain the play, of which she speaks as if it were a completely unknown work:

D'ailleurs, si vous aviez entendu ce qu'elle disait, je ne connais qu'une scène, mais je ne crois pas qu'on puisse imaginer quelque chose de pareil: cela s'appelle *les Sept Princesses.*

—*Les Sept Princesses,* oh! oïl, oïl, quel snobisme! s'écria M. d'Argencourt. Ah! mais attendez, je connais toute la pièce. L'auteur l'a envoyée au Roi qui n'y a rien compris et m'a demandé de lui expliquer. (II, 229)

Twenty pages later they are back on the subject, with no more progress in their comprehension. The Duchesse is speaking:

Ce sont des gens qui cherchent à avoir l'air obscur et au besoin qui s'arrangent d'être ridicules pour cacher qu'ils n'ont pas d'idées. S'il y avait quelque chose dessous, je vous dirais que je ne crains pas certaines audaces . . . du moment qu'il y a de la pensée. Je ne sais pas si vous avez vu la pièce de Borelli. Il y a des gens que cela a choqués; moi, . . . j'avoue que j'ai trouvé cela infiniment curieux. Mais *les Sept Princesses!* (pp. 249–50)

The tone of these discussions is enough to invalidate the opinions of the same speakers on the subject of Rachel's talent. Whatever the merits of Maeterlinck's early play, these people seem unlikely to appreciate them or their interpretation. Rachel herself begins to seem the more admirable in this mild reversal of the values of society and those of art.

In the discussion of the actual performance, the wit of the Guermantes seems stale and contrived, if sometimes nonetheless tepidly amusing. The whole discussion is brought on when Bloch, who is working on a drawing-room production for Mme de Villeparisis, offers the services of Rachel, which are refused: "Il avait même proposé en plus une tragédienne 'aux yeux pers, belle comme Héra,' qui dirait des proses lyriques avec le sens de la beauté plastique. Mais à son nom Mme de Villeparisis avait refusé, car c'était l'amie de Saint-Loup" (II, 217). This, incidentally, is the first intimation which the reader has had that Rachel has become a tragic actress; her last appearance, aside from the drawing room, was as a "walk-on." The Duchesse, although scornful, is nevertheless pleased to be able to lay some claim to possession: "Comment, vous ne savez pas qu'elle a joué chez moi avant tout le monde? je n'en suis pas plus fière pour cela, dit en riant Mme de Guermantes, heureuse pourtant, puisqu'on parlait de cette actrice, de faire savoir qu'elle avait eu la primeur de ses ridicules" (p. 223). The Duke's contributions are equally lofty and scornful: "Ah! ce n'est pas ce que nous appelons une comédienne de la grande lignée. . . . C'était même drolatique . . . " (p. 227).

The account of the rehearsal is one of Oriane's set pieces, which meets with her usual success:

—D'abord la veille il y eut une espèce de répétition qui était une bien belle chose! . . . Imaginez qu'elle disait une phrase, pas même, un quart de phrase, et puis elle s'arrêtait; elle ne disait plus rien, mais je n'exagère pas, pendant cinq minutes. . . .

. . . Et elle m'a repondu textuellement: "Il faut toujours dire une chose comme si on était en train de la composer soi-même." Si vous y réflechissez c'est monumental, cette réponse!

—Mais je croyais qu'elle ne disait pas mal les vers, dit un des deux jeunes gens.

—Elle ne se doute pas de ce que c'est, répondit Mme de Guermantes. Du reste je n'ai pas eu besoin de l'entendre. . . . J'ai tout de suite compris qu'elle n'avait pas de talent quand j'ai vu les lis!

Tout le monde rit. (II, 230)

When next the paths of the Duchesse and Rachel cross, in *Le Temps retrouvé*, the Duchesse is pleased to be able to claim the friendship of the celebrated actress, and has completely revised her opinion of the performance in her drawing room.

Although there is no intervening material about Rachel's theater career, and very little more about her personal life, the preparation for the final reversals is skillfully made in the fiasco episode.

Proust's plotting is not entirely unlike that of the detective-story writer, in which the reader may learn to be suspicious of the surface effect and to look for contrary evidence which may fall into place later, when the surprise must seem both surprising and inevitable. So carefully has the ground been laid and the adjustments managed, that Proust is able to add extra reversals without destroying the fabric. The intention to have Rachel turn out to be a successful actress preceded, as will be seen, the extension of this into the violent contrast between Rachel and Berma. Although Rachel does not take Berma's place in Marcel's artistic hierarchy, he has presented sufficient evidence to justify her success in the theater. He has announced that he was mistaken in thinking her untalented, and has attributed to her the humility that he associates with great talent. He has shown her, however maliciously, upholding standards of ability and taste. He has described, however backhandedly, her stage presence, and the way in which the stage brings out beauty not evident in closer circumstances. Finally, in the Guermantes treatment of Maeterlinck, he has shown her by contrast as evidencing intelligence in her choice of material, if not in the audience to which she presents it. Illusions about her come into play in both her private and public life, and with Proust, when illusions are created, revelations must follow.

BERMA AND RACHEL

The material about Berma and Rachel worked into the account of the last Guermantes reception includes at least four reversals of previous situations, part of the *coup de théâtre* by which everything is turned topsy-turvy, enabling Marcel to proceed with the writing of the novel which shall capture it all. With the two actresses, we are shown the change in the Duchesse's social position which has led her to be pleased by the friendship of Rachel (and of other actresses); her consequent about-face on her opinion of the performance of *Les Sept Princesses* and of the play itself; the arrival of Rachel in Berma's high position in the theater; and the violent contrast in their social positions.

The reversal of positions does not constitute for Marcel a reversal on artistic grounds, but merely a reversal in popularity or success. He writes of "l'extraordinaire ignorance de ce public" (III, 1002) before whom Rachel has her success, and announces flatly that "la Berma était, comme on dit, à cent pics au-dessus de Rachel, et le temps . . . avait surfait une médiocrité et consacré un génie" (p. 1003). Rachel, despite her success, is shown as unchanged in her malice and in a coarseness which Marcel attributes to theatrical life (although Berma appears to be free of it). Rachel speaks patronizingly of Berma in the same feline terms which she had used earlier: "Elle n'a pas été je ne dirai pas sans talent, car ce n'était pas au fond du vrai talent, elle n'aimait que des horreurs, mais enfin elle a été utile, certainement; elle jouait d'une façon plus vivante que les autres, et puis c'était une brave personne, généreuse, elle s'est ruinée pour les autres." Rachel continues, more personally, ". . . Je vous dirai que mon âge ne m'a permis de l'entendre, naturellement, que tout à fait dans les derniers temps et quand j'étais moi-même trop jeune pour me rendre compte. [Marcel has described Rachel as "une affreuse vieille femme" whom he did not recognize (p. 991).]—Elle ne disait pas très bien les vers? hasarda l'ami de Bloch pour flatter Rachel, qui répondit: — Oh! ça, elle n'a jamais su en dire un; c'était de la prose, du chinois, du volapük, tout, excepté un vers" (pp. 1002–1003).

Marcel sees no reason to be surprised at this, adding, "Qu'une femme du monde de la plus haute intelligence, de la plus grande bonté, se fasse actrice . . . on s'étonnera . . . d'entendre non son langage à elle, mais celui des comédiennes, leur rosserie spéciale envers les camarades, ce qu'ajoutent à l'être humain, quand ils ont passé sur lui, 'trente ans de théâtre.' Rachel les avait et ne sortait pas du monde" (p. 1003).

Rachel's calculation is shown in her cultivation of the Duchesse:

> Quant à Rachel, si elle s'était en réalité donné une grande peine pour se lier avec la duchesse de Guermantes . . . sans doute cela tenait d'une façon générale à la fascination que les gens du monde exercent à partir d'un certain moment sur les bohèmes les plus endurcis. . . . Mais le désir de Rachel pouvait avoir une raison plus particulière. C'est chez Mme de Guermantes, c'est de Mme de Guermantes, qu'elle avait reçu jadis sa plus terrible avanie. Rachel l'avait peu à peu non pas oubliée, ni pardonée, mais le prestige singulier qu'en avait reçu à ses yeux la duchesse ne devait s'effacer jamais. (p. 994)

The effect of the reminder of her fiasco at this juncture is obvious in underlining the irony.

Rachel's calculation is even more painful as she shows her awareness of her assertion of power, when Berma's children wait at the Princesse's door, and her spiteful vision of patronizing Berma to her face:

> . . . Elle fit dire au jeune couple d'entrer, ce qu'il fit sans se faire prier, ruinant d'un seul coup la situation sociale de la Berma comme il avait détruit sa santé. . . . Rachel cependant

composait déjà dans sa tête la phrase gracieuse dont elle accablerait le lendemain la Berma, dans les coulisses: "J'ai été navrée, desolée, que votre fille fasse antichambre. Si j'avais compris! Elle m'envoyait bien cartes sur cartes." Elle était ravie de porter ce coup à la Berma. (pp. 1014–15)

Clearly, Rachel's character has not improved with her career and her status; leadership in the theater and acceptance by society have not sweetened her. Her artistic life and her personal life remain separate, and playing tragic roles has done nothing to develop her own nobility.

Berma's fate seems more closely to intertwine her personal and public lives. "Les grandes tragédiennes," Marcel observes, "meurent souvent victimes des complots domestiques noués autour d'elles, comme il leur arrivait tant de fois à la fin des pièces qu'elles jouaient" (p. 1015). Marcel's summary, when Berma's single guest leaves her alone, is this:" . . . Il se leva et partit, laissant Phèdre ou la mort, on ne savait trop laquelle des deux c'était, achever de manger, avec sa fille et son gendre, les gâteaux funéraires" (p. 999). By contrast, the last personal appearance of Rachel shows her protesting, untruthfully, her innocence of malice; her last professional appearance is not on stage, or in drama, but reciting Victor Hugo and La Fontaine in a drawing room.

This is the unattractive creature who has stolen Berma's fame, and whose friendship pleases the once lofty Duchesse:

Car la duchesse . . . se passait la fantaisie de déjeuner avec telle ou telle actrice qu'elle trouvait délicieuse.

. . . .

La duchesse hésitait encore, par peur d'une scène de M. de Guermantes, devant Balthy et Mistinguett, qu'elle trouvait adorables, mais avait décidement Rachel pour amie. Les nouvelles générations en concluaient que la duchesse de Guermantes, malgré son nom, devait être quelque demi-castor qui n'avait jamais été tout à fait du gratin. . . . Mais cette intimité avec Rachel pouvait signifier aussi que l'intelligence était, en réalité, chez la duchesse, médiocre, insatisfaite. . . . (pp. 992–94)

The Duchesse has acquired some of the coarseness of theatrical life that Marcel mentions in connection with even society women turned actresses. When she speaks of Gilberte as "une cochonne," Marcel observes, "Une telle expression était rendue possible à Mme de Guermantes par la pente qu'elle descendait du milieu des Guermantes agréables à la société des comédiennes . . . " (p. 1028). Berma, be it noted, is still among the "tragédiennes," Rachel among the "comédiennes." In adopting the theater into her society, the Duchesse has not taken the best of it.

Having taken Rachel as a friend, she adjusts her aesthetic opinions to suit the altered relationship. Marcel shows, by his description of Rachel's performance and the audience's reaction to it, that Rachel is still as open to derision as when she performed in *Les Sept Princesses*. This time the description, which echoes the earlier one, is not secondhand or prejudiced, but given by Marcel himself, immediately after the description of the deserted Berma:

Nous fûmes interrompus par la voix de l'actrice qui venait de s'élever. Le jeu de celle-ci était intelligent, car il présupposait la poésie que l'actrice était en train de dire comme un tout existant avant cette récitation et dont nous n'entendions qu'un fragment. . . .

L'annonce de poésies que presque tout le monde connaissait avait fait plaisir. Mais quand on vit l'actrice, avant de commencer, chercher partout des yeux d'un air égaré, lever les mains d'un air suppliant et pousser comme un gémissement chaque mot, chacun se sentit gêné. . . . Car on se figure que c'est grotesque, mais après tout c'est peut-être magnifique, et on attend d'être fixé.

Néanmoins, les auditeurs furent stupéfaits en voyant cette femme, avant d'avoir émis un seul son, plier les genoux, tendre les bras, en berçant quelque être invisible, devenir cagneuse, et tout d'un coup, pour dire des vers fort connus, prendre un ton suppliant. (p. 999)

So baffled is the audience, so close the possibility of disaster, that Rachel's success on this occasion, before another ignorant audience, is due to the weight cast in her favor by her social supporters, who are like Marcel when he allowed others to persuade him of Berma's greatness:

. . . En écoutant l'actrice, chacun attendait, la tête baissée et l'œil investigateur, que d'autres prissent l'initiative de rire ou de critiquer, ou de pleurer ou d'applaudir. . . . Mais comme c'était chez elle . . . [la princesse] faisait la claque. Elle provoquait l'enthousiasme et faisait la presse en poussant à tous moments des exclamations ravies. . . .

. . . La duchesse de Guermantes sentit le léger flottement et décida de la victoire en s'écriant: "C'est admirable!" au beau milieu du poème, qu'elle crut peut-être terminé. Plus d'un invité alors tint à souligner cette exclamation d'un regard approbateur et d'une inclinaison de tête, pour montrer moins peut-être leur compréhension de la récitante que leurs relations avec la duchesse. (pp. 1000–1001)

Following the *coup de théâtre* passage, in which the members of society have seemed to Marcel to resemble all that is false and stagey in the theater, the behavior of the audience and the Duchesse underlines the reversal of values of society and art, with society incompetent even to comprehend art, let alone survive it. The "consecrated" genius of Berma appears as the most permanent and valid element in the pattern of

179

shifts and reversals, and the work which Marcel would produce is placed on the same plane.

The Duchesse continues to praise the performance after it is over: "On peut dire ce qu'on veut, c'est admirable, cela a de la ligne, du caractère, c'est intelligent, personne n'a jamais dit les vers comme ça" (p. 1003). She praises it to Marcel, dangling Rachel as a personal possession: "Mais si belle qu'elle ait été, elle ne se donne pas devant ce public-là. Je vous ferai déjeuner seul avec elle. Alors vous verrez l'être que c'est. . . . Et après le déjeuner elle vous dira du Verlaine" (p. 1026).

The necessity for the Duchesse to adjust not only her present behavior but the past as well produces a pleasant passage of comedy—with a sting in the tail when the Duchesse, sneering at her new cousin, ends up in a piece of action that irresistibly recalls Mme Verdurin and the piano in the old days:

Si les jugements que la duchesse porta sur Rachel étaient en eux-mêmes médiocres, ils m'intéressèrent en ce que, eux aussi, marquaient une heure nouvelle sur le cadran. Car la duchesse n'avait pas plus complètement que Rachel perdu le souvenir de la soirée que celle-ci avait passée chez elle, mais ce souvenir n'y avait pas subi une moindre transformation. . . . " . . . Je l'ai dénichée, appréciée, prônée, imposée à une époque où personne ne la connaissait et où tout le monde se moquait d'elle. Oui, mon petit, cela va vous étonner, mais la première maison où elle s'est fait entendre en public, c'est chez moi! . . . Je l'avais trouvée intéressante et je lui avais fait offrir un cachet pour venir jouer chez moi devant tout ce que nous faisons de mieux comme gratin. . . . Je n'ai pas besoin de vous dire, reprit-elle, que cet intelligent public qui s'appelle le monde ne comprenait absolument rien à cela. On protestait, on riait. . . . C'est comme la chose qu'elle jouait, c'était une chose de Maeterlinck, maintenant c'est très connu, mais à ce moment-là tout le monde s'en moquait, eh bien, moi je trouvais ça admirable. . . . Naturellement je n'aurais pas su dire pourquoi, mais ça me plaisait, ça me remuait; tenez, Basin, qui n'a rien d'un sensible avait été frappé de l'effet que ça me produisait. Il m'avait dit: 'Je ne veux plus que vous entendiez ces absurdités, ça vous rend malade.'" (pp. 1012–13)

The circles have come full turn; "plus ça change. . . . " Rachel has spiraled above the Duchesse.

As Milton Hindus writes:

Morel and Rachel, in spite of their being among Proust's most egocentric and morally obtuse characters, are partially redeemed for us by the fact that they are serious about their art if about nothing else. . . . It is this standard of values which, in spite of all her viciousness, cruelty, and prostitution, raises her in Proust's pages far above the fine but vapid society women who fancy themselves her superiors.[17]

But if Rachel is as single-minded about her art as Hindus maintains, Berma has been placed a hundred times higher than Rachel, as a real genius. And Berma is simply forgotten, except by Rachel and Marcel.

Until these final passages, as has been noted earlier, the personal life of Berma has been omitted, except for Marcel's brief speculations about her lovers, while the greater part of the material about Rachel has been about Rachel as mistress. The introduction of the episode of Berma's tea party and her desertion by all her so-called friends, including Marcel, in favor of the Guermantes reception, is a late addition to the manuscript.[18] So is the episode in which Rachel exercises her social power: "Tout le développement sur Rachel et les enfants de la Berma . . . est une addition."[19] So, too, is Proust's decision to have Rachel's blow seemingly result in

Berma's broken-hearted death: "Le Ms. prouve en effet qu'il a beaucoup varié au sujet de la date de la mort de la Berma, et on y relève sur ce point de nombreuses contradictions." [20] In the passage in which Rachel speaks disparagingly of Berma, the choice is between "she is in the greatest misery," or "she died in the greatest misery," the former being followed to fit her death after the reception. It is evident that Proust wished to make the contrasts between the new and old first ladies of the theater as striking as possible, and to weight the sympathies of the reader heavily in favor of Berma, both as artist and as person—the effect being to make society the more unfeeling, fickle, and uncomprehending.

Berma, who has not figured in the action for almost two thousand pages, reappears as an old friend who invites Marcel to her tea (III, 856), and as a "grande artiste" (p. 995). For this great artist, "Rachel était restée une grue qu'on laissait figurer dans les pièces où elle-même, la Berma, jouait le premier rôle, parce que Saint-Loup lui payait ses toilettes pour la scène . . . " (p. 995). The destruction of her health, fortune, and fame have not stilled Berma's faith in herself, nor her scorn for her successful rival: " . . . Ayant conscience du génie qui était en elle, ayant appris dès son plus jeune âge l'insignifiance de tous ces décrets de la mode, elle était quant à elle restée fidèle à la Tradition qu'elle avait toujours respectée, dont elle était l'incarnation, qui lui faisait juger les choses et les gens comme trente ans auparavant, et par exemple juger Rachel non comme l'actrice à la mode qu'elle était aujourd'hui, mais comme la petite grue qu'elle avait connue" (p. 997). But Berma's pride in herself and her art is almost all she has left.

Suffering from a fatal disease, she forces herself to perform (like Bernhardt after the loss of her leg), making her health even worse to gain the money so greedily required by her daughter and son-in-law. Her daughter reports only part of the doctor's advice, when he weakly says this can do her no harm—since the disease is incurable anyway (pp. 995–96). Berma's training enables her to delude the audience, including the doctor: "La Berma n'était pas une moins vieille habituée de la scène, aux exigences de laquelle ses organes étaient si parfaitement adaptés qu'elle pouvait donner en se dépensant avec une prudence indiscernable pour le public l'illusion d'une bonne santé troublée seulement par un mal purement nerveux et imaginaire. Après la scène de la déclaration à Hippolyte, la Berma avait beau sentir l'épouvantable nuit qu'elle allait passer, ses admirateurs l'applaudissaient à toute force, la déclarant plus belle que jamais" (p. 996).

The money that she so painfully and fatally earns is used by her family for redecorating, which destroys all her rest, and for entertaining, at which she must appear as the family's lion (pp. 996–97). She is forced even to compete with Réjane, embarking on foreign tours, although she must take morphine injections, which almost kill her (p. 997). The final description of Berma is of a figure of tragedy: "La Berma avait, comme dit le peuple, la mort sur le visage. . . . Ses artères durcies étant déjà à demi pétrifiées, on voyait de longs rubans sculpturaux parcourir les joues, avec une rigidité minérale. Les yeux mourants vivaient relativement, par contraste avec ce terrible masque ossifié, et brillaient faiblement comme un serpent endormi au milieu des pierres" (p. 998).

It would be too ironic to describe the final inhumane treatment of Berma by her children and by Rachel as a *coup de grâce*, though the results are fatal. The children take advantage of the fact that she has to retire to her room, spitting blood (p. 1013), to dress, sneak out, and invade the Guer-

mantes reception for which, they believe, Rachel has issued
the invitations. Rachel, as has been seen, is all too glad to
take advantage of the opportunity offered by their treason:
"Elle était ravie de porter ce coup à la Berma. Peut-être eût-
elle reculé si elle eût su que ce serait un coup mortel. On
aime à faire des victimes, mais sans se mettre précisément
dans son tort, en les laissant vivre. D'ailleurs où était son
tort? Elle devait dire en riant quelques jours plus tard: 'C'est
un peu fort, j'ai voulu être plus aimable pour ses enfants
qu'elle n'a jamais été pour moi, et pour un peu on m'accuserait
de l'avoir assassinée'" (p. 1015).

Berma, Rachel, and the Duchesse finish the action which
has involved the two actresses for so long. The genius which
Marcel took years to comprehend is dead at the hands of
a malicious inferior viciously applying social power, while
the Duchesse is called on as approving witness. The values
of art and society that Marcel so painfully acquired through
the years are, so far as the world is concerned, topsy-turvy
and crumbled. "Here a mighty mammoth lies, fouled to
death by butterflies." Berma and the Duchesse, whom Marcel
admired equally, if differently, have over the years gone quite
separate ways in his admiration. Only by true art and dedication to it can Marcel remain not disillusioned. Like the illusion of Rachel that Saint-Loup created out of his love, the
illusion of Odette that Swann created, and the illusion of
Albertine that Marcel created, Marcel's illusion about the
Duchesse de Guermantes—and all she represents—is finally
shattered. The myriad pieces are reassembled in the only thing
that matters, a work of art, free from time because, like
Berma's genius, it exists out of time. The end of *Le Temps*

retrouvé includes not one, but several *coups de théâtre,* of which the one involving Rachel and Berma is not the least.

OTHERS

The remaining actresses in Proust's novel are not important for their artistic careers, which are barely mentioned, but for their associations—particularly as they affect Marcel's jealousy—with promiscuity, Lesbian or otherwise. The term "actress" operates much like the term "artiste" in Middle Eastern passport control; it is a convenient *nom de guerre,* covering a multiude of sins and availabilities. The young actress at Balbec with her lover and his two friends seems at first view to be merely another theater cocotte; but later, Charlus offers assertions of more intricate complications. On first description, she appears only to be involved in a rather odd *ménage à quatre.* The actress, described as "plus connue d'ailleurs à cause de son élégance, de son esprit, de ses belles collections de porcelaine allemande que pour quelques rôles joués à l'Odéon," constitutes with her three young men a "bande à part"—they dine together after the other guests have finished, and spend the day playing cards in their own room (I, 680). Marcel is mildly pleased, later, to become acquainted with the actress and two of her friends (p. 952).

Later still, he is astonished at Charlus' description of the faces behind the masks in this sexual masquerade:

M. de Charlus m'étonna beaucoup en citant parmi les invertis "l'ami de l'actrice" que j'avais vu à Balbec et qui était le chef de la petite Société des quatres amis. "Mais alors cette actrice?"— Elle lui sert de paravent, et d'ailleurs il a des relations avec elle, plus peut-être qu'avec des hommes, avec qui il n'en a guère.—Il en a avec les trois autres?—Mais pas du tout! Ils sont amis pas du tout pour ça! Deux sont tout à fait pour femmes. Un en est, mais n'est pas sûr pour son ami, et en tous cas ils se cachent l'un de l'autre. (III, 297)

Whether Charlus is reporting facts or this is another part of his massive smokescreen, the novel's ambiguous associations with actresses are made no less equivocal by his remarks.

If Marcel "collects" actresses, Bloch's female relatives collect Lesbian actresses, of whom Léa becomes the type, and the focus of Marcel's jealousy and suffering over Albertine: "Et une de leurs cousines qui n'avait que quinze ans scandalisait le Casino par l'admiration qu'elle affichait pour Mlle Léa, dont M. Bloch père prisait très fort le talent d'actrice, mais que son goût ne passait pas pour porter surtout du côté des messieurs" (I, 903). Marcel, talking to Albertine, makes light of such relationships, attributing stories about them to malicious gossip: "Ainsi, tenez, ces relations dont vous parliez l'autre jour à propos d'une petite qui habite Balbec et qui existeraient entre elle et une actrice, je trouve cela ignoble, tellement ignoble que je pense que ce sont des ennemis de la jeune fille qui auront inventé cela et que ce n'est pas vrai. Cela me semble improbable, impossible" (I, 941–42).

But improbable or impossible though it seems to Marcel, the Bloch women continue to become involved: in *Sodome et Gomorrhe*, he has to report, " . . . la plus jeune, la cousine, vivait, au su de tout le monde, avec l'actrice dont elle avait fait la connaissance pendant mon premier séjour. Andrée, sur une allusion qu'on fit à mi-voix à cela, me dit: 'Oh! là-dessus je suis comme Albertine, il n'y a rien qui nous fasse horreur à toutes les deux comme cela'" (II, 802); and he adds, "quant à Albertine . . . elle avait tourné le dos aux deux jeunes filles de mauvais genre." Only a few pages later, Bloch's sister is involved in outright scandal at the Balbec hotel. Engaged in an affair with an elderly actress, she takes perverse pleasure in public manifestations of her Lesbianism, to the point that two officers complain to the management of the hotel. Her uncle's influence protects her because the management does not wish to lose his patronage (he lunches there every day in order to continue his own affair with a young waiter). Marcel describes this in theatrical metaphor: "Aussi M. Nissim Bernard entretenait-il avec le directeur de ce théâtre qu'était l'hôtel de Balbec, et avec le metteur en scène et régisseur Aimé—desquels le rôle en toute cette affaire n'était pas des plus limpides—d'excellentes relations" (p. 845).

The outcome is satisfactory for M. Bernard, his niece, and the old actress:

Et un soir où je sortais du Casino à demi éteint, avec Albertine, et Bloch que nous avions rencontré, elles passèrent enlacées, ne cessant de s'embrasser, et, arrivées à notre hauteur, poussèrent des gloussements, des rires, des cris indécents. Bloch baissa les yeux pour ne pas avoir l'air de reconnaître sa sœur, et moi j'étais torturé en pensant que ce langage particulier et atroce s'adressait peut-être à Albertine. (II, 850–51)

It is little wonder that Marcel is jealous and suspicious at any suggestion of a relationship between Albertine and actresses, particularly Léa, and subsequent events show that his suspicions are justified.

In the unfolding of these events, the arts of the theater and drama play no part. Simply, when Albertine attends the theater, it seems to mean bad luck for her lover. When she goes, on his recommendation and with his ticket, to see *Phèdre*, he rushes home in order to receive her after the theater, only to get a telephone call to say that she had misread his note. She did not understand that she was expected, and wishes, if there is to be so much fuss, that she had not gone to the theater at all (II, 645, 709, 726, 731–32).

The second time, it is Marcel who wishes that Albertine had not gone, although his excitement turns out to be something of a false alarm. When she is to go to a special matinée at the Trocadéro (III, 119), he is delighted to know that she is going with Andrée, whom he feels he can trust (pp. 131–32, 136). The only professional information about Léa which appears in the novel throws him into a panic. When he sees in the paper that Léa is appearing that afternoon as Nérine in the *Fourberies de Nérine*, he recalls that "Léa, c'était la comédienne amie des deux jeunes filles qu'Albertine, sans avoir l'air de les voir, avait, un après-midi, au Casino, regardées dans la glace" (III, 144). Marcel, in panic and suspicion, although not certain whether Albertine does or does not know Léa, sends Françoise to summon her to him. To his relief, all is well: she has not met Léa (pp. 144–57); but the "narrow escape" continues to stick in his memory for years. He is reminded of it on numerous occasions: when he hears that Léa has undertaken a new part (p. 465); on the anniversary of the event (p. 559); and several other times (pp. 225, 295, 346, 485, 876).

His suspicions are sharply intensified upon hearing that Albertine had once been on a three week trip with Léa, a fact which she feels she should confide in him (pp. 350–52, 373, 374). The idea of Léa throws him into fits of retroactive jealousy: "Ainsi il y avait plusieurs années, comme on parlait de son peignoir de douche, Albertine avait rougi. . . . Cela m'avait d'autant plus préoccupé qu'on m'avait dit que les deux jeunes filles amies de Léa allaient à cet établissement balnéaire de l'hôtel et, disait-on, pas seulement pour prendre des douches" (p. 491). Nor is the picture of Léa's private life made any more attractive, or any less complex or equivocal, by the description of one of her letters to Morel: " . . . Sa lettre à Morel (que M. de Charlus ne soupçonnait même pas la connaître) était écrite sur le ton le plus passionné. Sa grossièreté empêche qu'elle soit reproduite ici. . . . Et dans cette lettre il était question de plusieurs autres femmes qui ne semblaient pas être moins amies de Morel que de Léa" (III, 215).

Even Gilberte is connected with Léa, if in a contradictory passage. Several times Marcel describes seeing Gilberte walking with an unidentified young man (I, 623, 625, 626, 630), and several times he recalls the episode. In the opening pages of *Le Temps retrouvé* he asks her about it: "C'était Léa habillée en homme. Elle savait qu'elle connaissait Albertine, mais ne pouvait dire plus. Ainsi certaines personnes se retrouvent toujours dans notre vie pour préparer nos plaisirs et nos douleurs" (III, 695 n.). But of this identification of Léa with Albertine and Gilberte the Pléiade editors write, "Nous isolons en bas de page un passage qui contredit le reste du texte, et qui dans le Ms. constitue un béquet marginal, évidemment inséré après coup." [21] The plan, however, to tie the knot or add the grace note, makes clear the intention surrounding the treatment of Léa, and the aura that the actress is meant to provide, in which her professional life, unlike that of Berma, is of miniscule importance. The Duchesse's latter-day friendships do not raise her to the aesthetic heights of Berma, but lower her to the personal depths of Rachel or Léa. The theatricalization of society in the *coup de théâtre* at the Guermantes reception slides society in the same direction, as well as emphasizing its falseness and deceptiveness.

The whole association of Odette with things of the theater is in line with the equation between *soi-disant* actresses and cocottes, without the strong Lesbian overtones attached to Léa. As with Léa, Odette's professional career is of little moment. But the entire history of the Miss Sacripant portrait serves to keep her within the pattern of theatrical promiscuity. Swann met her at a theater—whether as an actress or as one of the audience is not stated—(I, 195), and Charlus first met her as an actress: "Je l'avais trouvée charmante dans son demi-travesti, un soir qu'elle jouait Miss Sacripant . . ." (III, 299). This is the only indication of any part she has played; her career on the stage must have been brief, and a makeshift. The focus is kept on Odette as theatrical cocotte, starting with Marcel's boyish observation just before his meeting with her at his uncle's: "Or mon oncle en connaissait beaucoup, et aussi des cocottes que je ne distinguais pas nettement des actrices" (I, 75). He is surprised that she does not carry the badge of what she is: "Je ne lui trouvais rien de l'aspect théâtral que j'admirais dans les photographies d'actrices, ni de l'expression diabolique qui eût été en rapport avec la vie qu'elle devait mener. J'avais peine à croire que ce fût une cocotte et surtout je n'aurais pas cru que ce fût une cocotte chic . . . " (p. 77).

Years later, when young Morel brings to Marcel his uncle Adolphe's collection of photographs, the equation between the stage and the illicit bed is maintained: "C'étaient les photographies des actrices célèbres, des grandes cocottes que mon oncle avait connues, les dernières images de cette vie de vieux viveur . . . " (II, 264). In her later appearances in the novel,

Odette's theater career is all but forgotten, except in a few indications of her tastes in theater, which suggest that her aesthetic judgment is no better than that of actresses, who are better at performing than at choosing roles. Swann convinces himself that her tastes are depraved; in any case, they are not given as lofty. At great length he sarcastically requests her not to see Victor Massé's *Une Nuit de Cléopâtre*, resenting the necessity to soil his lips with the abject title (I, 289–91). When Odette marries Forcheville, the social and intellectual values of old are still further overturned, two worlds intermingled in a way that would have seemed impossible to the young Marcel, and still seems astonishing to him now. The greatest actress of them all is forgotten; the Rachels and Odettes have risen to the level of the Guermantes; and the Léas have left their sooty touch across the scene. What is best in the theater is neglected; what is worst in the life of the theater has triumphed.

While the actresses in the novel are professionals and *soi-disant* professionals, the playwrights who figure in the action are drawing-room playwrights. Even Bergotte, professional as a novelist, is associated as a playwright with the salon. The emphasis falls more on the hostesses as patronesses than on playwrights as artists, leaving the real art of playwriting to Racine and Molière. Dramaturgy is for the most part an amateur and dilettante exercise, of the sort summed up in actual life by George Painter's remark about Proust's friend Bibesco: "Antoine, having written a never-to-be-staged play, *La Lutte*, and made friends with the rising Jewish dramatist Henri Bernstein, was engrossed in an affair with an actress." [22] Even Marcel can be mistaken, by a stupid man, for a possible playwright (II, 430–31). His Uncle Adolphe, who expects great things of his young nephew, is not sure whether to hope for poet, poet-dramatist, or historian—a Hugo or Vaulabelle (I, 79), a Racine or Vaulabelle (II, 264–65).

The Duchesse de Guermantes dabbles in playwrights, and she acts as an advisor on drama: "Parfois même, sans prétentions, avec pertinence et simplicité, elle donnait à un auteur dramatique académicien quelque conseil sagace, lui faisait atténuer une situation ou changer un dénouement" (II, 209). Bloch maintains a place in the salon of Mme de Villeparisis in his capacity as "jeune auteur dramatique" (II, 189), and even becomes the object of a drawing-room rivalry between Mme de Villeparisis and three old ladies (II, 196–98). Bloch's position does not extend so far as to be able to use Rachel for his performance, but his drawing-room dramaturgy guarantees his own social acceptance.

Bergotte as dramatist is of trifling importance; the salon reduces his stature. In one instance, the Prince de Guermantes is reported to have been offended by a "take-off" in a play of Bergotte's given at the Swanns', and Swann to have assured him, "Mais, pas du tout, cela ne vous ressemble en rien, vous êtes bien plus ridicule que ça!" (II, 675). Swann, however, later denies having said this (p. 702). And that is all we are told of Bergotte's play. Bergotte, of course, becomes Odette's particular lion, the attraction of her salon, and her putative collaborator:

Elles étaient persuadées qu'Odette, intime de Bergotte, avait plus ou moins collaboré à ses œuvres. . . . A une répétition générale d'une pièce de Bergotte . . . ce fut un vrai coup de théâtre quand on vit dans la loge de face, qui était celle de l'auteur, venir s'asseoir à côté de Mme Swann, Mme de Marsantes et celle qui, par l'effacement progressif de la Duchesse de Guermantes . . . était en train de devinir la lionne, la reine du temps, la comtesse Molé. (II, 745–46)

The playwrights who, in any case, play a very minor role as playwrights, are used simply as social pawns and servitors, fulfilling no major function in the development of the novel.

Another minor character who works in the theater illustrates a different point, one already implied in society's willingness to believe Odette capable of offering artistic assistance to Bergotte. The career of Andrée's friend Octave shows society's inability to accept the artistic accomplishments of people who seem to be like themselves. As Georges Piroué writes, "The lightly-sketched character of Octave is that of a man who, before becoming one of the leading theatrical producers of the century, was known only as a golfer." [23] Marcel writes, "Ce jeune homme fit représenter de petits sketches, dans des décors et avec des costumes de lui, et qui ont amené dans l'art contemporain une révolution au moins égale à celle accomplie par les Ballets russes. Bref les juges les plus autorisés considérèrent ses œuvres comme quelque chose de capital, presque des œuvres de génie, et je pense d'ailleurs comme eux, ratifiant ainsi, à mon propre étonnement, l'ancienne opinion de Rachel" (III, 605). But other judges hold other views:

Les personnes qui l'avaient connu à Balbec . . . pensèrent que peut-être ses œuvres étaient d'Andrée qui par amour voulait lui en laisser la gloire, ou que plus probablement il payait . . . quelque professionnel génial et besogneux pour les faire (ce genre de société riche . . . croyant volontiers que tous les gens du monde qui écrivent, composent ou peignent, font faire leurs œuvres et payent pour avoir une réputation d'auteur comme d'autres pour s'assurer un siège de député). Mais tout cela était faux; et ce

jeune homme était bien l'auteur de ces œuvres admirables. . . .
Il était déjà un homme de génie, peut-être distrait de son génie.
. . . Pour Octave les choses de l'art devaient être quelque chose
de si intime, de vivant tellement dans les plus secrets replis de
lui-même, qu'il n'eût sans doute pas eu l'idée d'en parler. . . .
(III, 605–6)

Octave represents a reverse snobbery and the superiority of
the artist, but like the playwrights his contribution to the
main flow of the novel is minor—a brief variation on a theme.

Although terms of the drama—"comic," "tragic," "scene,"
"coup de théâtre"—may be usefully applied to Proust's treatment of his material, his profuse employment of theatrical
material has not carried over to the structure or organization
of the novel. Germaine Brée, for example, writes, "Alors,
comme dans une tragédie classique, le drame de toute sa vie
se dénoue en vingt-quatre heures, en passant par deux solu-
tions possibles, celle du désastre, celle de l'accomplissement.
A l'inverse de la tragédie classique toute-fois, ce n'est point la
première qui l'emporte." [24] And Jacques Nathan discusses
Proust's peripeteias as compared to those of classical drama:

[Parce que] Proust ne décrit pas seulement les périodes de crise,
comme on le fait dans les tragédies et les romans courts, on
pourrait croire que les coups de théâtre sont rares et qu'ils sont
seulement amenés, comme dans les œuvres du grand siècle, par
les sentiments des personnages. Nous allons voir qu'il n'en est
rien, que tous ces personnages si stables et si bien défendus
subissent constamment les coups du sort, et qu'en apparence tout
au moins, Proust fait souvent appel à un ressort qu'on croirait
incompatible avec ses intentions: l'intérêt de curiosité.
En apparence, disons-nous; car cette conception ne résiste pas
à l'examen. La multiplicité même de ces coups de théâtre toujours
dirigés dans le même sens fait qu'ils ne surprennent plus personne,

et Proust était un romancier beaucoup trop avisé pour ne pas s'en apercevoir.[25]

It might be said that although the events that Marcel describes constitute *coups de théâtre*, they are *coups de théâtre* for him and from his point of view. His analytical and personal way of describing them is the antithesis of the dramatic method. Drama is action; Proust's aim is the analysis of action.

6

The Pattern of Theater Metaphors in "A la recherche du temps perdu"

PROUST USES the familiar metaphor *coup de théâtre* to describe the effect produced on Marcel at the moment he enters the drawing room where the crucially significant, final Guermantes reception is being held. Proust has chosen no casual isolated metaphor: he has, in this context, brought a well-worn metaphor to new life. The sounding of the word *théâtre* at this particular point begins a passage that is to echo the undertones and overtones, and recall the themes and variations on drama and theater that have been so carefully developed throughout the whole of the vast work. The theater, in metaphor and fact, constantly figures in the pages following the key phrase, with fact and metaphor lending strength to each other, and establishing links with the past. In this section of the novel, we are shown the changes in the reputations of Berma and Rachel. Her friendships with actresses are here shown to have offset the Duchesse's earlier social eminence. Proust refers in the same pages to at least two previous passages concerned with the theater: the celebrated comparison between the theater audience and aquarium denizens in *Le Côté de Guermantes* (II, 39–41), and the occasion of Rachel's first, unsuccessful attempt at drawing-room theater (III, 223–30). And in the thirty-odd pages following the *coup de théâtre* phrase, Proust has included more than twenty additional metaphors of varied lengths, drawing on the theater, the drama, and the stage.

It would indeed be surprising if this were merely an isolated cluster of theatrical references and metaphors, a structural accident quite untypical of Proust's methods. André Maurois writes of one of Proust's extended metaphors, "Whether it be from nature or from art that the second term of a metaphor is borrowed, Proust is always at great pains to prepare us for its entry. . . . Even before the first phrase of the metaphor has been sounded, Proust has been careful to scatter, here and there, a number of adjectives designed to herald its approach. The classic example of what I mean is his account of that evening at the Opera, when he saw the theater in terms of a submarine aquarium."[1] The *coup de théâtre* section, in which the surviving members of society are seen as elaborately disguised actors in an incredible play, must be one of Proust's most extended metaphors, and the preparation for it consists not of the adjectives to announce it, but of a sustained series of metaphors, begun in *Du côté de chez Swann,* and steadily maintained—except in the penultimate volume, where the comparative paucity of these metaphors provides a kind of relief—to the "end," which is also the beginning.

A close examination reveals that these theatrical metaphors provide a useful perspective on Proust's grand plan, a plan which he clearly intended should be examined not from one, but from several related viewpoints, like the church steeples which shifted and rearranged themselves while remaining always the same. Only a few pages before he enters the drawing room, Marcel, thinking of the book which is to be the novel we are reading, observes of truth and metaphor, " . . . La vérité ne commencera qu'au moment où l'ecrivain prendra deux objets différents, posera leur rapport . . . et les enfermera dans les anneaux nécessaires d'un beau style; même, ainsi que la vie, quand, en rapprochant une qualité commune à deux sensations, il dégagera leur essence commune en les réunissant l'une et l'autre pour les soustraire aux contingences du temps, dans une métaphore" (III, 889). An elaborate cluster of metaphors so soon after this passage should—unless Proust was here uncharacteristically careless and unthinking in his profusion—cast some illumination across the vast landscape of the novel, as well as on his metaphorical method.

In his use of theater metaphors, as with theater allusions and quotations, Proust, in *A la recherche*, was developing to its highest pitch and usefulness a device that he had begun naturally in his letters, and had experimented with in his earlier fiction. It is in the metaphors drawn from drama and theater that Proust's letters show the closest parallels to the theater material in *A la recherche*. In discussing both his personal and his public life, terms of theater come most naturally to his pen. Even the breaking of his glasses becomes, ironically, a drama.[2] In a more serious vein, he writes of "le drame obscur qu'est une maladie cachée."[3] In another allusion to his state of health, he wrote: "Je me rappelle des gens qui ont 'traîné' des années. On avait l'air de croire qu'ils avaient joué la comédie."[4] To Walter Berry he wrote of "la dernière péripétie catastrophique de la tragédie grecque à laquelle vous compariez ma vie présente." [5]

In his letters, as in the novel, Proust treats the Dreyfus affair as a drama. In 1899 he wrote to Mme Straus, "Je ne vous ai plus vue depuis que l'Affaire de si balzacienne . . . est devenue si shakespearienne avec l'accumulation de ses dénouements précipités." [6] Again to Mme Straus, 1906: "D'ailleurs je ne sais qui dans cette réparation est le metteur en scène des derniers 'tableaux.' Mais il est incomparable et même émouvant. Et il est impossible de lire le 'dernier tableau' de ce matin: 'Dans la cour de l'École militaire, avec cinq cents figurants' sans avoir les larmes aux yeux." [7] Later the same year, he wrote, "Le rideau est tombé et il est rentré dans la vie." [8] Of Dreyfus' lawyer, Proust wrote Lauris in 1905, "Quelle tristesse de voir Labori faire de l'affaire Humbert la parodie de l'affaire Dreyfus où lui-même joue le rôle de l'État-major avec des absurdes secrets toujours promis." [9] In a passage in *Le Côté de Guermantes*, Labori, along with Charlus, is criticized by Marcel for a kind of insincerity and theatricality that he finds in actors and lawyers:

Je m'avisai que non seulement par les choses qu'il disait, mais par la manière dont il les disait, M. de Charlus était un peu fou. La première fois qu'on entend un avocat ou un acteur, on est surpris de leur ton tellement différent de la conversation. . . . Tout au plus pense-t-on d'un acteur du Théâtre-Français: "Pourquoi au lieu de laisser retomber son bras levé l'a-t-il fait descendre par petites saccades coupées de repos, pendant au moins dix minutes?" ou d'un Labori: "Pourquoi, dès qu'il a ouvert la bouche, a-t-il émis ces sons tragiques, inattendus, pour dire la chose la plus simple?" (II, 379–80)

As is characteristic, the assumption conveyed by the casual metaphor in the letter is developed and analyzed in the novel

—not that Proust necessarily had the former in mind when he wrote the latter.

As Marcel later does, Proust compares himself to characters in drama. In one letter, he writes: "Mon cher Gaston, je sens, comme Phèdre, que ma force m'abandonne et je ne peux plus que vous dire toute mon affection." [10] Montesquiou was the recipient of several such comparisons, sometimes hinging on rather ambiguous transpositions, as in this example: "J'espérais tellement venir hier! Dès 11 heures du matin je m'étais lavé et baigné, comme Esther pour paraître devant le 'Souverain roi.'" [11] To Daudet he wrote, "J'avoue que j'ai été en colère comme les personnages de Molière quand ils disent: 'Morbleu,'" and, "Après ce marivaudage amical, je te dirai simplement qu'en apprenant la *visite* . . . que tu me dénonce, j'aurais simplement voulu, comme dit le tragique Grec, 'ne pas être né.'" [12]

Proust finds specific theater metaphors equally useful in describing others than himself. He compliments Mme Straus: "Vous allez vous sentir comme un enfant de Maeterlinck avec des sensations d'une fraîcheur exquise pour toutes les choses naturelles et bonnes." [13] In 1918 he wrote to her, "Les descriptions qu'ils rapportent de votre hôtel font penser aux *Sept Princesses*." [14] One may wonder if he would have thought of this rather unimportant one-act play of Maeterlinck's had it not played so important a part in the career of Saint-Loup's Rachel. Proust requires three dramatists to help him make an adequately flattering remark to Montesquiou: "Comme à Corneille, par les 'examens,' à Molière par les 'critiques,' à tant d'autres et à Hugo, une attaque vulgaire a été pour vous l'occasion d'un nouveau chef-d'œuvre." [15] His terms of comparison for Antoine Bibesco are even more flattering: "Tous ceux qui disent 'prince' à ce jeune diplomate d'un si grand avenir, se font à eux-mêmes l'effet de personnages de Racine, tant avec son aspect mythologique il fait penser à Achille ou à Thésée." [16] He can go further: "Pourquoi es-tu si gentil pour moi? Etant déjà Ibsen et Carlyle, prétendrais-tu devenir Jésus?" [17]

Proust used theater metaphors in his letters and conversation to clarify ideas as well as people. Georges de Lauris cites a witticism: "Et il reprochait même à Renan d'avoir écrit, par places, lorsqu'il cherchait à trop bien et trop aisément expliquer les faits tenus pour miracles par les croyants, une *Belle Hélène* du Christianisme." [18] This must have been one of the very few times when Renan was compared to Offenbach. To Robert Dreyfus, on September 7, 1888, Proust wrote, "Car nous ne construisons dans notre esprit un caractère que d'après quelques lignes, par nous vues, qui en supposent d'autres. Mais cette construction est très hypothétique. *Quare* si Alceste fuit les hommes, Coquelin prétend que c'est par mauvaise humeur ridicule, Worms par noble mépris des viles passions. *Item* dans la vie." [19] To Jacques-Emile Blanche, in 1919, Proust made one of his observations that is paralleled in the novel: "Je trouverais donc idiot de déclarer vos secondes versions inférieures. Je me ferais [sic] l'effet des gens qui aiment dans Molière, non *le Misanthrope* mais *l'Étourdi*, dans Musset, non *les Nuits* mais *la Ballade à la Lune*, c'est-à-dire tout ce que Molière et Musset ont tâché d'abandonner pour des formes plus hautes." [20]

Proust continued his use of theater metaphors through his short-stories, essays, and novels. Those in *Les Plaisirs et les jours* are usually familiar and directly illustrative of particular points, without balancing the values of life and art as Marcel does in *A la recherche*. "Joue-t-il la comédie?" Alexis wonders of his uncle (p. 23); and "Mon Dieu! s'écria intérieurement Alexis, ce rôle est au-dessus de ses forces" (p. 23). In two instances in the "Comédie italienne" section, the conventionality of the theater is hinted at, the first instance raising the later discussed question of type-casting: "Ce public, égaré par la psychologie conventionelle du théâtre . . . se refuse à reconnaître que la flatterie n'est parfois que l'épanachement de la tendresse et la franchise la bave de la mauvaise humeur" (p. 82). And the author-narrator inquires of Olivian, "Vos amis n'ont-ils pas plus d'esprit que Pantalon, Scaramouche ou Pasquarello?" (p. 91).

The theatrical and dramatic metaphors in *Pastiches et mélanges* (and the *Nouveaux mélanges*) are also almost all conventional and neutral. In "L'Affaire Lemoine," events in a Balzac plot are presented in terms of "la comédie qui venait de se jouer" (p. 15), or "le drame qui va suivre, et la scène que nous venons de raconter" (p. 16). The Goncourt piece mentions a "dénouement à la Sarcey" (p. 39). In "Sentiments filiaux d'un parricide," Proust three times refers to the murder as a "drame," (pp. 211, 215, 221), and once as a "drame de la folie" (p. 218). He also writes of "les cruelles émotions de l'homme d'État et de l'acteur" (p. 217), and speaks of "vils comédiens" (p. 217). The shortness of the sections in *Les Plaisirs* and the *Pastiches* and *Mélanges* precludes the patterning and interrelationship of metaphors that is to come later.

Contre Sainte-Beuve includes only half a dozen theater metaphors. It is too fragmentary to make organic use of such a device, but those Proust uses do mirror some of his later attitudes. In one of the more neutral ones, Proust does stress slightly the better side of theater: "Plus tard, quand ces mêmes personnes furent devenues pour moi des personnes ennuyeuses

. . . le reste de ce que je voyais n'étant qu'un sorte de coulisse où l'on ne peut rien soupçonner de la beauté de la pièce et du génie de l'actrice" (p. 93). Derogation by theater metaphor, to be used so extensively and so carefully in *A la recherche,* is here used in three instances, obviously not enough for the developed structural use that appears later. In criticism of Balzac, Proust writes, "Mais presque tous les personnages de Balzac sont rangés là autour du narrateur comme dans les 'à-propos,' ces 'cérémonies' que la Comédie-Française donne à l'occasion d'un anniversaire, d'un centenaire," and he lists a number of characters who "viennent successivement dire leur mot, comme les sociétaires, défilant à l'anniversaire de Molière devant le buste du poète, y déposent une palme" (pp. 212–13). With similar detachment and pleasant irony, he views the Guermantes domain: "Comme dans ma lanterne magique, comme dans Shakespeare ou dans Maeterlinck, 'à gauche, il y a une forêt.' Elle est peinte sur la colline qui domine Guermantes, elle a velouté de vert tragique le côté ouest. . . . Elle est 'la forêt' qui est 'à gauche' dans le drame" (p. 286). He also describes his brother as a princess of tragedy: "[Mon frère] avait les yeux rouges, la gorge oppressée de se falbalas, comme une princesse de tragédie pompeuse et désespérée. . . . Il relevait ses cheveux sur sa tête avec l'impatience de Phèdre. 'Quelle importune main en formant tous ces nœuds,/ A pris soin sur mon front d' assembler mes cheveux'" (p. 293).

Jean Santeuil includes more than fifty metaphors whose source is the drama or theater, but the method of using metaphors in *A la recherche* is present only in embryo. The metaphors function separately, whereas those in *A la recherche* function organically, and, as will be seen, in a complex pattern that creates a cumulative stream of significance, and which gradually reverses the weight of the metaphors. If we consider theater as a standard against which life may be measured, we may divide the metaphors as "neutral," "favorable," or "derogatory." (Examples may clarify these terms: *neutral*—the curtain fell on this social scene; *favorable*—she moved with a ballerina's grace; *derogatory*—he ranted, and used theatrical gestures.) Following this classification in *Jean Santeuil* is convenient, but no particular pattern emerges. In *A la recherche*, neutral or derogatory metaphors are more frequent in the early portions, favorable metaphors more important toward the end.

The metaphors in *Jean Santeuil* are seldom used either to denigrate or to elevate the drama. Among the neutral metaphors are obvious and often brief examples of the kind so frequent in Proust's letters, dealing with little "dramas," or characters "playing parts" in social contexts. We find "les drames de la société" (I, 170), "tous drames naturels" of the weather (I, 225), and Proust has his "reader" remark, "Vous prétendez nous peindre la vie, me direz-vous, et c'est de plus en plus à une pièce que vous nous faites assister" (III, 31). Although some of Proust's metaphors are drawn from "out front," dealing with the behavior of theater audiences rather than with theater as art, they are presented without irony. A habit of one character is explained in terms which will be recognizable to anyone who has attended foreign motion pictures; in his conversation he imitates "ces étrangers qui, écoutant une pièce de Molière ou de Musset, restent tout le temps de la représentation le sourire à la bouche, de peur qu'une des innombrables finesses dont le dialogue est sans doute semé pût paraître leur avoir échappé" (III, 32–33). (Proust might find much material for metaphor in the modern "art" cinema.)

In two examples, Proust presents the theater as seen by the playwright. In one, he gives a playwright's-eye view of history: ". . . [Il] maudit dans son cœur la république . . . pareil à cet auteur dramatique qui, joué pour la première fois le deux Décembre, gardait rancune à l'Empire d'avoir le soir de son avènement empêché le public, plus attentif aux nouvelles qu'à la pièce, de témoigner à l'auteur ce qu'il en pensait" (I, 266). The second example also emphasizes, but in a different way, the rather special viewpoint of the playwright: "A vrai dire ce n'était pas une découverte pour la duchesse de Réveillon qui en avait donné ce matin l'idée au cuisinier. . . . L'auteur d'une pièce qui réussit n'a pas comme le spectateur ignorant encore du dénouement des plaisirs de curiosité. Mais les applaudissements lui en causent un autre qui n'est pas non plus à dédaigner" (II, 18).

In a metaphor that prefigures several in *A la recherche*, Proust uses a detailed description of an aged actress to emphasize Jean's reaction to his parents, and the passage of time:

Et les seuls chocs ineffables que nous ayons entendus au théâtre, c'est par une actrice vieille, quand le corps est déjà fragile et que la bouche, les regards, la mémoire trahissent la personne qui leur pardonne, mais aussi où l'âme peut jouer librement dans les ruines du corps, comme elle ne le faisait pas quand une bouche fraîche et ferme, quand deux yeux perçants témoignaient du plaisir de vivre. . . . Il y a quelque chose dans la vie (plus qu'au théâtre) d'un ineffable dans ces yeux d'un père ou d'une mère. . . . (I, 83–84)

Metaphors of similar content and intent add to the effect of the grand *coup de théâtre* in *A la recherche*, where they are used more sharply and are combined in significant clusters.

Even into those metaphors that are seemingly "neutral" there creeps a possible tinge of irony. In a combination of the "play-player" metaphors, Proust writes of "une maîtresse de maison qui ne se contente pas de recevoir mais qui jouera dans la comédie qu'elle donne à ses invités, l'obligation de se mêler en robe de ville avant le moment de se montrer sur les planches, son rôle ne comportant pas de robe decolletée" (I, 232). Of Bergotte he writes, "Mais lui ne répondit pas à mon sourire, soit prudence, soit parce qu'à force de jouer son rôle il n'avait plus l'impression de jouer un rôle" (III, 199–200). When M. Marie is on trial, his behavior is presented in theater terms:

On se demandait presque si c'était bien de sa vie qu'il était question, si ce n'était pas un petit acteur jouant la terreur de Saint-Just, dans une séance révolutionnaire insuffisament reconstituée, sur un théâtre où des faibles murmures des figurantes ne donnaient pas une idée exacte de la fureur de la Convention. (II, 84)

A similar idea is caught up in a later passage: "Y a-t-il un homme au monde qui dans les soirées d'hiver ne puisse nous dire: 'Moi aussi, j'ai assisté, j'ai joué mon rôle dans un véritable roman?' . . . Car l'autre acteur dort à jamais sous une pierre lointaine, ou vit dans un autre pays" (II, 106–107). The irony in such metaphors never denotes more than the obvious suggestion of insincerity implied by merely placing life and the theater in juxtaposition.

The irony may be slightly more explicit in a cluster of metaphors applied to Bergotte:

Aussi était-il convenu que c'était pour le maître Bergotte qu'il venait, comme c'était pour lui que des acteurs du Théâtre-

Français vinrent jouer un autre soir une pièce nouvelle, que Fauré une autre fois encore se fit entendre. . . . Il s'adressait . . . à Loisel au milieu du silence des autres auditeurs, qui, réduits au rôle de chœur antique quand le discours de Bergotte était fini, reprenait d'un air d'assentiment: "C'est admirable." . . . Bergotte, comme un claqueur chargé quand on rappellera Sarah Bernhardt de dire: "Non, tous, tous," disait: "Non, tout, tout." . . . Cette fois Bergotte comme un critique dramatique qui ne va pas au théâtre pour les pièces dont il n'a pas à rendre compte n'écoutait plus du tout, puisque les mots à dire étaient trouvés. (III, 195–97)

These metaphors about Bergotte seem designed to provide overtones as well as to clarify particular points, but the irony is well short of that connected with the theater metaphors in *A la recherche.*

Other characters are described, with less irony, as speaking or behaving like actors: "Et quand M. de Valtognes disait un de ces mots, qui, ressemblant aux mots des maris de théâtre, donnaient à ceux qui les écoutaient l'illusion d'être des auteurs dramatiques observant la réalité . . . " (III, 174). This is the only instance in *Jean Santeuil* in which Proust emphasizes the contrast between art illusion and reality, a contrast which becomes crucial in his handling of the theater metaphors in *A la recherche.*

Almost none of the metaphors in *Jean Santeuil* establish a favorable atmosphere for the theater. (In *A la recherche,* such an atmosphere is required, if only so that Proust can change it, the theater—like life—taking on shifting values.) A metaphor alluding to the splendor of an actress is made ironic by its emphasis on falseness, and by its application to a woman greeting a group of boys arriving at a brothel: "Jean s'étonnait d'un regard cruel à travers le henné des cils, un eczéma sous la poudre de riz, et avec la vulgarité d'un voyou, la scélératesse d'un escroc parmi la splendeur fantastique et douce d'une actrice" (I, 131). Several other metaphors also use the theater to downgrade actuality. "Le nuage chargé de pluie vous apparaît comme dans un décor de théâtre, comme quelque chose qui vous laisse indifférent et sur quoi on peut dire seulement un joli mot à celui qui est monté à côté de vous" (I, 224). More unfavorable, and based on a backstage view, is this: "Elle gardait ses sabots. Mais ce dernier reste de la chrysalide brisée ne déplaisait pas plus que chez un Hector ou une Andromaque au théâtre se promenant dans la coulisse la coiffure à la Bressant qu'ils portent encore, réservant leur perruque pour le dernier moment, . . . " (I, 232). Later, Proust has a character speak with "exagération comme au théâtre" (III, 24).

Jean Santeuil seems to show Proust moving in the direction of *A la recherche* in the number and variety of its theater metaphors, and in the method of applying these metaphors in isolated places; but *Jean Santeuil* has no *coup de théâtre* in which the metaphors can explode to greater, more organized significance.

One metaphor apparently struck some chord for Proust, since it occurs three times, in *Jean Santeuil, Contre Saint-Beuve,* and *A la recherche.* It is the comparison, conventional enough, of an outside view of a lighted room with a stage setting, and is duplicated in the sections of the novels with the protagonists' military experiences, shortly before the comparisons of theater and military hierarchies, which also appear in both novels. In *Jean Santeuil*, Jean is walking through a village street, looking into the windows:

Que n'arrivait-il là jouer son rôle dans l'apparition, laissant voir sans s'en douter chacun de ses mouvements et sans voir Jean invisible dans la nuit, comme c'est la coutume dans ces fragments d'une existence qu'un magicien nous fait apparaître au théâtre. (II, 262)

In *Contre Sainte-Beuve*, in the section entitled "Chambres," Proust wrote:

Une boutique éclairée de l'intérieur . . . nous montrait sous sa paroi de verre des personnages prolongés par de grandes ombres qui . . . ignorant que nous les regardions, mettaient toute leur attention à jouer pour nous les scènes éclatantes et secrètes de leur vie usuelle et fantastique. (p. 71)

In *A la recherche*, the same experience is developed at greater length:

La vie que menaient les habitants de ce monde inconnu me semblait devoir être merveilleuse, et souvent les vitres éclairées de quelque demeure me retenaient longtemps immobile dans la nuit en mettant sous mes yeux les scènes véridiques et mystérieuses d'existences où je ne pénétrais pas. Ici le génie du feu me montrait en un tableau empourpré la taverne d'un marchand de marrons où deux sous-officiers . . . jouaient aux cartes sans se douter qu'un magicien les faisait surgir de la nuit, comme dans une apparition de théâtre. (II, 96)

This comparison seems to have lost its metaphorical force and become an autobiographical fact of Proust's life.

Proust uses one metaphor in *Jean Santeuil* that he repeats in *A la recherche*, but which serves more complex purposes in the later book. A comparison of the passages casts light on the differences between the treatments of theater metaphor in the two novels. Not only the metaphor, but the circumstances in which it occurs are directly similar. In his treatment of Jean's conversation with military friends, Proust writes: "Dès qu'on lui disait un nom sortant de l'obscurité, un officier moins connu, confirmant une renommé aux dépens d'autres, ou trouvant un mérite plus grand à un officier généralement déprécié, Jean se sentait envahi d'un véritable enthousiasme, comme quand autrefois—le théâtre était alors sa passion—il éprouvait une secousse quand un camarade amateur du théâtre lui disait quel était à son avis le premier comédien . . . " (II, 267). In *A la recherche*, Marcel's passion for theater and his recollection of it, in the parallel between theater and military hierarchies, are given more than a thousand pages apart. In *Du côté de chez Swann*, the first reference appears:

A cette époque j'avais l'amour du théâtre, amour platonique, car mes parents ne m'avaient encore jamais permis d'y aller. . . .
. . . .
Plus tard, quand je fus au collège, chaque fois que pendant les classes je correspondais . . . avec un nouvel ami, ma première question était toujours pour lui demander s'il était déjà allé au théâtre et s'il trouvait que le plus grand acteur était bien Got, le second Delaunay, etc. . . .
Mais si les acteurs me préoccupaient ainsi . . . la vue du visage d'une femme que je pensais être peut-être une actrice, laissait en moi un trouble plus prolongé. . . . Je classais par ordre de talent les plus illustres: Sarah Bernhardt, la Berma, Bartet, Madeleine Brohan, Jeanne Samary, mais toutes m'intéressaient. (I, 73–75)

The two full pages from which these passages have been selected are directly followed by the episode of Marcel's meeting with the lady in pink at his uncle's, thus setting the whole cluster of theater material clearly in place for the past reference of the later comparison, as it appears in *Le Côté de Guermantes*: "Car je continuais à leur demander avidement de classer les différents officiers dont je savais les noms, selon l'admiration plus ou moins grande qu'ils leur semblaient mériter, comme jadis, au collège, je faisais faire à mes camarades pour les acteurs du Théâtre-Français. . . . J'éprouvais la même surprise heureuse que jadis quand les noms épuisés de Thiron ou de Febvre se trouvaient refoulés par l'épanouissement soudain du nom inusité d'Amaury" (II, 128). The differences between the treatments of the comparison in the two novels are characteristic. In *Jean Santeuil*, the metaphor serves a single purpose, at the point where it is introduced. In *A la recherche*, it not only clarifies the point being made, but forces the reader's memory to work in tandem with Marcel's—at the same time casting an ironic overtone—by first comparing the real life of the military with the theatrical life of the actors; and second, by using in widely separated incidents the same boyish kinds of standards. In *Jean Santeuil*, the past reference must be established parenthetically and awkwardly when the comparison is employed (explicitly, "—le théâtre était alors sa passion—"); in *A la recherche*, this reference is carefully and fully established some thousand pages earlier. Thus we can see part of the complex pattern that metaphors follow in the later work.

The largest cluster of derogatory theater metaphors (also the largest cluster of any sort of theater metaphors) in *Jean Santeuil* occurs in a five-page description of two women whom Jean sees on a train, dismisses as false and pretentious, and later discovers to be genuine. This is paralleled in *Sodome et Gomorrhe* by the scene when Marcel, on a train, first sees the

Princess Sherbatoff as a fat lady about whom he idly and somewhat maliciously speculates. In *Jean Santeuil*, the impression of the falsity of the two women is given by the use of derogatory metaphors and in much the same way that Proust was to use more subtly in various passages of *A la recherche*:

> Jean reconnut une cocotte, une actrice. Mais de celles qui n'ont de nom dans aucune ville, actrice à qui on a promis un engagement à l'Opéra-Comique. . . .
>
> Mais la personne subalterne . . . exagérait encore la mauvaise impression que Jean eut de sa voisine. . . . Peut-être était-ce tout simplement une camarade de l'actrice . . . à qui l'habitude de jouer durant sa vie tant de rôles et dans chacun de donner à ses traits ridicules une signification nouvelle de laideur ou de stupidité leur en avait ôté à peu près toute, jusqu'à leur laisser seulement ce quelque chose de bestial et d'incertain, de louche, que prennent des traits réduits à eux-mêmes, n'ayant plus aucune expression. Il en est souvent ainsi des traits des acteurs. . . .
>
> Quel ne fut pas l'étonnement de Jean en voyant le bicycliste partir avec elles deux. . . . Sans doute comme amant de cette femme, il est obligé de jouer son rôle dans les scènes de dédain, de prétention, de vulgarité, de charlatanisme. . . . Il doit donner tort au directeur qui ne l'engage pas, faire cause commune dans ses ineptes jalousies contre ses camarades, être l'ami des acteurs les plus grossiers. . . .
>
> Mais Jean . . . avait déjà oublié . . . ces figures grotesques ou belles que nous avons vues dans un lieu public, dans un wagon de chemin de fer, un omnibus chargé de monde, veritables chariots de Thespis où nous nous amusons comme Jean venait de la faire tout à l'heure à reconnaître l'Isabelle, le pédant, la Zerbinette, acteurs tout grimés, ayant déjà sur la figure la mine de leur emploi, sur la langue des bouts de leur rôle, mais dont nous ne connaissons ni la nature véritable ni même la comédie qu'ils vont jouer. (II, 200–204)

In *A la recherche*, Proust is almost never this explicit or this extended in a derogatory description of an aspect of the theater to which life may be compared and made to seem tawdry. Many of the same assumptions about theater life appear in the later novel, but in briefer flashes.

When dealing with the similar situation on the train in *Sodome et Gomorrhe*, Proust does not repeat the theater material, but causes Marcel's speculating to deal even more harshly, if much more briefly, with the princess: "Malgré sa vulgarité, elle était prétentieuse dans ses gestes, et je m'amusai à me demander à quelle catégorie sociale elle pouvait appartenir; je conclus immédiatement que ce devait être quelque tenancière de grande maison de filles, une maquerelle en voyage. Sa figure, ses manières le criaient" (II, 858). He is later more amused than otherwise to discover how far wrong his speculations were: "Apprendre le surlendemain quelle était la personne à côté de qui on a voyagé dans le train sans parvenir à trouver son rang social est une surprise beaucoup plus amusante que de lire dans la livraison nouvelle d'une revue le mot de l'énigme proposée dans la précédente livraison" (p. 892). The shift of the terms of the speculation, abandoning the theater material, may be attributed to the fact that such explicit use of this material would not fit the pattern and organization of the theater metaphors in *A la recherche*. When Proust merely wants to make a specific point in a single place, as he does in *Jean Santeuil*, the question of interrelationships and balance does not arise.

A comparison to Oscar Wilde finds its way both into a letter to Dreyfus and into *Contre Sainte-Beuve*, and finally, into *A la recherche*. In the letter, May 16, 1908, the phrase is: " . . . comme Oscar Wilde disant que le plus grand chagrin qu'il avait eu, c'était la mort de Lucien de Rubempré dans Balzac, et apprenant peu après, par son procès, qu'il a des chagrins plus réels." [21] He explicitly develops the irony of this at some length in *Contre Sainte-Beuve*:

Oscar Wilde, à qui la vie devait hélas apprendre plus tard qu'il est de plus poignantes douleurs que celles que nous donnent les livres, disait dans sa première époque: ". . . Le plus grand chagrin de ma vie? La mort de Lucien de Rubempré dans *Splendeurs et Misères des Courtisanes*." Il y a d'ailleurs quelque chose de particulièrement dramatique dans cette prédilection et cet attendrissement d'Oscar Wilde, au temps de sa vie brillante, pour la mort de Lucien de Rubempré. . . . On ne peut s'empêcher de penser que, quelques années plus tard, il devait être Lucien de Rubempré lui-même. Et la fin de Lucien de Rubempré . . . n'était que l'anticipation—inconnue encore de Wilde, il est vrai—de ce qui précisément arriver à Wilde. (pp. 217–18)

In its final appearance, the allusion is a passing one and becomes vaguer, but the irony, if the allusion is grasped at all by the reader, is increased by the fact that the remark is put into the mouth of Charlus, who says, "Je ne rappelle plus quel homme de goût avait eu cette réponse, à qui lui demandait quel événement l'avait le plus affligé dans sa vie: 'La mort de Lucien de Rubempré dans *Splendeurs et Misères*'" (II, 1050). Could Proust possibly have expected the reader to seize the reference to Wilde? Proust seems almost to be suppressing the source of the reference in Charlus' remark, especially as the original observation was not made by Wilde himself, but was, as the English translator of *Contre Saint-Beuve* points out, "said by Vivian in Wilde's *The Decay of Lying*." [22] The irony of Wilde's fate is made more obvious in *Contre Sainte-Beuve* by attributing the remark to Wilde himself, but there is no way to tell whether in *A la recherche* Proust sought to be more accurate or, assuming the reader's familiarity equal to his own, more allusive. In any event, the relevance of the remark, from its triple repetition, would seem to be more applicable to Proust than to Charlus—if, on this point, they are separable. It is easy to see why Wilde's fate would have interested either of them.

From his early letters to the later *Jean Santeuil*, Proust's use of theater metaphors, sometimes of the same metaphors, seems to have been an unconscious preparation for the grand controlling metaphor of *A la recherche*. Just as the meaning of Marcel's life is crystallized by the revelation and his subsequent decision at the last Guermantes reception, so is Proust's mastery of his key metaphor crystallized in the description of the reception, the last *coup de théâtre*.

The *coup de théâtre*, of course, consists of the discovery that all the people of his world have been so remarkably and unexpectedly altered by Time that they seem more like actors playing parts than like the "real" people Marcel remembers; and the second, even more shattering realization that the years have done the same to him: "Alors moi qui, depuis mon enfance, vivais au jour le jour, ayant reçu d'ailleurs de moi-même et des autres une impression définitive, je m'aperçus pour la première fois, d'après les métamorphoses qui s'étaient produites dans tous ces gens, du temps qui avait passé pour eux, ce qui me bouleversa par la révélation qu'il avait passé aussi pour moi" (III, 926–27). In a letter to Louis de Robert, Proust reports the same experience as having actually happened to him—backstage at a theater:

Il est vrai que je suis allé à la répétition générale de *Kismet,* assistant je pense pour la première fois depuis quinze ans ou même vingt-cinq à une cérémonie de ce genre. . . . Si par hasard on me voit et on me reconnaît (ce qui est encore plus rare), il faut expliquer que je ne suis pas mort, m'en excuser, mille complications. Et chose inouïe, n'ayant pas voulu quitter Mme Straus, je l'ai conduite sur la scène où elle allait parler à Guitry. Mais pour ne pas "paraître" je suis resté à l'entrée de "sacristie," me dissimulant auprès d'un vieillard de l'Orestie tremblant et d'une figure charmante. Or c'était Lemaître! Et chose plus inouïe, car je suis plus changé que lui, Lemaître, jouant son rôle de vieillard de l'Orestie, m'a reconnu! [23]

Whether the experience was actually the seed of the novel's conclusion,[24] or merely offers one example of a kind of experience to which Proust became increasingly sensitive, the description of the last Guermantes reception is a detailed rendering of the same recognitions on a grand scale.

The three paragraphs which follow the significant phrase immediately solidify the *coup de théâtre* image:

Au premier moment je ne compris pas pourquoi j'hésitais à reconnaître le maître de maison, les invités, et pourquoi chacun semblait s'être "fait une tête," généralement poudrée et qui les changeait complètement. Le prince avait encore en recevant cet air bonhomme d'un roi de féerie que je lui avais trouvé la première fois mais cette fois . . . il s'était affublé d'une barbe blanche et, traînant à ses pieds, qu'elles alourdissaient, comme des semelles de plomb, semblait avoir assumé de figurer un des "Ages de la Vie." A vrai dire je ne le reconnus qu'à l'aide d'un raisonnement et en concluant de la simple ressemblance de certains traits à une identité de la personne. . . . A la première personne que je parvins ainsi à identifier, en tâchant de faire abstraction du travestissement et de compléter les traits restés naturels par un effort de mémoire, ma première pensée eût dû être, et fut peut-être bien moins d'une seconde, de la féliciter, d'être si merveilleusement grimée qu'on avait d'abord, avant de la reconnaître, cette hésitation que les grands acteurs, paraissant dans un rôle où ils sont différents d'eux-mêmes, donnent, en entrant en scène, au public qui, même averti par le programme, reste un instant ébahi avant d'éclater en applaudissements.
A ce point de vue, le plus extraordinaire de tous était mon ennemi personnel, M. d'Argencourt, le véritable clou de la matinée. Non seulement, au lieu de sa barbe à peine poivre et sel,

217

il s'était affublé d'une extraordinaire barbe d'une invraisemblable blancheur, mais encore. . . . c'était un vieux mendiant qui n'inspirait plus aucun respect qu'était devenu cet homme dont la solennité, la raideur empesée étaient encore présentés à mon souvenir et qui donnait à son personnage de vieux gâteux une telle vérité que ses membres tremblotaient, que les traits détendus de sa figure, habituellement hautaine, ne cessaient de sourire avec une niaise béatitude. Poussé à ce degré, l'art de déguisement devient quelque chose de plus, une transformation complète de la personnalité. . . . M. d'Argencourt, dans son incarnation de moribond-bouffe d'un Regnard exagéré par Labiche, était d'un accès aussi facile, aussi affable que M. de Charlus roi Lear qui se découvrait avec application devant le plus médiocre salueur. . . . Je ne félicitai pas M. d'Argencourt d'offrir un spectacle qui semblait reculer les limites entre lesquelles peuvent se mouvoir les transformations du corps humain.

Alors, dans les coulisses du théâtre ou pendant un bal costumé, on est plutôt porté par politesse à exagérer la peine, presque à affirmer l'impossibilité, qu'on a à reconnaître la personne travestie. Ici au contraire un instinct m'avait de les dissimuler le plus possible; je sentais qu'elles n'avaient rien de flatteur parce que la transformation n'était pas voulue. . . . (III, 920–23)

Within this single passage appear three of the devices which Proust constantly uses to add reverberation to his metaphors.

First, the metaphors should remind the reader of numerous other passages, hundreds or even thousands of pages earlier. The reference to Charlus as King Lear throws us back almost fifty pages to an earlier comparison, just after an explicit reference to the theater, which in its turn echoes material from *Du côté de chez Swann*:

. . . Les rues par lesquelles je passais en ce moment étaient celles, oubliées depuis si longtemps, que je prenais jadis avec Françoise pour aller aux Champs-Élysées. . . . Il était d'ailleurs fait de tant de passés différents qu'il m'était difficile de reconnaître la cause de ma mélancolie, si elle était due à ces marches au-devant de Gilberte . . . à la signification de vanité philosophique que semble prendre un chemin qu'on a suivi mille fois . . . comme celui où, après le déjeuner, je faisais des courses si hâtives, si fiévreuses, pour regarder, toutes fraîches encore de colle, l'affiche de *Phèdre* et celle du *Domino noir.* (III, 858–59)

With this memory of his childhood fresh in mind, Marcel sees Charlus and Jupien in another carriage: "C'était . . . M. de Charlus convalescent d'une attaque d'apoplexie que j'avais ignorée . . . et qui . . . avait plutôt, comme en une sorte de précipité chimique, rendu visible et brillant tout le métal que lançaient et dont étaient saturées, comme autant de geysers, les mèches, maintenant de pur argent, de sa chevelure et de sa barbe, cependant qu'elle avait imposé au vieux prince déchu la majesté shakespearienne d'un roi Lear" (p. 859). And on the following page, another tragedy is drawn upon for comparison: "Car le baron vivait toujours, pensait toujours; son intelligence n'était pas atteinte. Et plus que n'eût fait tel chœur de Sophocle sur l'orgueil abaissé d'Œdipe, plus que la mort même et toute oraison funèbre sur la mort, le salut empressé et humble du baron à Mme de Saint-Euverte proclamait ce qu'a de fragile et de périssable l'amour des grandeurs de la terre et tout l'orgueil humain" (p. 860). Thus, the casual reference to Charlus in his King Lear role brings to mind a train of associations that recapitulates his entire downfall, and, with the reference to theater posters, returns the reader to Marcel's earliest years, more than two thousand pages back.

In the second place, throughout the novel as in these paragraphs, Proust mingles the metaphorical with the actual, so that life clarifies art as much as art clarifies life. Characteristic of the method are the allusions, in a context of theatrical metaphor, to real theater, with the names of Regnard and

Labiche; and possibly to drama, with the "Ages de la Vie" (p. 921). A similar effect is obtained by the mixture of direct and explicit comparison with the suggestiveness of metaphor, in the passages about the actor and the wings of a theater (p. 967). Proust so frequently crosses from metaphor to comparison, and from comparison to metaphor that vehicle and tenor are all but coalesced. In the *coup de théâtre* passage, life is compared to the theater, and the theater to life, so frequently and in such a way that life is no longer *like* theater, but *is* theater, with all the theater's glamor and falsity, seen simultaneously from the audience and from backstage.

In the third place, Proust uses the metaphors subtly to lower the reader's estimation of the characters. The references in the quoted paragraphs are almost never to the higher kinds of drama and theater. The King Lear allusion is an obvious exception; the only other one in this part of the novel is to Shylock, but hardly in a way that elevates the subject of the comparison: "De près, dans la translucidité d'un visage où, de plus loin et mal éclairé, je ne voyais que la jeunesse gaie . . . se tenait le visage presque effrayant, tout anxieux, d'un vieux Shylock attendant, tout grimé, dans la coulisse, le moment d'entrer en scène, récitant déjà le premier vers à mi-voix" (III, 966–67). Other references are to comedy and burlesque, Punch and Judy, figures in an exposition pageant, or transformation scenes and fairy plays. The portrait of M. d'Argencourt breaks down in the following anticlimactic fashion:

Si M. d'Argencourt venait faire cet extraordinaire "numéro" qui était certainement la vision la plus saisissante dans son burlesque que je garderais de lui, c'était comme un acteur qui rentre une dernière fois sur la scène avant que le rideau tombe tout à fait au milieu des éclats de rire. . . . C'était trop de parler d'un acteur, et, débarrassé qu'il était de toute âme consciente, c'est comme une poupée trépidante, à la barbe postiche de laine blanche . . . comme dans un guignol à la fois scientifique et philsophique. . . .

Des poupées, mais que, pour les identifier à celui qu'on avait connu, il fallait lire sur plusieurs plans à la fois, . . . quand on avait devant soi ces vieillards fantoches, car on était obligé de les regarder, en même temps qu'avec les yeux, avec la mémoire. Des poupées baignant dans les couleurs immatérielles des années, des poupées extériorisant le Temps. . . . (III, 923–24)

Just before concluding this development, Proust, by another metaphor, again recalls the earliest pages of the novel, referring to the "lanterne magique" of Time that makes d'Argencourt "aussi immatériel que jadis Golo sur le bouton de porte de ma chambre de Combray." Then the description ends, "Dans les éléments nouveaux qui composaient la figure de M. d'Argencourt et son personnage, on lisait un certain chiffre d'années, on reconnaissait la figure symbolique de la vie non telle qu'elle nous apparaît, c'est-à-dire permanente, mais réelle, atmosphère si changeante que le fier seigneur s'y peint en caricature, le soir, comme un marchand d'habits" (p. 924).

Although M. d'Argencourt receives the fullest treatment, as the "hit" of the afternoon, others are also reduced to comedy and lower drama. One is the old woman who realized that "l'indéfinissable et mélancolique sourire qui avait fait son charme ne pouvait plus arriver à irradier jusqu'à la surface ce masque de plâtre que lui avait appliqué la vieillesse. . . . Trouvant plus spirituel de se résigner, elle s'en servait comme d'un masque de théâtre pour faire rire" (p. 947). Odette is brought even lower in the scale of comparison, since Marcel attributes to her no awareness of what she is doing, and even less effectiveness than the old woman: "Elle avait l'air . . . de l'Exposition de 1878 . . . venant débiter son couplet dans une revue de fin d'année, mais de l'Exposition de 1878 représentée par une femme encore jeune" (p. 948). Proust again recalls the distant past of *Du côté de chez Swann* by adding the qualification, "Pour moi, du reste, elle ne semblait pas dire: 'Je suis l'Exposition de 1878,' mais plutôt: 'Je suis l'allée des Acacias de 1892'" (p. 950). Here the metaphor works in all three typical ways, establishing a reference to time past, mingling theater and life, and referring to lower aspects of theater.

The same purposes are served, in the pages following the *coup de théâtre* paragraphs, by three comparisons based on fairy plays, and their transformation scenes. Finishing off the account of d'Argencourt, Marcel reflects, "Alors la vie nous apparaît comme la féerie où on voit d'acte en acte le bébé devenir adolescent, homme mûr et se courber vers la tombe" (p. 926). Later, again in general terms, Marcel reports, "Mais pour d'autres, et pour des hommes aussi, la transformation était si complète, l'identité si impossible à établir . . . que plus même qu'à l'art de l'acteur, c'était à celui de certains prodigieux mimes, dont Fregoli reste le type, que faisaient penser ces fabuleuses transformations" (pp. 946–47). The "transformation" here is not literally the same as the theatrical principle in "transformation scenes," but in the context; and following a number of instances where the two are brought together, it is all but impossible to insist upon the distinction.

The third and most important "fairy play" metaphor leads us to the Duchesse. Of Mme d'Arpajon, Marcel points out,

"Cet aspect était si différent de celui que je lui avais connu qu'on eût dit qu'elle était un être condammé, comme un personnage de féerie, à apparaître d'abord en jeune fille, puis en épaisse matrone, et qui reviendrait sans doute bientôt en vieille branlante et courbée" (p. 937). Only thirteen lines later, we are brought to focus on a more important character, with the discerning of "une trace de vert-de-gris" in the cheeks of the Duchesse de Guermantes. This parallels the earliest description of her, when the young Marcel, in the Combray church, tried to identify the real Duchesse with the romantic vision he had associated with her name, and presents a parallel in the use of metaphor: " . . . Tout, jusqu'à ce petit bouton qui s'enflammait au coin du nez, certifiait son assujettissement aux lois de la vie comme, dans une apothéose de théâtre, un plissement de la robe de la fée, un tremblement de son petit doigt, dénoncent la présence matérielle d'une actrice vivante, là où nous étions incertains si nous n'avions pas devant les yeux une simple projection lumineuse" (I, 175)—this, in the first description of the Duchesse who, years and pages later, is to decline to dependence on the friendship of actresses!

Another thread of transformation scenes and other theater metaphors, clearly related to the same system, is concerned with Odette. Very near the end of *Du côté de chez Swann* occurs the following sequence: "Quant à elle [Odette], elle ne m'avait jamais vu avec Gilberte, elle ne savait pas mon nom, mais j'étais pour elle . . . un des personnages secondaires, familiers, anonymes, aussi dénués de caractères individuels qu'un 'emploi de théâtre,' de ses promenades au bois. Certains jours où je ne l'avais pas vue allée des Acacias . . . " (I, 421). Again, early in *Sodome et Gomorrhe* Marcel has related Odette to the theater and to a transformation scene, this time more directly, when she is seen by one of her guests in a "salle magique où, comme grâce à un changement à vue dans une féerie, elle reconnut dans ses figurantes éblouissantes . . . appelant la maîtresse de maison par son petit nom, les altesses, les duchesses qu'elle-même, la princesse d'Épinoy, avait grand'peine à attirer chez elle. . . ." (II, 745). The theatrical atmosphere attached to Odette is underlined in the same paragraph with literal references to her habit of taking her guests, with Bergotte, to interesting first nights, and to the really dramatic moment of the dress rehearsal of a play by Bergotte: the appearance of Mme de Marsantes and the Comtesse Molé in Bergotte's box.[25]

The transformation-scene metaphors underline one of the main effects of Proust's use of theatrical metaphors in the *coup de théâtre* passage: the way in which they establish direct and indirect references to time past—from Charlus as King Lear back to the playbills in *Du côté de chez Swann*; from d'Argencourt in Time's magic lantern back to Golo on the Combray doorknob; from Odette as a pageant figure back to the Allée des Acacias, when her daughter was Marcel's childhood playmate and Odette was the socially undesirable wife of Swann; again, from Odette as mother of a grown daughter back to Odette as a successful hostess; and from the Duchesse, aged almost beyond recognition, back to the Duchesse of Marcel's earliest memories. All these metaphors interconnect with the past and the present at the precise point in the novel when Marcel is deciding that the way to recapture the lost past is to catch it in the novel he and the reader are finishing together, when "en rapprochant une qualité commune à deux sensations, il dégagera leur essence commune en les réunissant . . . dans une métaphore" (III,

889). The theater metaphors at this juncture pick out and intertwine in one process the threads of lost time.

This process, and another, are both illustrated in the remaining *coup de théâtre* metaphors, all of them based on a backstage, or inside, view of the theater—the view which is not deceived by stage illusions, but rather looks on them objectively with a technician's eye: "Une jeune femme que j'avais connue autrefois, maintenant blanche et tassée en petite vieille maléfique, semblait indiquer qu'il est nécessaire que, dans le divertissement final d'une pièce, les êtres fussent travestis à ne pas les reconnaître" (III, 926).[26] The make-up artist's tone of this is intensified a few pages later: "A un visage linéairement le même il suffisait, pour qu'il semblât autre, de cheveux blancs au lieu de cheveux noirs ou blonds. Les costumiers de théâtre savent qu'il suffit d'une perruque poudrée pour déguiser très suffisamment quelq'un et le rendre méconnaissable" (p. 938). Marcel reduces two views of the same woman to stock characters of well-made drama: " . . . Ce nom était peut-être la seule chose qu'il y avait de commun entre ces deux femmes, plus différentes (celle de ma mémoire et celle de la matinée Guermantes) qu'une ingénue et une douairière de pièce de théâtre" (p. 939).

Other characters are diminished to mere players of roles: " . . . Il faisait partie du nouveau cabinet, dont le chef lui avait donné un porte-feuille, un peu comme ces directeurs de théâtre confient un rôle à une de leurs anciennes camarades, retirée depuis longtemps, mais qu'ils jugent encore plus capable que les jeunes de tenir un rôle avec finesse . . ." (p. 949). Marcel, complimenting her on her youthful appearance, thinks that "Odette eût pu jouer encore" (p. 950); and certain snobbish ladies "toutes ces dernières années, avant que Mme Verdurin ne fût princesse de Guermantes, avaient dit en ricanant 'la duchesse de Duras,' comme si c'eût un rôle que Mme Verdurin eût tenu au théâtre" (p. 955). This awareness of theatrical life—literal and figurative— in the midst of social occasions is sustained in the description of Oriane's unexpected arrival at a party: " . . . C'était une plus grande fête pour la vieille grande dame qui donnait la soirée qu'autrefois, pour un directeur de théâtre, que Sarah Bernhardt, qui avait vaguement promis un concours sur lequel on ne comptait pas, fût venue et eût, avec une complaisance et une simplicité infinies, récité, au lieu du morceau promis, vingt autres" (p. 959 n.).

The same tendency to present the characters through a backstage eye is also observable in metaphors previously examined: guests who "semblait s'être 'fait une tête,'" "merveilleusement grimée," and "véritable clou de la matinée" (pp. 920–21); d'Argencourt "dans son incarnation de moribond-bouffe" (p. 922), and again in "cet extraordinaire 'numéro' . . . dans son burlesque" (p. 923); the transformation so complete that "plus même qu'à l'art de l'acteur, c'était à celui de certains prodigieux mimes . . . que faisaient penser ces fabuleuses transformations" (p. 947); the Exposition "venant débiter son couplet dans une revue de fin d'année" (p. 948); and, combining the implications of several of the foregoing, Bloch like "un vieux Shylock attendant, tout grimé, dans la coulisse, le moment d'entrer en scène, récitant déjà le premier vers à mi-voix" (p. 967). The majority of the theatrical metaphors in the *coup de théâtre* section of the novel have this implication of falsity and illusion recognized from behind the scenes, or through knowledge of what goes on there that the audience does not see.

The treatment of theatrical material in the *coup de théâtre* section is not only consistent with, but necessarily arises directly from, the way in which the same kind of material is handled throughout the novel. In the whole novel, Proust includes upward of 270 metaphors drawn from the theater, varying from the shortest possible length to several of a page or more. Of the more than two hundred theater metaphors in the bulk of the novel before the *coup de théâtre*, over a hundred allude to popular drama and theater, about sixty are "neutral," (referring to "the theater" or "an actor"), and about sixty more have the classical repertoire or other admirable subjects as their vehicle. But more than half of the latter group are used only to clarify particular points, by providing quick terms of metaphorical reference that cannot be described as elevating the characters or their society. A score of these same metaphors are used ironically, like the "transpositions" mentioned by Pierre-Quint, to show the "real" world at a disadvantage. Only half a dozen are favorable in their terms of comparison, while two are flatly derogatory. Of the hundred-odd metaphors drawn from popular theater, the majority create the effect of theatrical falsity, often emphasized by a backstage view. The tendency of these metaphors to lower the reader's estimate of theater—or at least to expose its illusory side—is such as to attract to it even the "neutral" comparisons. Merely on this sequence of metaphors, one might base an argument against those who would dismiss Proust as a snob who takes this dying society too seriously. By the time the final great comparison of society and theater is reached, no reader should be tempted to suppose that Marcel is confusing his moribund mimes with the great figures of great drama.

In the course of the metaphors, Marcel alludes to many of the great figures: dramatists such as the Greeks, Shakespeare, Corneille, Racine, and Molière; plays such as the *Menaechmi, A Midsummer Night's Dream, Esther, Andromaque, Le Malade imaginaire,* and *Hernani;* characters like Oedipus, Orestes, Hamlet, Lear, Romeo and Juliet, Harpagon, Mephistopheles and Faust; and such actors and actresses as Bernhardt, Bressant, Thiron, Réjane, and Reichenberg. But only half a dozen of these are used to present favorable comparisons. In *Sodome et Gomorrhe,* Marcel writes of an image, "conservée vivante au fond de moi—comme Oreste dont les Dieux avaient empêché la mort pour qu'au jour désigné il revînt dans son pays punir le meurtre d'Agamemnon—pour mon supplice, pour mon châtiment . . ." (II, 1115). Other allusions are more casual: Marcel's family trying to imitate Norpois "comme ils auraient fait pour quelque intonation de Bressant ou de Thiron dans *l'Aventurière* ou dans *le Gendre de M. Poirier*" (I, 483); or, Marcel's inability to notice social differences "pas plus que je n'avais vu le premier jour les différences qui séparaient la Berma de ses camarades" (II, 415). A handful of such mildly honorific comparisons can do little against the weight and number of scores of ironic and derogatory allusions.

Similarly, little counterbalance to the prevailing tendency is provided by those references to well-known and admired plays and playwrights that merely clarify a point by providing a ready means of comparison. These include such metaphors as a toothache transformed in sleep to a line of Molière that we repeat to ourselves without stopping (I, 28), a social confusion which is "victime d'une ressemblance comme celle qui fait le fond des *Ménechmes*" (p. 566), girls appearing like

228

Mephistopheles to Faust (p. 855), Charlus quoting his nurse's "patois moliéresque" (II, 289), or Robert like a character in *Le Malade imaginaire* (p. 509).

Once Proust explicitly uses a theatrical figure to emphasize the inferiority of her audience ("une radiation télépathique, comme celles qui déchaînaient des applaudissements dans la foule ignorante aux moments où la Berma était sublime" [I, 420]), but more often the contrast is less clearly made, or left to the working of irony. Some of these are brief, such as vegetables "dans leurs farces poétiques et grossières comme une féerie de Shakespeare" (p. 121), or the allusion to Fran-çoise, who "avait pour les liens invisibles que noue entre les membres d'une famille la circulation d'un même sang, autant de respect qu'un tragique grec" (p. 53). Françoise is also described as "capable de rivaliser avec la Berma elle-même dans l'art de faire parler les vêtements inanimés et les traits du visage" (II, 735). In similar transpositions of the comic and serious, or "real" and theatrical, the arrival of the doctor to treat Marcel's grandmother made one imagine oneself "chez Molière" (p. 342); and the feud of the Capulets and Mon-tagues is a standard for the obstacles inverts must overcome in their loves (p. 627). One of the most elaborate of these metaphorical transpositions is the comparison between the activities in the Balbec hotel lobby and the composite scene from *Athalie* and *Esther*.

Those metaphors whose material is neither honorific nor derogatory—those which have been called "neutral"—are not rendered useless by their neutrality. Aside from their specific purposes in context, they also maintain the continuity of theatrical metaphor throughout the novel, and underline the importance of the theater in Proust's milieu. Several of his metaphors draw upon the social aspects of theatergoing: the difficulties of gaining admission, the lending of one's box, the problems of seating, and meeting in the lobby. In *La Prisonnière*, he writes, "Personne n'eût plus pensé à se faire présenter à Mme Verdurin qu'à l'ouvreuse d'un théâtre où une grande dame a, pour un soir, amené toute l'aristocratie" (III, 266–67), and describes Albertine as "comme une personne qui, faisant passer sa suite, toute une société, au contrôle devant elle, la fait entrer au théâtre" (p. 386). At least ten more such metaphors are scattered through the novel, emphasizing the social side of the theater, and contributing to the continual sounding of the theatrical note. Another twenty-five of these neutral metaphors allude briefly to acting or the stage. Without the larger context they would not in themselves be very significant, since they present such common terms as "chacun est un mauvais acteur" (I, 855), "ils faisaient de sa vie une comédie d'une complication scintillante" (II, 668), or "la triste comédie que j'avais jouée" (III, 361). Such metaphors as these, for all their casualness (and even partly because of it), also make their contributions to the orchestration with a note here and there, to prepare for the crashing *coup*.

The largest group of metaphors is made up of those which, by constant reference to the "inside" backstage view and by emphasis on the falsity of stage illusion, lead most directly to the implications of the theatrical material in the conclusion. These are the metaphors which draw most frequently on popular and contemporary theater, and deal most often with the resemblances between social behavior and stage acting, or with the methods of producing stage splendors. The faces of girls are compared to the stage properties in Russian ballet, made beautiful by lighting effects (I, 946); or the splendors of private houses to stage splendors produced "en dirigeant un rayon factice sur un pourpoint de grosse toile semé de bouchons de verre" (II, 881). He casts a similar backstage glance at his own emotions, analyzing them like a stage director: "Néanmoins, comme un récitant qui devrait connaître son rôle et être à sa place depuis bien longtemps mais qui, arrivé seulement à la dernière seconde et n'ayant lu qu'une fois ce qu'il a à dire, sait dissimuler assez habilement, quand vient le moment où il doit donner la réplique, pour que personne ne puisse s'apercevoir de son retard, mon chagrin tout nouveau me permit . . . de lui parler comme s'il avait toujours été le même" (II, 768). Almost all these comparisons are presented through the eyes of the undeluded spectator who, though not involved in the stage action, either actually is—or observes as if he were—separate from the naïve audience that is uncritically involved. Occasionally the stage is ironically made to seem more real than life: "Je le lui fis avec une simplicité et une franchise dignes du théâtre" (II, 828). Marcel, referring to an actual conversation, writes of "cette forme de véritable mise en scène où je l'avais poussée" (III, 359), and one wonders whether the Guermantes reception is a "real" scene, or a real "scene."

Marcel's reference to his own play acting is only one of numerous instances of characters assumed to be playing roles. Marcel observes that "certains rôles favoris sont par nous joués tant de fois devant le monde, et repassés en nous-mêmes, que nous nous référons plus aisément à leur témoignage fictif qu'à celui d'une réalité presque complètement oubliée" (I, 595). Parties and receptions are treated as stage productions. Mme de Villeparisis regards parties as "une sorte de répétition" for her memoirs (II, 216). The comparison is applied from footmen to kings and queens: one of the Guermantes servants "jouait-il son rôle sans soupçonner qu'on le lui eût confié" (II, 588); and Marcel meets "reines qui jouent à la reine, et parlent non selon les habitudes de leurs congénères, mais comme les reines dans Sardou" (p. 426). Mme de Villeparisis is more fully treated in the same fashion: "Elle voulut donc signifier à Bloch qu'il eût ne pas revenir et elle trouva tout naturellement dans son répertoire mondain la scène par laquelle une grande dame met quelqu'un à la porte de chez elle, scène qui ne comporte nullement le doigt levé et les yeux flambants que l'on figure. . . . Elle avait fait le jeu de grand dame qu'elle désirait, lequel fut universellement admiré et commenté le soir même dans divers salons, mais d'après une version qui n'avait déjà plus aucun rapport avec la vérité" (II, 248–49). Saint-Loup is equated with his uncle, as a member of an acting family: "A une autre génération, sur une autre tige, comme un acteur qui reprend le rôle joué jadis par Bressant ou Delaunay, il était comme un successeur . . . de M. de Charlus" (III, 761).

Through Saint-Loup, Marcel is enabled to see these same metaphorical relationships in reverse, from the actor's viewpoint:

Depuis que les acteurs n'étaient plus exclusivement pour moi, les dépositaires, en leur diction et leur jeu, d'une vérité artistique, ils m'intéressaient en eux-mêmes . . . et ainsi, surtout grâce aux renseignements que Saint-Loup me donnait sur la vie privée des artistes, je voyais une autre pièce, muette et expressive, se jouer sous la pièce parlée, laquelle d'ailleurs, quoique médiocre, m'intéressait; car j'y sentais germer et s'épanouir pour une heure, à la lumière de la rampe, faites de l'agglutinement sur le visage d'un acteur d'un autre visage de fard et de carton, sur son âme personnelle des paroles d'un rôle. . . . (II, 172)

Life is like the stage, the stage like life, and even Marcel seems hardly able to tell which is which. After his massive preparation, the *coup de théâtre* is a grand climax in his life, far more than a melodramatic surprise.

Beyond the purposes already mentioned, an even more important purpose is served in the *coup de théâtre* passage, not merely by the frequent and interrelated use of theatrical metaphors, but by the very reliance on metaphor to sustain this crucial passage. Such reliance plays an important part in the grand structure and theme of the whole novel. The constellation of *coup de théâtre* metaphors follows directly after the series of physically small but psychologically tremendous experiences which, uniting past and present in a single sensation by the workings of involuntary memory, have defined for him the purpose of his life and work. Stumbling on a paving block, hearing the clink of a spoon and feeling the texture of a napkin, hearing the noise of a hot-water pipe—all have revived within him sensations that have revealed him to himself as a person outside of time, who must try to interpret these sensations. His purpose and his material have been defined for him: "Il me fallait rendre aux moindres signes qui m'entouraient . . . leur sens que l'habitude leur avait fait perdre pour moi. . . . Alors, moins éclatante sans doute que celle qui m'avait fait apercevoir que l'œuvre d'art était le seul moyen de retrouver le Temps perdu, une nouvelle lumière se fit en moi. Et je compris que tous ces matériaux de l'œuvre littéraire, c'était ma vie passée. . . . Ainsi toute ma vie jusqu'à ce jour aurait pu et n'aurait pas

233

pu être résumée sous ce titre: Une vocation" (III, 897–99). But he enters the drawing room to a *coup de théâtre* that "allait élever contre mon entreprise la plus grave des objections . . . par l'exemple cent fois répété de la consideration la plus propre à me faire hésiter . . . " (p. 920).

Yet after the experience with Bergsonian time at the reception, largely expressed in the theater metaphors of this passage, Marcel has solved his problem. His meeting with Mlle de Saint-Loup, Gilberte's daughter, has revealed to him how the book must be written. She has shown him how the innumerable threads of time may be woven into the work which he contemplates. In the first instance, she demonstrates the pattern of his life: she is the crossroads at which the paths of his life meet, where the two "ways" ended. In the second instance, time has for a capturable moment stood still in her. But in addition to defining his material and showing him how it may be disposed, the meeting and the whole experience of the reception has provided Marcel with the impetus to execute the work. And, significantly, the same passage which expresses his joy in the new-found work also shows his recognition of the kind of metaphor necessary to execute it: "Que celui qui pourrait écrire un tel livre serait heureux, pensais-je, quel labeur devant lui! Pour en donner une idée, c'est aux arts les plus élévés et les plus différents qu'il faudrait emprunter des comparaisons . . . " (p. 1032). The end has become the beginning.

What has happened to Marcel? Not a social recognition or an intellectual perception; not even an emotional shock. What has happened includes all these, but is something more: a spiritual or intuitive and aesthetic recognition whose seed was planted in the theatrical metaphors. With Marcel's new op-

234

timism has immediately come the need to resort to comparisons with the arts, to comparisons which transform experience into aesthetic or symbolic forms. The effect of the whole episode is similar to that of two of the most striking incidents in the novel. Proust in these very pages has Marcel allude to the moment when he lost his grandmother—really many months after he had actually lost her—and this same experience occurs with the second most important character in the novel. As Charlotte Haldane writes:

Albertine *has to die twice*: the first time, in the flesh, as the result of her riding accident; the second time, as the consequence of the inexorable action of Time on her lover's mind. . . . Before he can win back his own peace of mind he has to reconstitute her, recreate her, synthetically, in order to be able to destroy her in his memory as she was destroyed by death. . . . When he has succeeded in doing this, but only then, can he find some kind of emotional release, regain his emotional equilibrium.[27]

Marcel has the same need to destroy society and recreate it synthetically in order to deal with it in the novel.

Pierre-Quint has written of the *coup de théâtre* passage: "Dans la scène finale du *Temps Retrouvé*, où tous les personnages du roman tellement vieillis, tellement changés, se 'retrouvent' chez le prince de Guermantes, il ne reste presque plus rien de mobile et de vivant en eux; les habitudes, les tics, les locutions toutes faites, le mécanisme a peu à peu envahi tout leur être. La nature . . . '[les] a immobilisés dans le mouvement accoutumé,' première forme de la mort. . . . Ici le symbole remplace la réalité." [28] J. M. Cocking describes the general pattern that expresses Proust's need to transpose "reality" in his imagination in order to see it in terms of art: "The falling rhythm of the loss of childhood impressions is counterpointed by the rising rhythm of the growing sense of vocation; the loss of imaginative spontaneity is counterbalanced by a gain of imaginative insight, culminating in the 'revelation' provided by involuntary memory. This final upward swing is foreshadowed in a recurring local pattern: imagination clashes with reality, and disintegrates; then, usually under the guidance of an artist, it reawakens in forms compatible with reality." [29] In the *coup de théâtre* passage, which brings to a focus all the theater material of the novel, Marcel himself is the artist who guides the material to its awakening, in a transformation which turns life into art. Just as Marcel cannot deal emotionally with his grandmother and Albertine until their death is a reality as well as a fact, he cannot deal artistically with the society in which he has lived until it is dead. The "reality" must become a symbol, the materials for which have been laid down throughout the novel. Proust has crystallized society in a metaphor, so that Marcel may control it as art.

Notes

Notes

CHAPTER I

1. "Goethe," in *Contre Sainte-Beuve, suivi de nouveaux mélanges* (Paris, 1954), p. 404.

2. *Axel's Castle* (New York, 1953), p. 158.

3. "Tone in *A la recherche du temps perdu*," in *Forms of Modern Fiction*, ed. William Van O'Connor (Minneapolis, 1948), pp. 208-9.

4. Robert Dreyfus, *Souvenirs sur Marcel Proust* (Paris, 1926), pp. 59–60.

5. *Lettres à Walter Berry [et al.]* (*Correspondance générale de Marcel Proust*, Vol. V [Paris, 1935]), p. 134.

6. Bibliography in *Lettres à la NRF* (*Les Cahiers de Marcel Proust*, Vol. VI [Paris, 1932]).

7. *Lettres à la Comtesse de Noailles, 1901-1919* (*Correspondance générale de Marcel Proust*, Vol. II [Paris, 1937]) pp. 70–72.

8. André Maurois, *Proust: Portrait of a Genius* (New York, 1950), p. 44.

239

9. Proust, *Lettres à P. Lavallée* [*et al.*] (*Correspondance générale de Marcel Proust*, Vol. IV [Paris, 1933]), p. 128.

10. Princess Bibesco, *Au bal avec Marcel Proust* (*Les cahiers de Marcel Proust*, Vol. IV [Paris, 1928]), p. 19.

11. *Lettres à P. Lavallée*, p. 114.

12. *Lettres à la NRF*, p. 263.

13. *Ibid.*, p. 139.

14. Maurois, *Proust: Portrait of a Genius*, p. 11.

15. *Introduction to Proust: His Life, His Circle and His Work* (London, 1940), p. 27.

16. *Souvenirs*, p. 16.

17. *Proust: The Early Years* (Boston, 1959), p. 56.

18. Proust, *Correspondance avec sa mère*, ed. Philip Kolb (Paris, 1953), p. 13.

19. *Ibid.*, p. 43.

20. Maurois, *Proust: Portrait of a Genius*, p. 38.

21. *Autour de soixante lettres de Marcel Proust* (*Les Cahiers de Marcel Proust*, Vol. V [Paris, 1929]), p. 15.

22. *Souvenirs*, pp. 59-60, 61. The footnote identified by the first asterisk is as follows: "Francisque Sarcey, qui, lorsqu'une pièce l'avait amusé, écrivait invariablement dans son feuilleton du *Temps*: 'des fusées de rire ont traversé la salle.'" The double asterisk refers the reader to the following note: "Encore un réminiscence de Sarcey."

23. *Introduction to Proust*, p. 91.

24. *Ibid.*, p. 217.

25. *Ibid.*, p. 36.

26. *Lettres à P. Lavallée*, p. 20.

27. Leon, *Introduction to Proust,* pp. 54–55.

28. E. Clermont-Tonnerre, *Robert de Montesquiou et Marcel Proust* (Paris, 1925), p. 74.

29. *Lettres à la Comtesse de Noailles,* pp. 31–32.

30. Painter, *Proust: The Early Years,* p. 353.

31. *Introduction to Proust,* p. 57.

32. *Ibid.,* p. 62.

33. *Lettres à Robert de Montesquiou (Correspondance générale de Marcel Proust,* Vol. I [Paris, 1930]), p. 3.

34. *Proust: The Early Years,* p. 102.

35. *Souvenirs,* pp. 122–25.

36. *Ibid.,* p. 123.

37. *Introduction to Proust,* p. 89.

38. *Souvenirs,* p. 250.

39. *Lettres à P. Lavallée,* pp. 107–8.

40. *Introduction to Proust,* p. 48.

41. Painter, *Proust: The Early Years,* p. 390.

42. *Ibid.,* p. 94.

43. *Lettres à Madame et Monsieur Emile Straus (Correspondance générale de Marcel Proust,* Vol. VI [Paris, 1936]), p. 107.

44. *Marcel Proust et Jacques Rivière, Correspondance (1914-1922),* ed. Philip Kolb (Paris, 1955), p. 110.

45. *Introduction to Proust,* p. 231.

46. "Creative Agony," in *Proust: A Collection of Critical Essays,* ed. René Girard (Englewood Cliffs, N. J., 1962), p. 16.

47. Proust, *Deux amitiés féminines de Marcel Proust* (*Lettres et vers à Mesdames Laure Hayman et Louisa de Mornand*), ed. Georges Andrieux (Paris, 1928), p. 10.

48. *Ibid.*, pp. 46–47.

49. Maurois, *Proust: Portrait of a Genius*, p. 91.

50. *Lettres à Walter Berry*, p. 168.

51. *Ibid.*, p. 169.

52. *Ibid.*, pp. 188–89, 204.

53. *Ibid.*, pp. 172–75.

54. *Ibid.*, pp. 186–87.

55. Leon, *Introduction to Proust*, p. 72.

56. Maurois, *Proust: Portrait of a Genius*, p. 68.

57. *Autour de soixante lettres*, p. 19.

58. *Correspondance avec sa mère*, p. 13.

59. *Ibid.*, p. 180.

60. *Lettres à Robert de Montesquiou*, pp. 36, 90–91, 97–98.

61. *Ibid.*, pp. 88, 111; Clermont-Tonnere, *Robert de Montesquiou et Marcel Proust*, p. 29.

62. Preface to Proust, *A un ami* (Paris, 1948), p. 28.

63. *Ibid.*, pp. 168–69.

64. *Ibid.*, p. 208.

65. *Ibid.*, p. 209.

66. *Introduction to Proust*, p. 135.

67. *Lettres à Madame et Monsieur Emile Straus*, p. 128.

68. *Ibid.,* p. 150.

69. *Marcel Proust et Jacques Rivière,* p. 13.

70. *Lettres à M. et Mme Sydney Schiff* [*et al.*] (*Correspondance générale de Marcel Proust,* Vol. III [Paris, 1932], p. 66.

71. *Lettres à Madame et Monsieur Emile Straus,* p. 129.

72. *Ibid.,* pp. 161–62.

73. *Lettres à Walter Berry,* p. 20.

74. *Proust et Jacques Rivière,* p. 113.

75. *Ibid.*

76. *Lettres à la NRF,* p. 226.

77. *Lettres à Madame et Monsieur Emile Straus,* p. 234.

CHAPTER II

1. (Paris, 1953).

2. He discusses the second question in his "thèse principale," *La Morale de Proust* (Paris, 1953).

3. *Citations,* pp. 3–4.

4. *Ibid.,* pp. 9–10.

5. *Ibid.,* pp. 12–13.

6. The distinction between author and narrator will be maintained in subsequent discussion by invariable use of "Proust" as author and "Marcel" as narrator.

7. *A la recherche du temps perdu,* eds. Pierre Clarac and André Ferré (Paris, 1954), III, 240. All references are to this Pléiade edition.

8. *La Morale de Proust,* pp. 27–28.

9. *Ibid.,* p. 28.

10. Virginia Cowles, *Gay Monarch: The Life and Pleasures of Edward VII* (New York, 1956), p. 83.

11. Proust, *Les Plaisirs et les jours* (Paris, 1924), pp. 22–23.

12. Proust, *Jean Santeuil* (Paris, 1952), III, 95.

13. Theaters named in the novel include the Ambassadeurs, the Comédie Française (Théâtre Français), the Eden, the Folies Bergères, the Gymnase, the Odéon, the Opéra, the Opéra Comique, the Palais Royal, and the Trocadéro.

14. J. Brander Matthews, *The Theatres of Paris* (New York, 1880), p. 187.

15. *Citations,* p. 8.

16. The name appears thus in both passages, although other sources omit the final *t.*

17. Nathan, *Citations,* Erratum, and p. 36. The allusion is lost in the English translation, which reads, "It is all very well your coming to see Gilberte. I should like you to come sometime for my sake, not to my 'kettledrums,' which would bore you . . . but on the other days," *Remembrance of Things Past,* trans. C. K. Scott Moncrieff and Frederick Blossom (New York, 1934), I, 450.

18. *Ibid.,* p. 102. The allusion is again lost in the English translation, which reads, "Middle-class comedy is stilted. I must have either the princesses of classic tragedy or the broad farce of the common people. *Phèdre* or the clowns—nothing in between!" (II, 965).

19. *Ibid.,* p. 81.

20. Frank Wadleigh Chandler, *The Contemporary Drama of France* (Boston, 1920), p. 66.

21. A connection between Mérimée and Proust is indicated by Lewis Galantière: "Across half a century of time a bond between Mérimée

and Marcel Proust existed in the person of Mme de Beaulincourt, whom young Proust used to call on in the rue de Miromesnil in 1895-96, who served as a model for his Mme de Villeparisis, and to whom Mérimée wrote just before his death and just after the necessary tragedy of Sedan. . . . "—"Biographical Repertory," *The Goncourt Journals* (New York, 1937), p. 340.

22. Jacques Nathan confirms the Duchesse's accuracy: "Il y a dans *l'Arlésienne* un personnage d'innocent" (*Citations*, p. 61).

23. *Proust and Literature: The Novelist as Critic* (Cambridge, Mass., 1957), p. 196. Strauss refers the reader to Mouton's *Le Style de Marcel Proust*, p. 60.

24. *Pastiches et mélanges* (Paris, 1921), pp. 44–47.

25. "Chronologie de Marcel Proust," *A la recherche*, I, xxxix.

26. *The Contemporary Drama of France*, p. 326.

CHAPTER III

1. *If Memory Serves* (Garden City, 1935), p. 69.

2. *Citations*, p. 43. The passage in English appears thus: "His speech ended as a rule in some pleasantry of a less Homeric kind: 'See, draw closer your pepla with fair clasps, what is all that I see? Does your mother know you're out?'" (*Remembrance of Things Past*, I, 582).

3. *Du temps perdu au temps retrouvé* (Paris, 1950), p. 35.

4. *La Morale de Proust*, pp. 238–39.

5. What has usually been discussed is not so much the chronology of the novel as the chronology of the writing of the novel. Albert Feuillerat is, of course, aware that the variant versions of the novel bring about confusions and inconsistencies, but his emphasis is on the differences of

versions as they affect plot and characterization, as his title indicates: *Comment Marcel Proust a composé son roman* (New Haven, 1934). Robert Vigneron also is concerned with the chronology of the writing, and the structure of the resulting work: "Structure de *Swann*: Prétentions et défaillances," *Modern Philology,* XLIV (November, 1946), 102–28; "Structure de *Swann*: Combray ou le cercle parfait," *Modern Philology,* XLV (February, 1948), 185–207. Neither writer devotes particular comment to the points raised here. Several writers have touched on the question in passing: "Proust's chronology is extremely difficult to follow, the succession of events spasmodic, and his characters and themes . . . are presented and developed with a fine Dostoievskian contempt for the vulgarity of a plausible concatentation" (Samuel Beckett, *Proust* [London, 1931], p. 62); "It would be idle to worry over the historical chronology of Proust, to tie him down too closely to the central point of the second Dreyfus trial, to reconcile that date with the references to the Russo-Japanese war or the aeroplane that is seen by Marcel and Albertine" (D. W. Brogan, "Proust as a Social Historian," *French Personalities and Problems* [New York, 1947], p. 22); "There is a basic inconsistency in the time scheme [of *Jean Santeuil*], far more serious than those in *A la Recherche,* which the reader accepts as mysterious but credible loops in the dimensions of Time" (Painter, *Proust: The Early Years,* p. 246). Willy Hachez in his working out of the chronology, "La Chronologie et l'âge des personnages de *A la recherche du temps perdu,*" *Bulletin de la Société des Amis de Marcel Proust et des Amis de Combray,* No. 6, (1956), 198–207, proceeds from the references to historical occurrences, in some instances confirming the present study, in others presenting some disagreement, and in others not overlapping. In one of the main points made here there is agreement: "En gros, le narrateur a dix ans de moins que Proust" (p. 204). See also Wolf Albert Traeger's "Temps et souvenir: A propos d'un livre allemand sur la *Recherche du temps perdu,*" *Bulletin de la Société des Amis de Marcel Proust . . . ,* No. 8 (1958), 490–505. The previous view closest to that of the present study is in Clive Bell's *Proust* (New York, 1929), in which Bell writes, "Proust deals with time as modern painters deal with space. The painter will not allow scientifically ascertained spatial relations and laws of perspective to restrict his imagination. And Proust in his first volumes does not hesitate to make the hero sometimes an old and sometimes a young man. . . . Do not try to establish a satisfactory chronology: events of a post-war complexion are made to take their place in nineteenth-century settings. . . . That scene *chez la princesse,* in the last volume, cannot be placed earlier than 1932, since we are given to understand that fifteen years have elapsed since last we met some of the characters whom last we did meet towards the end of the war" (pp. 56–57). In sum, "He juggles with time. And with time he can juggle because time is the material in which he works" (p. 64).

6. *Comment Marcel Proust a composé son roman,* pp. 260–62.

7. Painter indicates that Proust actually was confused about the age of one of the originals of Gilberte: "As Proust remembered her long afterwards, she was fifteen when he fell in love with her, and perhaps he was right; for although according to Gotha she was born at Pavlovsk on 12 July 1874, and would therefore only have been twelve, Gotha is known to be less fallible on the ages of princes than on those of princesses, particularly when these belonged before their marriages only to the minor nobility" (p. 57).

8. *Comment Marcel Poust a composé son roman,* p. 29.

9. Justin O'Brien, "Albertine the Ambiguous: Notes on Proust's Transposition of Sexes," *PMLA,* LXIV (December, 1949), 933–52.

10. *Proust,* p. 62.

11. *Du côte de Marcel Proust* (Paris, 1929), pp. 166–67.

CHAPTER IV

1. A footnote in the Gallimard edition (I, 960 n.) informs the reader, "Le vers de Corneille (*Mort de Pompée,* 1072), est exactement: 'O ciel, que de vertus vous me faites haïr!'" Another quotation from Corneille is attributed (not by Marcel) to Voltaire (see note 20 below).

2. *Citations,* p. 9.

3. *Citations,* p. 4; *Proust: Portrait of a Genius,* p. 8.

4. Dreyfus, *Souvenirs,* p. 16.

5. *Correspondance avec sa mère*, p. 23.

6. *Ibid.*, p. 31.

7. *Ibid.*, p. 58. The lines cited are from *Richard III*, Act I, scene 2.

8. *Ibid.*, p. 92. Kolb's note: "Cf. Molière, les *Précieuses ridicules*, scène ix."

9. *Ibid.*, p. 101. Kolb's note: "La pièce de Marivaux dont il s'agit est *la Surprise de l'amour;* l'héroïne est une comtesse plutôt qu'une marquise."

10. *Lettres à Montesquiou*, p. 4.

11. *Ibid.*, p. 240.

12. *Ibid.*, pp. 20, 96.

13. *Lettres à Mme et M. Straus*, p. 94.

14. *Souvenirs*, p. 340.

15. *Lettres à la Comtesse de Noailles*, pp. 178–79.

16. *Lettres à Mme et M. Straus*, p. 37.

17. *Lettres à Montesquiou*, p. 64.

18. *Souvenirs*, p. 196.

19. Nathan identifies it as line 175 of the dedication of *La Coupe et les lèvres* (*Citations*, p. 53). The notes to *A la recherche* identify it as from the dedication of *Spectacle dans un fauteuil* (III, 1181).

20. Errata in *Citations*.

21. *Contre Sainte-Beuve*, p. 13.

22. *Citations*, p. 5.

23. *Ibid.*, p. 119.

24. P. 125.

25. *Lettres à Montesquiou*, p. 64.

26. *Le Misanthrope,* the sonnet scene.

27. Nathan, who identifies the quotation from Molière, is unable to find this phrase in the Sévigné letters (*Citations,* p. 54).

28. *Marcel Proust, sa vie, son œuvre* (Paris, 1935), pp. 137–38.

29. *Ibid.,* p. 292.

30. *Proust* (New Haven, 1956), p. 26. See also Strauss, *Proust and Literature: The Novelist as Critic,* p. 37.

31. "Proust's memory has furnished him with two passages from the first scene of *Amphitryon,* which he has put together. . . . " Marcel Proust, *On Art and Literature, 1896–1919,* trans. Sylvia Warner Townsend (New York, 1958), p. 401 n. 5.

32. "Here the quotation is slightly manipulated by the speaker. . . . " *Ibid.,* p. 401 n. 7.

33. "Proust's memory has recalled the last line first. . . . " *Ibid.,* p. 401 n. 9.

34. *Lettres à Montesquiou,* p. 253.

35. Proust has made some minor changes, omitting one couplet in the middle, and changing "jeter d'effroi" to "jeter d'émoi," "de vos yeux" to "de ses yeux." The changes indicate not so much that he alters quotations to suit his own purposes as that he relies on his memory. See *A la recherche,* III, 1092 n.

36. Proust has slightly altered the orginal text to bridge the omission of an interverning line:

> Le Roi, jusqu'à ce jour, ignore qui je suis:
> Celui par qui le ciel règle ma destinée
> Sur ce secret encor tient ma langue enchaînée.
> —*Esther,* Act I, scene 1.

37. *Citations,* p. 12.

38. "Un peuple florissant," Nathan points out (*Ibid.,* p. 70), is a combination of two lines from *Athalie:* "Le peuple saint en foule inondait les portiques," Act I, scene 1, and "le peuple florissant," Act II, scene 8.

39. *Athalie*, Act II, scene 7. The question is "Quel est tous les jours votre emploi?" The "vague" reply of Joas is: "J'adore le Seigneur; on m'explique sa loi;/Dans son livre divin on m'apprend à la lire,/Et déjà de ma main je commence à l'écrire."

40. *Athalie*, Act I, scene 3. The exact line of Josabeth, presenting the chorus, is: "O filles de Lévi, troupe jeune et fidèle."

41. *Du temps perdu*, p. 160.

42. *Athalie*, Act II, scene 9.

43. *Ibid.*, Act I, scene 2. Nathan points out (*Citations*, p. 73) that the exact phrase is "Sous l'aile du Seigneur dans le temple élevé." The change might be due either to faulty memory, or a deliberate omission of the reference to the Lord in this particular context.

44. *Ibid.*, Act IV, scene 2. Nathan points out (*Citations*, p. 73) that the exact lines are "Un roi sage, ainsi Dieu l'a prononcé lui-même,/Sur la richesse et l'or ne met point son appui." Again, the omission of the reference to God might be a matter of tact.

45. *Ibid.*, Act II, scene 9.

46. *Ibid.*, Act I, scene 2. Nathan points out (*Citations*, p. 73) that the original reads "pour me caresser," and "je me sentis presser."

47. *Ibid.*, Act II, scene 9; Act III, scene 8. In the last four lines, Proust has made two minor changes, from "les honneurs" to "l'honneur" and "basse obéissance" to "douce obéissance."

CHAPTER V

1. *The Mind of Proust* (Cambridge, 1949), p. 37.

2. Matter of the theater and the drama figures more or less importantly in the action of *Jean Santeuil*—to the extent to which it may be thought to have action. Jean is described as a playwright, presumably of the

drawing-room variety, in an invitation issued by the Duchess of Réveillon: "Henri complote avec son ami M. Santeuil, un garçon remarquable dont l'esprit vous enchantera, une petite comédie qui est ma foi fort gentille" (II, 240). Nothing more is made of this; like most of the events or actions in *Jean Santeuil*, it is disjunctive. The theater passages run in separate short sections, the longest being a set piece of five pages (II, 149–54) in which Jean goes backstage at the Opéra Comique to see the director, on an errand for the Duc de Réveillon. The reader receives a backstage description through the point of view of a young dramatist observing the activities, which seem at first quite inadequate to his own vision of his play, then become a kind of ordered chaos of which his play is the real center. Jean does not even get to see the director, except in a brief announcement that he has had a sleepless night. Contrasted to Marcel's backstage visit with Saint-Loup and Rachel, the whole episode is chiefly remarkable for its irrelevance—or as autobiography. Unlike the episode in *A la recherche*, it casts no light on the characters and establishes no standards of comparison; it does not seem to *mean*, but merely *is*. Proust seems content to present the anecdote, where in the later novel he would have used it. Each point of comparison makes *Jean Santeuil* seem more bound to fact, like a notebook, rather than having been created as a novel.

3. *The Proustian Vision* (New York, 1954), pp. 36–37.

4. *Proust's Way*, trans. Gerard Hopkins (Fair Lawn, N.J., 1958), pp. 20–21.

5. *Ibid.*, pp. 7-8.

6. *The Proustian Vision*, p. 194.

7. *Ibid.*, pp. 37–38.

8. *Proust: The Early Years*, p. 285.

9. *Proust*, pp. 48–49.

10. *Ibid.*, p. 51. See also *Mind of Proust*, pp. 367–68.

11. *Citations*, p. 96.

12. *La Morale de Proust*, p. 83.

13. *Proust* (New York, 1929), p. 95.

14. *Du temps perdu au temps retrouvé*, p. 226.

15. *The Two Worlds of Marcel Proust* (Philadelphia, 1948), p. 155.

16. *Proust: The Early Years*, p. 388.

17. *The Proustian Vision*, pp. 37–38.

18. Feuillerat, *Comment Marcel Proust a composé son roman*, p. 244.

19. *A la recherche*, III, 1146, n. 2 for p. 1015.

20. *Ibid.*, III, 1145, n. 6 for p. 1002.

21. *Ibid.*, III, 1118, note for p. 695.

22. *Proust: The Early Years*, p. 365.

23. *Proust's Way*, p. 20.

24. *Du temps perdu*, p. 45.

25. *La Morale de Proust*, pp. 78-79.

CHAPTER VI

1. *Proust: Portrait of a Genius*, pp. 184–85.

2. *Lettres à la NRF*, p. 132; *Lettres à M. et Mme Sydney Schiff*, p. 192.

3. *A un ami*, p. 104.

4. *Lettres de Marcel Proust: Comment parut "Du Côté de chez Swann,"* ed. Léon Pierre-Quint (Paris, 1930), p. 58.

5. *Lettres à Walter Berry*, p. 58.

6. *Lettres à Mme et M. Straus,* p. 17.

7. *Ibid.,* pp. 48–49.

8. *Ibid.,* p. 67.

9. *A un ami,* p. 84.

10. *Lettres à la NRF,* p. 216.

11. *Lettres à Montesquiou,* p. 177.

12. *Autour de soixante lettres,* pp. 145, 149.

13. *Lettres à Mme et M. Straus,* p. 23.

14. *Ibid.,* p. 190.

15. *Lettres à Montesquiou,* p. 31.

16. *Au bal avec Marcel Proust,* p. 21.

17. *Ibid.,* p. 23.

18. *A un ami,* p. 24.

19. *Souvenirs,* p. 38.

20. *Lettres à M. et Mme Schiff,* p. 139.

21. *Souvenirs,* p. 241.

22. Warner, *On Art and Literature,* p. 409, n. 4.

23. Louis de Robert, *Comment débuta Marcel Proust* (Paris, 1925), pp. 37–38.

24. Albert Feuillerat reports that Proust's brother informed him that the idea did indeed come from this experience (p. 237).

25. Two other references to transformation scenes are almost a relief, so without reverberation are they. One is a description of soldiers in the booth of a chestnut seller "sans se douter qu'un magicien les faisait surgir

de la nuit, comme dans une apparition de théâtre" (II, 96). The other refers to the man who is to marry Mme Verdurin: "Et, en effet, le prince, faisant comme dans une apothéose de théâtre, de cirque, ou dans un tableau ancien, faire front à son cheval, adressait à Odette un grand salut théâtral et comme allégorique" (I, 640).

26. As a further example of Proust's economy, it might be noted how "divertissement final" has worked in its suggestion, as did the description (p. 923) of d'Argencourt "sur la scène avant que le rideau tombe tout à fait."

27. *Marcel Proust* (London, 1951) pp. 106–9.

28. *Marcel Proust, sa vie, son œuvre,* p. 283.

29. *Proust,* p. 29.

Bibliography

Bibliography

BARKER, RICHARD. *Marcel Proust: A Biography.* New York: Criterion, 1958.

BECKETT, SAMUEL. *Proust.* London: Chatto & Windus, 1931.

BELL, CLIVE. *Proust.* New York: Harcourt Brace, 1929.

BELL, WILLIAM STEWART. *Proust's Noctural Muse.* New York: Columbia University Press, 1962.

BERNHARDT, LYSIAN. *Sarah Bernhardt: My Grandmother.* London: Hurst & Blackett, 1948.

BIBESCO, PRINCESSE [MARTHE]. *Au bal avec Marcel Proust.* (*Les Cahiers de Marcel Proust,* Vol. IV.) Paris: Gallimard, 1928.

BRÉE, GERMAINE. *Du temps perdu au temps retrouvé.* Paris: Belles Lettres, 1950.

BROGAN, D. W. "Proust as a Social Historian," *French Personalities and Problems.* New York: Knopf, 1947.

CHANDLER, FRANK WADLEIGH. *The Contemporary Drama of France.* Boston: Little Brown, 1920.

CLERMONT-TONNERRE, ELISABETH (DE GRAMONT). *Robert de Montesquiou et Marcel Proust.* Paris: Flammarion, 1925.

COCKING, J. M. *Proust.* New Haven: Yale University Press, 1956.

COWLES, VIRGINIA. *Gay Monarch: The Life and Pleasures of Edward VII.* New York: Harper, 1956.

CRÉMIEUX, BENJAMIN. *Du côté de Marcel Proust.* Paris: Lemarget, 1929.

DAUDET, LUCIEN. *Autour de soixante lettres de Marcel Proust.* (*Les Cahiers de Marcel Proust,* Vol. V.) Paris: Gallimard, 1929.

DREYFUS, ROBERT. *Souvenirs sur Marcel Proust.* Paris: Grasset, 1926.

FEUILLERAT, ALBERT. *Comment Marcel Proust a composé son roman.* New Haven: Yale University Press, 1934.

FISER, EMERIC. *L'Esthétique de Marcel Proust.* Paris: Rieder, 1933.

GALANTIÈRE, LEWIS (ed.). *The Goncourt Journals.* Garden City: Doubleday, 1937.

GIRARD, RENÉ (ed.). *Proust: A Collection of Critical Essays.* Englewood Cliffs, N. J.: Prentice-Hall, 1962.

GREEN, F. C. *The Mind of Proust.* Cambridge: Cambridge University Press, 1949.

GUITRY, SACHA. *If Memory Serves.* Garden City: Doubleday, 1935.

HACHEZ, WILLY. "Chronologie du temps perdu et l'âge des personnages," *Bulletin de la Société des amis de Marcel Proust et des amis de Combray.* No. 6 (1956), pp. 198-207.

HALDANE, CHARLOTTE. *Marcel Proust.* London: Barker, 1951.

HINDUS, MILTON. *The Proustian Vision.* New York: Columbia University Press, 1954.

JOHNSON, C. W. M. "Tone in *A la recherche du temps perdu,*" *Forms of Modern Fiction,* ed. WILLIAM VAN O'CONNOR. Minneapolis: University of Minnesota Press, 1948.

258

LEON, DERRICK. *Introduction to Proust: His Life, His Circle and His Work.* London: Kegan Paul, 1940.

MARCH, HAROLD. *The Two Worlds of Marcel Proust.* Philadelphia: University of Pennsylvania Press, 1948.

MATTHEWS, J. BRANDER. *The Theatres of Paris.* London: Sampson Low, 1880.

MAUROIS, ANDRÉ. *Proust: Portrait of a Genius,* trans. GERARD HOPKINS. New York: Harper, 1950.

NATHAN, JACQUES. *Citations, références et allusions de Proust dans "A la recherche du temps perdu."* Paris: Nizet, 1953.

———. *La Morale de Proust.* Paris: Nizet, 1953.

O'BRIEN, JUSTIN. "Albertine the Ambiguous: Notes on Proust's Transposition of Sexes," *PMLA,* LXIV (December, 1949), 933–52.

PAINTER, GEORGE D. *Proust: The Early Years.* Boston: Little Brown, 1959.

PIERRE-QUINT, LÉON. *Marcel Proust, sa vie, son œuvre.* Paris: Sagittaire, 1935.

PIROUÉ, GEORGES. *Proust's Way* [*Par les chemins de Marcel Proust*], trans. GERARD HOPKINS. Fair Lawn, N. J.: Essential Books, 1958.

PROUST, MARCEL. *A la recherche du temps perdu.* 3 vols. Eds. PIERRE CLARAC and ANDRÉ FERRÉ. Paris: Gallimard, 1954.

———. *A un ami.* Preface by Georges de Lauris. Paris: Amiot-Dumont, 1948.

———. *Contre Sainte-Beuve, suivi de nouveaux mélanges.* Paris: Gallimard, 1954.

———. *Correspondance avec sa mère,* ed. PHILIP KOLB. Paris: Plon, 1953.

———. *Deux amitiés féminines de Marcel Proust* (*Lettres et vers à Mesdames Laure Hayman et Louisa de Mornand*), ed. GEORGES ANDRIEUX, with prefaces by ROBERT PROUST and FERNAND NOZIÈRE. Paris: Andrieux, 1928.

————. *Jean Santeuil.* 3 vols. Paris: Gallimard, 1952.

————. *Lettres à la Comtesse de Noailles, 1901–1919.* (*Correspondance générale de Marcel Proust,* Vol. II.), eds. ROBERT PROUST and PAUL BRACH. Paris: Plon, 1931.

————. *Lettres à la "N[ouvelle] R[evue] F[rançaise]* (*Les Cahiers de Marcel Proust,* Vol. VI.) Paris: Gallimard, 1932.

————. *Lettres à Madame et Monsieur Emile Straus.* (*Correspondance générale de Marcel Proust,* Vol. VI.), eds. SUZY PROUST-MANTE and PAUL BRACH. Paris: Plon, 1936.

————. *Lettres à M. et Mme Sydney Schiff* [*et al.*]. (*Correspondance générale de Marcel Proust,* Vol. III.), eds. ROBERT PROUST and PAUL BRACH. Paris: Plon, 1932.

————. *Lettres à P. Lavallée* [*et al.*]. (*Correspondance générale de Marcel Proust,* Vol. IV.), eds. ROBERT PROUST and PAUL BRACH. Paris: Plon, 1933.

————. *Lettres à Robert de Montesquiou.* (*Correspondance générale de Marcel Proust,* Vol. I.), eds. ROBERT PROUST and PAUL BRACH. Paris: Plon, 1930.

————. *Lettres à Walter Berry* [*et al.*]. (*Correspondance générale de Marcel Proust,* Vol. V.), eds. ROBERT PROUST and PAUL BRACH. Paris: Plon, 1935.

————. *Lettres de Marcel Proust: Comment parut "Du côté de chez Swann",* ed. LÉON PIERRE-QUINT. Paris: Kra, 1930.

————. *Marcel Proust et Jacques Rivière, Correspondance* (*1914–1922*), ed. PHILIP KOLB. Paris: Plon, 1955.

————. *On Art and Literature, 1896–1919,* trans. SYLVIA TOWNSEND WARNER. New York: Meridian, 1958.

————. *Pastiches et mélanges.* Paris: Gallimard, 1921.

————. *Les Plaisirs et les jours*. Paris: Gallimard, 1924.

————. *Remembrance of Things Past*. 2 vols. Trans. C. K. Scott Moncrieff and Frederick Blossom. New York: Random House, 1934.

Robert, Louis de. *Comment débuta Marcel Proust*. Paris: Gallimard, 1925.

Strauss, Walter A. *Proust and Literature: The Novelist as Critic*. Cambridge: Harvard University Press, 1957.

Traeger, Wolf Albert. "Temps et souvenir: A propos d'un livre allemand, sur *La recherche du temps perdu*," *Bulletin de la Société des Amis de Marcel Proust et des Amis de Combray*, No. 8 (1958), pp. 490–505.

Vignernon, Robert. "Creative Agony," *Proust: A Collection of Critical Essays*, ed. René Girard, pp. 13–27. Englewood Cliffs, N. J.: Prentice-Hall, 1962.

————. "Structure de *Swann*: Combray ou le cercle parfait," *Modern Philology*, XLV (February, 1948), 185–207.

————. "Structure de *Swann*: Prétentions et défaillances," *Modern Philology*, XLIV (November, 1946), 102–28.

Wilson, Edmund. *Axel's Castle*. New York: Scribner, 1953.

Index

Index